DATE DUE

		PRINTED IN U.S.A.

HELL ON TWO WHEELS

HELL ON
TWO
WHEELS

An Astonishing Story of
Suffering, Triumph,
and the **Most Extreme**
Endurance Race
in the World

AMY SNYDER

TRIUMPH
B O O K S

Library of Congress Cataloging-in-Publication Data

Snyder, Amy, 1960–
  Hell on two wheels : an astonishing story of suffering, triumph, and
the most extreme endurance race in the world / Amy Snyder.
     p. cm.
  Includes bibliographical references.
  ISBN 978-1-60078-525-2
  1. Race Across America. 2. Cycling—United States. 3. Extreme sports. I. Title.
  GV1049.2.R33S69 2011
  796.6'20973–dc22

                              2010052393

This book is available in quantity at special discounts for your group or organization. For further information, contact:

Triumph Books
542 South Dearborn Street
Suite 750
Chicago, Illinois 60605
(312) 939–3330
Fax (312) 663–3557
www.triumphbooks.com

Printed in U.S.A.
ISBN: 978-1-60078-525-2
Design by Patricia Frey; maps by Jill Petrowsky
Color photographs courtesy of the author unless otherwise indicated
Photographs of the Sonoran Desert on the title page, the staging area on p. xx, the four female racers on p. 22, Daniela Genovesi on p. 132, and Jim Rees on p. 142 courtesy of Brendon Purdy; photographs of Marko Baloh and Christoph Strasser on p. 10, Baloh on p. 50, Rees on p. 76, and Jure Robič on p. 166 and p. 202 courtesy of the author; photograph of Robič on p. 102 courtesy of John Foote; photograph of Gerhard Gulewicz on p. 182 courtesy of Alpine Photography

Contents

The woods are lovely, dark and deep.
But I have promises to keep,
And miles to go before I sleep,
And miles to go before I sleep.

—Robert Frost
"Stopping by Woods on a Snowy Evening"

Prologue

La Vale, Maryland, June 25, 2009, 5:30 AM

His legs were churning the pedals like massive pistons, pushing him along a quiet country road as the sun began to rise. His puffy, sun-scorched face was expressionless, and his lips were cracked and bleeding. He simply squinted down at the road through almost-shut eyes, barely able to turn his head as the pavement curved before him. There was nothing left physically. He was driving himself forward on sheer willpower. His crew chief radioed navigation instructions to him along with words of encouragement.

Left at the stop. Looking good.

He was digging so deeply he could taste his own bile. He'd been racing for almost eight days and nights with only a couple hours of sleep since leaving the Pacific coast on his transcontinental odyssey. Despite his staggering exhaustion he was managing a steady pace over rolling terrain approaching the exurbs of Baltimore–Washington, D.C. He'd already covered 2,800 miles; only 230 to go. He'd see the finish line in less than 15 hours. He was leading the race, but he was being hunted by a determined adversary, and his lead was shrinking.

A small climb ahead. Stay focused.

It was impossible to know what he was thinking. Was he present in the moment, or had his mind gone blank? Maybe he was somewhere else—perhaps in the mountains near his home, or playing a game with his young son. He turned a huge gear, and his slow cadence seemed poorly matched to the frantic mood out on the course. Through his radio came one more command, the only one that mattered now.

Go, go, go.

Introduction

The Race Across America (RAAM) is the most brutal organized sporting event you've never heard of and one of the best-kept secrets in the sports world. The scope of this epic event spans the continent, starting at the Pacific Ocean near San Diego, California, and ending at the Atlantic near Washington, D.C. It takes the winners about nine days to finish and the rest a couple of days more. The conditions are extreme and unpredictable, and nobody finishes the race unscathed.

Called "the toughest test of endurance in the world" by *Outside* magazine, RAAM is a bicycle race like no other. Once the starting gun goes off, the clock doesn't stop, so if you sleep, you lose. The first rider to complete the prescribed 3,000-mile route is the victor. A distance that's almost impossible to imagine traveling under one's own power, 3,000 miles is the equivalent of 114 marathon routes laid out end to end. Or 21 Ironman triathlon routes. Or the distance the average American will drive in two and a half months. During the race contestants climb more than 100,000 feet (nearly 20 miles straight up—three and a half times the height of Mount Everest), taking on the Rockies, the Ozarks, and the Appalachians in the process. Temperatures range from 125 degrees in the desert to 30 degrees atop mountain passes. Exposed to the elements day and night, racers must average between 230 and 250 miles every day just to make the time cutoffs placed every 1,000 miles along the course. The winners cover 350 miles each day and most survive on about an hour of sleep during each 24-hour cycle.

This race is nothing like its more famous cousin, the Tour de France. It offers none of the made-for-TV splendor of that grand European stage race. RAAM is decidedly less glamorous and far more savage. It takes participants to the limits of their physical and mental endurance, and in contrast to the compelling visuals of the Tour, it's often not a pretty sight.

As a lifelong cyclist and three-time Ironman finisher, even I was aghast when I first learned about RAAM. With a little bit of luck, a reasonably fit and determined person can finish an Ironman-length triathlon in less than three-quarters of a day. I knew I could never push myself beyond this, and that compelled me to discover how other athletes can and why they choose to do so. Then I learned that my friend George Vargas was preparing to compete in RAAM as part of a two-man team. After following George's progress across the continent and discussing his experience afterward, I realized that RAAM is much more than a race. I became convinced that this monster—this crucible—held lessons for us all.

Even with its stringent qualifying standards, I learned that half of all solo starters fail to finish RAAM. All are plagued by ghastly problems, including life-threatening respiratory emergencies, muscle and joint failure, nerve damage, heat stroke, and crashes caused by lack of sleep. Most racers get less than three hours of sleep during each day; those aspiring to win the race usually permit themselves only a brief power nap here and there. Sleep deprivation leads most racers to hallucinate, sometimes for hours on end.

So who are these people, and what drives them to endure such staggering amounts of punishment? To find the answers I spent time with a handful of contestants prior to the 2009 race. I got to know them and their families, then followed the race for two weeks in a minivan along with Les Handy, a longtime RAAM aficionado and an accomplished amateur bike racer. Watching this relentless contest unfold was considerably more disturbing than I expected. As it dragged on, I saw how RAAM transformed my new friends, brutalized them, and at times broke their spirits. I bore witness to their suffering, but it was their passion and grit that stuck with me most.

After two amazing weeks traveling the back roads of America from one coast to the other, I was forever changed by my experience of this race and its contestants. Everyone who encounters RAAM says it changes their own limiting thoughts and feelings. This is more than just a race—it's an allegory about overcoming personal limitations, self-discovery, and the power of the human spirit. And it's a story that needs to be told.

BUT I SOON DISCOVERED that telling the story of RAAM wouldn't be easy.

For one thing, it's almost impossible to comprehend what it feels like to propel oneself over a distance of 3,000 miles in a matter of days. Here's one way to think about it: it would take the average jogger who runs three miles a day, five days a week, nearly *four years* to cover this distance.

Another reason it's difficult conveying the monstrous nature of RAAM is because it shares little in common with some better-known extreme sporting challenges. Take the Tour de France. RAAM is half as long as that 23-day-long spectacle, but it's condensed into a far shorter time frame. Each of the Tour de France's daily stages calls for about five hours of racing, much of that time spent riding in a group sheltered from the wind in a 200-strong peloton of riders. At night, Tour contestants enjoy gourmet meals, physical therapy, and a decent night's sleep. RAAM cyclists, on the other hand, average 22 hours of racing each day. Unlike their ProTour brethren, they are forbidden from taking shelter behind their fellow racers or support vehicles. They ride alone. RAAM finishers proudly wear T-shirts proclaiming, "This Ain't No Tour."

How about Mount Everest? Three-time RAAM winner Wolfgang Fasching also climbed the world's highest mountain and said, "Everest is more dangerous, but the Race Across America is harder." True, there's one fatality for every 60 or so successful Everest summits, and Summit Day is a grueling 15-hour affair. But thanks to modern technology, as long as you avoid the most dangerous weather and catastrophic accidents, Everest isn't the torture chamber it once was. (K2 is actually twice as deadly.) The numbers tell the story: more than 3,000 people have stood on the roof of the world at the Everest summit, but only 200 men and women own a RAAM finisher's medal.

The Iditarod takes about the same amount of time as RAAM—the winners finish in roughly nine days. Like RAAM, it demands loads of preparation, equipment, and logistics. And the conditions are equally treacherous: steep mountain climbs, dense forests, frigid temperatures, fierce winds, and hours of darkness. But stating the obvious, Iditarod mushers are pulled along the 1,150-mile course by their dogs. In RAAM a racer's legs have to produce every watt of power necessary to propel him forward, making close to 1 million pedal revolutions during his transcontinental crossing.

The 135-mile Badwater Ultramarathon is one of the most challenging ultradistance running events in the world. It takes place in Death Valley in July, when temperatures hit 125 degrees and the pavement is hot enough to melt the soles of a racer's running shoes. Renowned ultramarathoner Dean Karnazes first entered Badwater in 1995. After running 72 miles in 120-degree heat, he collapsed on the side of the road suffering from hallucinations, diarrhea, and nausea. He went on to become one of the most accomplished ultramarathoners ever, and *Time* magazine named him one of the "Top 100 Most Influential People in the World." But he got shellacked in his first encounter with Badwater.

While Badwater is unquestionably brutal, RAAM takes almost *10 times* longer for the winners to complete. As a result, RAAM contestants suffer horrific effects that Badwater racers never experience. This is why RAAM rookie Michele Santilhano—who had finished Badwater the prior year—feared RAAM more. She described RAAM as "an animal, a beast not to be taken lightly, a beast I need to deal with."

THE TOLL THIS EVENT TAKES ON BODY AND MIND is equally difficult to convey.

During this relentless race, participants can gradually lose the use of their hands because of nerve compression in the wrists, neck muscles can fail because they must continually hold up one's head, life-threatening pulmonary infections and organ failure can hit at any moment, and muscles and joints can self-destruct.

Each year ambulances ply the race route as participants falter and finally succumb, but the ambulances' arrival only marks the culmination of a process that plays out over several days. Contestants can nurse the physical and emotional injuries they sustain during the race for months afterward. In the 2003 event, ultracycling great Marko Baloh (BAH low) raced for three days while battling breathing problems, then fevers, and finally searing chest pain before he ceased pedaling his bike and was rushed to the hospital. He was diagnosed with a potentially fatal pulmonary embolism that had to be surgically removed. He had pushed himself so hard he partially destroyed one of his lungs.

RAAM racers also experience a horrifying physical condition rarely seen anywhere else. After days of nonstop cycling spent hunched over on a bike, a racer's neck muscles can suddenly fail from the continuous strain of holding up his head. Known as Shermer's Neck, this condition causes a cyclist's head to flop forward like a rag doll's that has had its chin pinned to its chest. No matter how hard he tries, once his neck muscles fail, just like a newborn infant, a cyclist is as helpless to lift his head up. When one rider succumbed to this condition, a member of his crew said, "His head was flopping around like he had no bones in his neck."

Another way to comprehend how much effort RAAM demands is by considering the nutritional burden it places on racers. Participants consume more calories in a single day than the average adult gets in three or four. Despite this prodigious intake, many still lose five or more pounds of muscle mass during the race, as their bodies literally consume themselves to keep going. The racers' digestive systems are under such duress that many rely on bottles of Ensure and sports drinks, unable to stomach anything more adventurous. A daily diet might comprise five to 10 of each. Contestants can consume so much sugary, "fast" energy that they have to assiduously brush their teeth and use mouthwash or else their teeth can literally rot away during the race. One recent finisher returned home to discover five new cavities.

As the race drags on even seemingly inconsequential injuries become magnified. A spent racer can be driven to distraction by simple things like bug bites, nose bleeds, tendonitis, scratched corneas, and cracked lips. Saddle sores fall into this category, an ailment that plagues every racer at some point during RAAM. The repetitive, unremitting agony of these raw wounds can spell an early exit. Sitting on a bicycle seat for days after your private parts have been abraded and transformed into raw flesh is unimaginable to the average person, yet RAAM competitors view it as just another challenge to overcome. At least in an ultramarathon like Badwater, a contestant can use superglue to keep an open blister on his foot closed.

But a cyclist makes nearly 1 million pedal revolutions during RAAM, so even if he manages to avoid saddle sores until the halfway point, he still has to chafe himself 500,000 more times before reaching the finish line. Can you imagine enduring 100 pedal strokes in this condition? One thousand? Ten thousand?

The challenges RAAM presents to the mind and spirit are similarly difficult to fathom. Sleep deprivation has to be the most vexing condition experienced during RAAM. One recent finisher said that, "The effects of sleep deprivation and the mind-numbing enormity of RAAM are the greatest obstacles." Most racers shuffle into their motor homes in the middle of the night to get a massage, a shower, a nap, and some fresh cycling clothes. Because the clock never stops, to minimize time off the bike, almost everything else is (or should be) done while cycling. This includes eating, urinating, talking with family members, and brushing one's teeth.

Contestants who aspire to win the race usually make do with about an hour of sleep per day—just enough time to go through one brain-restoring REM cycle. Amnesty International would classify such severe sleep deprivation as torture. Cyclists' minds can be shattered by this lack of rest, which causes delayed reactions that can lead to violent crashes. Lack of sleep also induces behavioral problems, including depression, confusion, and anger. Riders often become paranoid and suggestible. Many eventually begin to hallucinate, seeing things that aren't there, conversing with animals, or jumping off their bikes deep into the night to do battle with invisible beasts.

BY NOW IT MIGHT SEEM AS THOUGH RAAM COMPETITORS are a different breed, invested with superhuman constitutions that help them overcome the unimaginable brutality that RAAM dishes out. But that's just not the case. These racers feel every ache and pain just like a normal person would, and they aren't masochists, either. They point out that persevering in this race is mostly a mental challenge. So how does a racer maintain the will to go on, sitting on a narrow bicycle saddle and churning his legs for up to 12 days straight, especially toward the end when physical discomfort blots out everything else and his sleep-deprived mind falters and sputters?

Actually, not a single racer fully maintains his resolve. Each comes close to quitting more than once. Racers sob and scream and curl up in fetal positions alongside the road, but then pull themselves together again and get back on their bikes. Late in the 2005 event, defending champion Jure Robič (YUR-eh ROH-bich) found himself in the lead almost a full day ahead of the nearest competitor. Even though he was set to win by a decisive margin, after seven days and nights of nonstop racing and almost no sleep, he was losing touch with reality. He began weeping and almost quit because he couldn't remember what his son's face looked like. As he crossed the finish line he held up a photo of his wife Petra and his infant son and kissed it. Even though his lips were so dry and cracked they made people cringe, he managed a big smile before falling to the ground.

In their bleakest moments on the road, each racer finds his own reason to keep going. Every reason is unique but all finishers share two things in common. The first is an unquenchable desire to challenge the limits of their own endurance. RAAM winner Franz Spilauer said, "What kept me going was my overall fascination with what I was doing and how it affected me, the testing of my body and seeing how far I could push myself." The second reason is the unfathomable sense of joy and fulfillment they experience while on their bikes. These fanatics just crave racing—the farther, the better.

These characteristics give racers determination, but they're insufficient to ensure success. There are two more pieces to the puzzle. One has to do with how RAAM finishers experience pain. The way ultradistance athletes relate to pain is different from you and me. They are able to dissociate from it, observe it, work with it, and calmly accept it as a necessary part of the race. To them, pain is information. The other crucial element is their unusual capacity to endure thousands of hours of grueling training, through all types of weather, at all hours of the day and night, and almost always alone.

Because these abilities are so hard to relate to for the vast majority of us who don't compete in ultradistance races, these athletes can seem masochistic, even nihilistic. But they keenly want to be understood as fully realized individuals.

Many race veterans explain how RAAM changed their lives and humanized them. Five-time finisher Rick Kent entered RAAM for the last time in 1994 and was later diagnosed with multiple sclerosis. "Competing in RAAM made me stronger, more confident, and able to handle my disease much better," he told me. Canadian RAAM veteran Lt. Col. Tony O'Keeffe credited the race with "opening me up emotionally. I cry now at weddings. I didn't realize I was so connected to other people's emotions until RAAM." This was a recurring theme I heard, especially from older male racers. Competing in RAAM makes it easier to feel, share, and be vulnerable with other people.

A sociological explanation for why ultradistance athletes do what they do goes something like this: in our modern age, we yearn for authentic experiences where our courage must be summoned. One way we do this is by willingly undertaking extreme physical challenges. Through these experiences, writer Nancy Soloman observes, "we drop our pretenses, ego, and arrogance in favor of truth and transformation…we fulfill our intention to be authentic."

Some racers explain that a race like RAAM demands so much that it peels everything away and lays them bare, reconnecting them to their simpler, animal selves. In this state of grace, athletes explain that they feel intensely alive and in touch with nature. Some claim to experience powerfully spiritual moments of transcendence.

All of this suggests that for ultradistance racers, the balance between pain and pleasure might not be as out of kilter as it first seems.

When Kirk Johnson ran Badwater, he was filled with "eye-opening wonder" while watching meteor showers in the night sky of the desert, when "the simple act of moving through was a source of joy." Johnson was a self-described "seeker" who thought "there might be a way—through the unfathomable post-apocalyptic wilderness of racing in Death Valley— to reach the veil and touch something beyond me and my life. A place where misery and transcendence were so deeply intertwined it couldn't be without meaning."

As RAAM began one sunny June day in Oceanside, California, 28 men and women started resolutely pedaling, driven by a force few of us can comprehend. They didn't know it at the time, but they had embarked on the closest and most controversial race in history. Through their ordeals, some racers would find the bliss they sought; others would be crushed by the crucible of RAAM. Moving steadily across the country, they would all learn important lessons about themselves as they traversed scorching deserts, ragged mountains, and open plains. It was the race of a lifetime.

The Race Day Scene

Oceanside Pier, June 17

This was the day each participant had circled on his or her calendar at least a year earlier. The men's race was set to begin at noon from a sunny beach in Oceanside, California, a short drive north of San Diego. The racers began arriving with about an hour to spare, peering expectantly from the windows of their support vehicles as they pulled into the shoreline parking lot. Their transports mixed with minivans ferrying vacationing families for a day at the beach, beat-up convertibles stuffed with bronzed teenagers, and tricked-out pickups belonging to Marines stationed at the nearby Camp Pendleton.

Surrounded by the other colorful Southern California subcultures drawn to the inviting shores of San Diego County, nobody paid any attention to a handful of elite ultradistance cyclists strutting around in colorful spandex and sporting $5,000 bikes.

The toughest cycling race in the world was about to start, but hardly any of the 20 million residents of Southern California seemed to care. There were no tickets sold, no journalists present, and no local politicians on hand to celebrate the event. In recent years, most local papers barely ran even the smallest mention. San Diego is a cycling and triathlon hotbed, but the local cycling and multisport communities were largely unaware of the race that was about to go off just up the coast.

The racers themselves—the best ultradistance cyclists in the world—weren't hounded by fans seeking autographs, nor were they escorted to the starting line in chartered buses. The athletes didn't even receive any help negotiating their trips from nearby hotels. Some of them even got lost, finally stumbling on the staging area only because they knew it was literally in the shadow of the towering Oceanside Pier, one of the longest on the West Coast, stretching almost a third of a mile into the blue waters of the Pacific.

No, these athletes had traveled from around the world to be here, but they had to scrape and scrounge to purchase plane tickets and deliver their crews to California. They maxed out their credit cards buying race supplies. They crammed their crew members into rooms in tired motels around town that normally catered to families visiting loved ones stationed at Camp Pendleton. To save money while waiting for the race to begin, they cooked their own meals in the motor homes most racers had rented to follow them across the country, vehicles that would soon double as their medical stations and command centers.

ULTRADISTANCE CYCLING IS AN OBSCURE SPORT in the U.S., and even though RAAM is the baddest race of them all, it is virtually unknown outside the ultracycling community. The race enjoyed far greater visibility years ago when ABC's *Wide World of Sports* televised the action in Emmy-winning broadcasts. But the TV crews are long gone, and with them the big-name sponsors have all vanished, too. Today there's almost no advertising or sponsorship money to be found. No prize money is awarded to the race winner. The only tangible reward the winner receives is the same medal every other finisher receives. In this sense, RAAM has more in common with, say, amateur rowing than with its cousin the Tour de France. Even the obscure Iditarod dog sled race is sponsored by large corporations, while ultradistance cycling—for better or worse—is imbued with the purest amateur spirit.

A Harvard rower once called his sport "a hermetically sealed world." In describing rowing's culture, the journalist David Halberstam writes, "Failing to get their deeds and names known to the world of outsiders, [rowers] become the custodians of their own honor, their own record-book keepers....Because their deeds were passed on by word of mouth rather than by book and newspaper, the sport gained a mythic aura."

The same is true for ultracycling. It's a small, eccentric subculture loosely governed by a sanctioning and record-keeping body run by a cabal of ultracyclists. The early RAAM pioneers did a decent job documenting the first few years of the race in book form, and today a RAAM finisher will occasionally write about his own experience. As far as media coverage goes, only the RAAM organization itself makes a sustained effort to chronicle the race, but it doesn't have the resources to do an in-depth job. Amateurish stories appear in a grab bag of cycling blogs, and glossy cycling magazines sporadically run pieces about RAAM or long-distance races held in Europe. General interest media hardly ever do.

Since nobody is around to document the races, ultracyclists pass down their stories and lore from one racer to another—just like ancient myths— and they are content with impressing only one another.

THE SCENE AT RAAM HEADQUARTERS THE DAY BEFORE the race began was even more low-key. There were no camera crews, no newspaper reporters, no crowds, and little fanfare. One had to work hard to pick out the registration area among all the beachgoers, surfers, and vacationers parading about. A "Race Across America" banner flapped in the breeze in front of some tables selling race merchandise, and that was that. Nobody paid it any mind.

All the action was taking place behind the scenes. Each of the 28 solo entrants was decamped at a local motel along with his or her crew, busily preparing vehicles, staging and testing bicycles and other equipment, and buying supplies. Each had spent years preparing body, mind, and soul for this moment, but in these last few days there was still a lot to do. All but eight starters had come from outside the U.S., and they faced added logistical and financial challenges.*

Each starter had earned the right to be in Oceanside by doing well in a sanctioned qualifying race. Their RAAM training regimens consumed ungodly amounts of time. Many logged more than 10,000 training miles

---

* Actually, there were more than 28 racers waiting to start in Oceanside. In addition to the solo racers, RAAM includes two-, four-, and eight-person teams, and other divisions as well. There's even a shorter race that travels the first third of the route and runs concurrently. All told, there were roughly 150 contestants and many more crew members on hand in 2009.

in the year leading up to their race, and some topped 25,000 miles—the circumference of the earth at the equator—sometimes riding for more than 24 hours straight. Racers from cold climates forced themselves to train indoors, spinning inside 100-degree saunas for hours at a time to acclimatize their bodies to the heat they'd have to endure during the race.

Each had invested tens of thousands of dollars in travel expenses, vehicles, equipment, food, and bicycles. Even more, they had to convince six to 12 of their dearest friends to devote up to three weeks supporting them—living without creature comforts, financial remuneration, or sleep—out of cramped support vehicles. The racers' spouses and family members make perhaps the biggest sacrifices of all.

Clearly these athletes had a lot on the line, and the pressure to not fail weighed heavily on them as they fell asleep in their hotel rooms the night before the race.

On their last day in Oceanside, solo racers reported to race headquarters to have their vehicles and bicycles inspected for safety. If you had managed to spy any of them milling around the Oceanside Pier that day, you never would have known it. They aren't easy to spot. One journalist observed that, "In cycling, which is all about enduring pain, a lot of the toughest riders…don't seem particularly tough at first glance…this is because they exist in a world beyond normal conventions of toughness. In their world… the toughest…is the one who is so deeply tough that he seems almost bashful, or in extreme cases, sleepy."

Take Slovenian racer Marko Baloh. Tall, lanky, and 42 years old, Baloh is a RAAM veteran and one of the most formidable ultracyclists in the world. While he comes across as soft-spoken and even a bit deferential, he doesn't hide his burning desire to succeed. Baloh will look you directly in the eye and declare slowly and confidently, "I've come here to win." Then with a slight shrug of his shoulders, he'll quickly glance away and flash a shy grin.

Baloh is a study in contrasts—at once humble, but also dignified and self-confident. He's easygoing, but also a fierce competitor. He's prepared to suffer to win the race, but wants to have fun in the process. Fittingly, his race moniker is Tweety Bird. But Baloh doesn't always act like a happy-go-lucky cartoon character. He is dead serious in his race preparation, sometimes heading out for all-night training rides after putting his children to bed. Baloh admits to having been excruciatingly shy as a boy, and even today you can see him struggle to find the right balance between modesty and ferocity.

Michele Santilhano's toughness is equally hard to spot. The 39-year-old South African has run 135-mile ultramarathons, swam the English Channel, and finished a quintuple Ironman, but there's no swagger in her. Being of average height and build, she doesn't look like the warrior goddess her athletic résumé implies. She settles into chairs gently, as if trying to occupy as little space as possible. She admits to being socially awkward, and sometimes it seems she doesn't want you to notice her.

RAAM soloists don't have to wear their toughness on their sleeves. Nevertheless, they're desperate for you to know how much it hurts to compete in this race. To the individual experiencing pain, the feeling is overwhelmingly present, yet the sufferer has difficulty conveying his experience of it. Pain is the most difficult of all human states to explain, in part because of its resistance to language. But describing a painful sensation to someone else helps diminish its intensity. This is one reason RAAM participants hunger to stay connected to the outside world while racing.

Close family members keep tabs through late-night phone calls, whispering tender words of encouragement to keep their loved ones pedaling in the middle of the night. A brief call from home creates a fleeting, private oasis that gives the racer a safe haven for releasing pent-up anxieties, an experience that often leaves him weeping. The best way for friends to let a racer know they're watching is by posting words of encouragement on his blog. Crew members access these posts from their support vehicles and read them to the racer as he peddles. Racers yearn for that extra burst of energy that can come from an encounter with someone who shows even the vaguest appreciation of what they are putting themselves through. Ultracyclists are tough as nails, but as human as can be.

ABOUT AN HOUR BEFORE THE START of the men's race, a small crowd milled around the staging area. Besides the racers' crew members, there were about a dozen RAAM staffers on hand, a few startled beachgoers who happened to get caught up in the mix, and maybe two dozen wizened ultracyclists and RAAM groupies.

As they waited, the old timers talked amongst themselves, handicapping the field and discussing rivalries as each racer's vehicle pulled into the parking lot. This year's field was considered to be the deepest in years.

When a race favorite pulled in, the crowd peeled away from other riders and moved toward the favorite's vehicles, cameras snapping. The favorites shared a few things in common. Most arrived sporting neatly shaven heads (a full head of hair just means more grooming and less ventilation). Like ProTour cyclists, they showed up looking unnaturally thin, with hollowed-out cheeks and legs so sculpted you could see the muscle and sinew as if you were looking at the illustrations in an anatomy book that had come to life.

Arriving early that morning was Gerhard Gulewicz (GOUL-eh-wits), a serious-minded 41-year-old Austrian back for his fourth time. Gulewicz finished third in 2007, the same year he set the world speed record for cycling across Australia. The following year this compact, powerfully built man was at the peak of his cycling career as RAAM began, but he was spirited off the course by a Navajo Nation ambulance after a bad crash near Tuba City, Arizona. He was forced to withdraw while second on the road. This year Gulewicz had unfinished business to take care of, and he came to win.

Christoph Strasser showed up next. At 26, golden boy Strasser was an ultracycling sensation making his rookie appearance at RAAM. When this young Austrian emerged from his vehicle, the old-timers in the crowd nodded appreciatively. Strasser sported the same yellow-and-white cycling kit that his mentor, Wolfgang Fasching, had worn when Fasching dominated RAAM years ago. Strasser was making a statement that he was Fasching's heir apparent. "Wolfgang was impressed by my passion and my serious approach to my sport. He says he recognizes himself in me," Strasser explained. As he stepped from his vehicle with long strips of bright blue Physio Tape adorning his powerful legs, Strasser was a sight to behold and seemed supremely confident for a rookie.

Strasser had burst onto the scene two years prior, beating veteran Baloh at the ultracycling world championship in Austria and becoming the youngest man to ever garner that title. He had wanted to do RAAM since the age of 15, when he watched Fasching win it on Austrian television. As a rookie, Strasser was realistic about his prospects, and as a student of the race he approached it with the respect and humility it deserved. The betting line was that he'd finish in the top five.

Next to arrive was Dani Wyss (VICE), a 39-year-old Swiss. Everybody was delighted he had returned because he won the 2006 race in his first RAAM appearance—only the second rookie to do so. Wyss was known as a savvy tactician and a cool character. One would never have known how much he had on the line just by looking at him. The slender, small-framed man had a finely featured face and soft, brown eyes that didn't give away his toughness. He seemed relaxed and self-assured as he readied himself at the start while his young, energetic crew members flitted about nervously.

Baloh also arrived looking calm. Like Gulewicz, this was his fourth time back, so the pre-race scene was a familiar one. As soon as this Slovenian ultracycling legend stepped from his vehicle, it was clear this man was a world-class athlete. His tall, wiry body was reminiscent of a cheetah's—taut and leggy, with the high-waisted look of an Olympic middle-distance runner. Baloh's entourage drew attention because it was quite the family affair. Two of his three children were accompanying their father on his cross-country journey, along with his wife and stalwart crew member Irma. I watched as Baloh clutched his kids in his long, slender arms, seeking their comfort in these last anxious moments. Days later, as Baloh plied the roads of rural Ohio, some of his crew members questioned whether having his family along was helping or hurting his bid to win the race.

Franz Preihs (PRICE), another Austrian like Gulewicz and Strasser, was difficult to miss. The 31-year-old full-time ultracyclist worked hard to cultivate a bad boy image, and he had a knack for self-promotion. When he stepped from his vehicle, it was impossible to miss his heavily tattooed arms and legs.

Preihs had burnished his tough guy image at RAAM the prior year. In the middle of the race he crashed into a road sign after dozing off and was rushed to the hospital with a broken collarbone. He returned to the race hours later and finished—in fourth place, no less.

But Preihs is a softie at heart. The night before his departure for Oceanside, he lay in bed in his wife Michaela's arms and asked her whether he really had to go. Couldn't he just stay here with her, safe and warm? Preihs needed his wife's encouragement to give him courage.

Preihs was gunning for a podium finish this time around, and his commitment was obvious—on the inside of his left forearm he sported a large, red tattoo of the RAAM logo.

The last favorite to show up this morning was reigning champion Jure Robič, the odds-on pick to win. The king of ultracycling was back for his seventh consecutive year. Having begun his love affair with RAAM in 2003, he was the most experienced racer in the field by far. Robič, a 44-year-old Slovenian Special Forces soldier, was the only man ever to win four solo championships. Robič was the Lance Armstrong of RAAM and a legend in his own right. Some called him the best endurance athlete in the world, and even well into his forties he still won most of the ultradistance cycling races he entered.

Robič's dedication to this race was a full-bore obsession. "I love RAAM," he explained. "Something inside this race, it's unique. It gets like a poison into you. It's the greatest and the toughest. It takes all your life. It takes everything."

The crowd surged toward his van as it pulled into the lot. It was adorned with dozens of sponsors' stickers, but one stood out. It read "Slovenian Armed Forces." First his crew members piled out, dressed in camouflage green and looking as intimidating as ever. Robič was supported by a large, dedicated cadre of fellow Slovenian soldiers, loyal to their racer and ready to do anything for him.

Finally, out climbed Robič. He quickly surveyed the scene, and with the slightest sigh, nodded in the direction of some acquaintances he recognized in the crowd. A good-looking man of medium height and build, Robič had a large, weathered face, a square chin, and a contagiously playful smile. The thick stubble he sported after a few days on the bike made him look like the Marlboro Man. He was easy to look at and attracted people like a magnet.

The first impression this champion gave was of a venerable, dangerous warrior. The way he carried himself, the crinkles in his forehead, the rippling musculature of his potent legs. These were all signs of the mythic weight of his suffering and of how hard this man struggled to prove his worthiness.

Before long, Robič was straddling his bike and patiently fielding banal questions from the small group of RAAM media and the Slovenian reporters who followed him everywhere. In the moments before the race clock started, he was trying to make people understand—always trying.

2

The European Onslaught

Southern California desert, early June

About two weeks before the race was set to begin, many of Europe's best ultracyclists began arriving at Los Angeles International Airport. They spilled off airplanes along with all manner of bicycle frames, wheels, gear bags, supplies, video equipment, and crew members. If you'd been in the terminal when one of them happened to land, you would have assumed you were seeing the arrival of a sizeable cycling team.

These men came to win. They had each arrived early to acclimatize to riding in the desert and to familiarize themselves with the part of the course they would race during the crucial first 24 hours.

Cycling is a top national sport and pastime in Europe, enabling a handful of European ultracyclists to eke out an existence as full-time professionals. Sponsors pitch in enough money supporting them that RAAM draws a highly international, elite field to Oceanside each June for the toughest test of them all. This year was no exception: only eight of the 28 solo racers were Americans.

Even though the Europeans had invented ultradistance bike racing, it was many years before elite European cyclists began to take note of, participate in, or win RAAM. Perhaps it's like everything quintessentially American: at first the Europeans didn't take it very seriously. Certainly in the first few years the Europeans were wary of RAAM, and they had every reason to be. The history of ultradistance cycling is littered with international disputes and controversies, and to compete in the U.S. the Europeans would have to race in "enemy" territory.

THE FIRST TRANSCONTINENTAL BIKE RACE on American soil—or any soil for that matter—was made possible not by some revolutionary new cycling technology, training innovation, or nutritional breakthrough. The catalyst was much more mundane. RAAM's inaugural race took place in 1982 thanks to the creation of a trustworthy, standardized, and repeatable approach for certifying the accuracy of finishing times.

Racers had to be confident their competitors had actually pedaled every mile of the course without doing anything devious like taking shortcuts, drafting their follow-vehicles, or jumping into crew cars for a few miles here and there.*

Cyclists had been competing in long-distance races for well over 100 years before RAAM came along. The first documented cycling race took place in 1868, but at 1,200 meters (less than a mile), it wasn't considered "long" even for the standards of the time. A longer race was held the following year, but truth be told, it was an embarrassment for the participants. Just after the Michaux company began mass producing the velocipede (a precursor to the modern bicycle), three Londoners rode a whopping 53 miles from Trafalgar Square to Brighton in 15 hours. A reporter who had witnessed this "extraordinary velocipede feat" wrote that mischievous boys along the route threw stones at the riders and grabbed at their machines in an effort to disrupt their progress.

Fifteen years later, in 1884, an intrepid soul named Thomas Stevens proved it was possible to travel much greater distances by bicycle. He took two and a half years to circumnavigate the globe. (In 2009 a Londoner named James Bowthorpe did it in 175 days—five times faster.) Stevens' odyssey began in the U.S., where he became the first person to make a transcontinental crossing, traveling from San Francisco to Boston over a 3,700-mile route.

As reported in *Harper's,* "Eighty-three and a half days of actual travel and twenty days stoppage for wet weather, etc., made one hundred and three and a half days occupied in reaching Boston." Stevens did all this

---

*Follow-vehicles are just that—vehicles driven directly behind the riders to shield them from passing cars. Drafting a vehicle or even another racer is forbidden because, depending on how fast a cyclist is moving, he can save up to 30 percent of his energy by riding in a slipstream. In fact, most of the power a cyclist generates goes into pushing against wind resistance.

on a black-enameled penny-farthing with nickel-plated wheels. When he struck out across the country it was reported he carried socks, a spare shirt, a raincoat that doubled as a tent and bedroll, and a .38-caliber Smith & Wesson.

Despite its dubious beginning in that hapless 53-mile affair, long-distance bike racing didn't die that day in 1868 in the British countryside. Not to be outdone by the British—and perhaps inspired by Stevens' circumnavigation—in 1891 the French Bordeaux Velo Club inaugurated a race from Bordeaux to Paris, upping the ante from a paltry 53 miles in England to 355 miles in France. The dawn of ultradistance bike racing had arrived, and so had the international rivalries that remain an enduring feature of this most international of sports. By the 1890s cycling was taking major cities in Europe—and even New York City—by storm. "It was the personal computer of back then," explained one historian. "That was the topic of the day. The bicycle was the hot thing."

To the horror of the local populace, a Briton named George Plinkton Mills won the inaugural 355-mile Bordeaux-to-Paris race, shocking everyone by riding through the night while his competitors slept. The top Frenchman finished a disappointing fifth. French cyclists were mortified, so in a bid to restore France's reputation as the most competitive cycling nation on earth, a few months later a French newspaper sponsored a competing club—the Audax Club Parisien—and put on a much longer, 1,200-kilometer (744-mile) event called Paris-Brest-Paris (PBP). It was conveniently limited to French cyclists. (PBP is still going strong today; the granddaddy of the ultracycling circuit, this quadrennial experience is now open to all comers and draws about 4,500 participants from around the world.)

Ever since that first PBP in 1891, the Audax Club Parisien has been happily certifying finishing times in a way that inspires confidence. But PBP is an event, not a race, so the stakes aren't nearly as high. It's also a much simpler affair to manage than RAAM, as the American event is more than four times the length of its French progenitor. To make an all-out transcontinental *race* practical, cyclists had to become much faster, and then someone had to devise credible race rules and a bulletproof approach for certifying finishing times. It took 91 years after that first PBP event for all these pieces to fall into place.

The first hurdle was cleared when *The Guinness Book of World Records* got into the act. In 1939 a Brit named Tommy Godwin pedaled 75,000 miles (three times around the world) in a single year. Godwin averaged more than 200 miles per day, riding day and night through all kinds of weather for 12 to 16 hours each day. At year's end he kept riding until he reached an even 100,000 miles, which he did in 500 days. Both marks were certified by Guinness World Records and remain unmatched today (Guinness won't recognize any attempts to break them, claiming they'd be too dangerous).

After Godwin's feat, there were some sporadic, time-certified transcontinental crossings over the next few decades. In 1972, Briton Peter Duker cycled from Santa Monica to New York, a crossing that was certified at a little over 18 days. The following year, American Paul Cornish set a transcontinental record that was also certified by Guinness World Records at 13 days, five hours, and 20 minutes.

Cyclists were now completing the crossing rapidly enough that the idea of a repeatable race became plausible. In 1976, John Marino, a middle-aged former college baseball player who had cycled throughout Europe as a young man, stumbled on Cornish's record while paging through *Guinness* trying to find a sport he could take up to burn off a few pounds. Audaciously, Marino set his sights on besting Cornish's 13-day record, and this launched him on a journey that would change his life forever.

Transforming his neglected body into a cycling powerhouse, Marino achieved his goal two years later. He was hooked, and ultradistance cycling became his undying passion. Under Marino's sure hand, an ultradistance record certification body was formed (now the UltraMarathon Cycling Association), and the blueprint and ground rules for the first transcontinental bike race fell into place by 1981.

The inaugural Great American Bike Race took place the following year with a four-man field recruited by and including John Marino, as well as superstar Olympic cyclist John Howard, seasoned ultracyclist Lon Haldeman, and Michael Shermer, a relative newcomer to the sport. Haldeman won going away, vanquishing even the formidable Howard.

Being a clever and confident promoter, Marino had convinced ABC's *Wide World of Sports* to film this first race for the world to see. The network did an inspired job, condensing the 12-day affair into an emotionally powerful broadcast and winning an Emmy for its efforts. Despite the fact that the race wasn't exactly spectator-friendly and couldn't be wrapped in a nice, glamorous package like the Tour de France, ABC proved it was possible to turn a long and sometimes ghoulish event into a compelling story about human perseverance.

Following some financial and legal hiccups, the Great American Bike Race evolved into the Race Across America in 1983, with a larger field and another ABC film crew on hand to broadcast the action. ABC's television audience was drawn by the monstrous challenge that RAAM represented, and was held spellbound by the racers' determination. Ultracycling had finally crossed into the mainstream, and the early races didn't disappoint. In 1984 the first two women contestants, Shelby Hayden-Clifton and Pat Hines, actually sprinted to the finish line, tied after more than 12 days and nights on the road. In 1985, Jonathan Boyer, a cocky ProTour stage racer and the first American ever to compete in the Tour de France, strutted onto the ultracycling stage, bringing an edge to a largely polite and decorous amateur sport. Like Howard a few years prior, Boyer was certain he could win RAAM thanks to his background in road racing, and he trashed ultracyclists as non-athletic plodders.

Even today ProTour cyclists consider ultradistance racers to be a lesser breed—just a bunch of kooky outcasts who could never make it on the pro circuit. So Boyer's challenge was an irresistible television moment, and again ABC televised the race. The field had swelled to 25 starters and Boyer beat them all, finishing utterly spent but validated in front of 1,000 cheering spectators. At one point during the race he almost relinquished his lead, as he had been sleeping a lot more than his competitors, then racing faster while on the bike. To eke out his victory, he was forced to ditch his race plan and go with hardly any sleep during the last third of the race. He was humbled by his experience and never trash-talked the ultra crowd again.

Boyer's win changed ultracycling forever. RAAM pioneer Michael Shermer explained that, "Boyer changed RAAM from an ultramarathon grind with a slow-as-you-go pace to an almost nonstop race where speed had become a prerequisite to winning."

AFTER BOYER'S 1985 PERFORMANCE CAPTURED THE ATTENTION of mainstream sports fans, ABC came back the following year and chronicled the effort of winner Pete Penseyres, who set an average speed record that still stands (though racers point out the course is more arduous today). ABC garnered another Emmy for its 1986 broadcast, but by then the economics of sports television had changed, and big, one-off productions were being shunned by the networks. When the economy softened, ABC discontinued its coverage.

After that, RAAM faded from popular view. In subsequent years it remained an almost entirely American pursuit enjoyed by an eccentric fringe who toiled in obscurity. Then in 1987 an Olympic-caliber road racer from Austria named Franz Spilauer came out of nowhere and finished third in his rookie attempt, using the same approach Boyer had pioneered two years earlier. "The only difference between me and other RAAM racers is my experience as a road racer in Europe," Spilauer explained. "I know...the proper time to attack." Because Spilauer was a respected road racer, elite European cyclists finally took notice of RAAM. The time for politesse and decorum had passed.

Spilauer returned to Austria, released a book and film documentary about his experience, and trained hard for his return the following year. He triumphed the second time around, pulling ahead of two others by banking sleep and attacking them late in the race—at just the right moment— somewhere in West Virginia.

But Spilauer's 1988 victory wasn't without international intrigue. When the battle for race leadership reached a crescendo in Ohio, Spilauer accused American RAAM officials of unfairly penalizing him for minor infractions, trying to fix the race in favor of his American rival, Rob Templin. Templin hurled cheating accusations of his own, charging that Spilauer had drafted his follow-vehicle. In the end, Spilauer vanquished Templin by more than seven hours, so their dispute became moot.

As European interest in RAAM grew, the race fell into obscurity at home, despite some incredible home-grown achievements. A woman named Seana Hogan piled up six victories during that time, and Floridian Rob Kish began his streak of 17 straight RAAM races without a single DNF ("did not finish"). But news of their exploits never made it outside the tightly knit ultracycling community.

Perhaps this was because racers like Kish didn't care to be discovered. Many of the early RAAM stars were introverted at best and reclusive at worst. Kish, for example, lived in anonymity in Florida. He rarely mixed with other ultracyclists and avoided pre-race festivities. He almost never raced in events other than RAAM and didn't do much to help raise the visibility of his sport. His living arrangements were unique, too: he and his wife tended more than 40 animals—including pigs, sheep, horses, and peacocks—which they rented out as "extras" in movies.

Then along came a dashing and publicity-hungry Austrian named Wolfgang Fasching, and he changed everything. Fasching won RAAM in 1997 and went on to notch two more championships, playing a pivotal role in the evolution of the race. He was a compelling and telegenic personality as well as an author, adventurer, and motivational speaker, so Austrian television jumped at the chance to chronicle his RAAM triumphs. Race organizers had finally found a compelling figurehead to play the role that race creator Haldeman had once played. The publicity that Fasching garnered was the spark that began the European onslaught, and only two Americans have won RAAM since.

ONCE THEY LANDED AT LAX ABOUT TWO WEEKS BEFORE the start of the 2009 race, the European contenders didn't linger long in Los Angeles. As soon as they set foot on the ground, the reality of the approaching event obliterated any interest in the bright lights of Hollywood.

Each man followed a similar routine, setting up shop in the desert valleys southeast of Los Angeles to begin his final training phase. Each brought a crew of 10 or more, and most brought professional videographers to capture the action. Crew members stayed busy during this time. They readied their vehicles, staged and tested bikes and equipment, honed their race plans, and supported their racers during their long, hot training rides in the scorching desert.

At home the top European ultracyclists trained and competed in temperate climates, so they needed to shock their systems into accepting the oven-like conditions they face during the first few days of the race. While their crews worked, the cyclists rode throughout the desert. The local townspeople who spotted these Europeans riding their fancy bikes in 100-degree temperatures just shook their heads as they sped by in the comfort of their air conditioned automobiles.

As in years past, Marko Baloh and his team camped out in a Palm Springs motel days before the race. Baloh, who always keeps his family close, was enjoying having his wife and kids along for this great adventure. "They help me go faster," he said. "I couldn't do it without them." Baloh did his training rides in the heat of the day, starting on the desert floor and climbing up the coastal range to the west. In the late afternoons, after Baloh had his massage and shower, Team Baloh relaxed by the motel pool and marveled at how the setting sun played off the jagged face of Mount San Jacinto, a 10,000-foot behemoth that towered above them. They all wore matching black "Marko Baloh" T-shirts, and every once in a while an American guest would hear them speaking in Slovenian and ask, "Are you here for a soccer match?" It was challenging explaining what they were up to, and their Slovenian accents didn't make it any easier.

Irma, Baloh's wife and loyal crew member, had her laptop with her poolside each evening, as it was her job to post daily updates on Baloh's website for his fans back home. While she typed, she kept one eye on her children as they splashed one another in the water. It was a pastoral scene—grownups lounging and bantering, kids frolicking in the pool, everybody looking relaxed, everything under control. But the adults were on edge; they knew they were about to be tested, and few of them knew exactly how.

A couple of Baloh's crew members were getting their first tastes of the U.S. Among these was Špela, Baloh's young, enthusiastic nutritionist. She was awestruck by how different the Mojave Desert was from her verdant Slovenia. She might as well have been on the moon. Bracing herself for what was to come, Špela suspected that her feeling of disequilibrium would stick with her for the duration.

Jure Robič, the fearsome king of ultracycling, was in town, too. The defending champion had visited Southern California just a few months earlier for his annual winter training camp. Since he had dominated RAAM for years now, Robič was known to a handful of professional American road racers who call Southern California home. During his winter trip, he sought out a few of them to ride with. Their plan this February morning was to meet for a long day in the saddle at Nytro, a popular bike shop on the coast just north of San Diego. The Americans were eager to test the Slovenian, curious to see if the 44-year-old Robič could keep pace with pros in their early thirties who had just completed the prestigious Tour of California.

As they began their ride eastward from the coast up to 6,000-foot Palomar Mountain and back, they faced a 120-mile day in the saddle. It was just Robič and four much younger American pros. The five of them stuck together until the nasty 12-mile Palomar climb, and as the road steepened and the switchbacks kicked in, the weaker ones began slipping back, leaving only David Zabriskie and Robič to race each other to the top. At 30 years old, Zabriskie was one of the most successful American cyclists on the pro circuit. He had even worn the coveted leader's jersey for three consecutive stages during the 2005 Tour de France. But none of this mattered to Robič. In the final push to the snow-capped Palomar summit, Robič dropped Zabriskie and arrived first.

Retelling the story, Robič flashed a sly smile. "Zabriskie congratulated me and said I was an animal," he said. "When we finished our ride, the other guys couldn't believe my age." Robič was accustomed to achieving the impossible. In his 2003 RAAM debut he found himself in third place, far behind second-place rider Rob Kish with only eight hours of racing to go (about 125 miles). Robič somehow managed to pass Kish to finish as the runner-up. "I went into a trance, and I felt no pain," he said. "I started going like a maniac. All I knew was that I had to dig deeper. I had to prove to everybody I was a decent guy."

That year Robič was in danger of losing more than the race; in his mind, he came dangerously close to losing his wife. As a member of his crew, Petra had watched Robič unravel during the final few days of the race—ranting, raving, hallucinating, and losing his mind. As he pushed himself up the leader board, his suffering became so acute that Robič said he would have put a gun to his head if he had had one. Petra was scared of the animal her husband had become, and Robič knew it. In his foggy brain, he thought if he finished strong everything would be all right again.

Golden boy Christoph Strasser, the zealous young Austrian, was the first of the European favorites to arrive in the California desert in June. The ambitious upstart knew he needed the extra time since he'd never raced in desert conditions before. Plus, he was eager to get a taste of the U.S. and to share an adventure with his friends.

He could hardly believe he had made it this far. He had worked hard to secure the sponsorships, make his plans, and do the training. Now he was plying the dusty roads of the Mojave Desert, far, far away from the alpine village he called home.

The year before, Strasser didn't think he would ever make it to RAAM. When he unexpectedly became the youngest ever to win the ultracycling world championship in 2007, he thought he'd be ready for RAAM that next year. But overconfidence led him to train too hard, and he learned a bitter lesson. "Two weeks before my title defense I felt tired, I was sick with a fever, and I had a stomach flu," he said. "I quit at the halfway point. I was cold, and I finished the first half of the race six hours slower than the previous year. After my withdrawal, I put the bike away and reflected on what I wanted to do next."

Following a self-imposed cooling-off period, he came back wiser and trained smarter. Now he was finally in Southern California. He handicapped his prospects with humility, but deep down he knew he had it in him to do very, very well.

Strasser's training plan called for riding the first 500 miles of the course from the coast all the way to Flagstaff, Arizona, cycling eastward over the coastal range, then through the desert, and finally up the formidable slopes of the central Arizona mountains. During his first encounter with desert heat, Strasser was able to fine-tune his techniques for staying cool. He wondered how difficult it was going to be to cross this foreboding terrain under race conditions.

After his long training ride into Arizona, Team Strasser decamped to Borrego Springs, a desert hamlet along the race route a few hours east of San Diego, and continued cycling. During their downtime Strasser and his young crew mates goofed off, listened to music, and took in the rugged beauty of the desert. They were having the time of their lives and bonding nicely as a team. One of Strasser's crew members was a professional photographer, and he kept their friends in Austria updated by posting his most picturesque shots on Strasser's blog. In the photos, everybody on Team Strasser is beaming.

About a week before the race was set to start, Strasser was on his bike somewhere north of Borrego Springs when he literally bumped into Baloh in the middle of the Mojave Desert. The two men knew each other from the European racing circuit, so they stopped to share some pleasantries and then continued in opposite directions.

People speculated that the Swiss challenger Dani Wyss was also training somewhere in the desert. He showed up at the starting line with deep tan lines that could only have come from spending time in the sun, as did the determined Gerhard Gulewicz and Franz Preihs, two of Strasser's countrymen. The deserts of California were swarming with top European ultracyclists a week before the start, all dreaming of how it would feel to cross the Annapolis finish line in first place on a pleasantly cool evening a few weeks hence.

3

The Deepest Field Ever

Boulder, Colorado, late May

Fred Boethling was feeling proud and justified as his eyes scanned the roster sheet for the 2009 race. The president and owner of RAAM was sitting in his Boulder, Colorado, race headquarters making final arrangements a few weeks before the start of the event. Boethling had been hard at work rebuilding the RAAM franchise ever since he had acquired it in 2006, just months after becoming its oldest solo finisher at the age of 61.

Before Boethling stepped in, RAAM was losing money and the previous owners were considering mothballing it. As an ultracyclist with a strong business background, Boethling was an ideal savoir. RAAM had turned Boethling's life around, so he was eager to pay back the favor. He explained that after a cancer diagnosis at the age of 52, "I made a list of things I wanted to do while I still could. I had raced bicycles as a young man and high on that list was competing in RAAM. I hadn't ridden in years, had put on weight, and knew I needed to get with the program." He triumphed in solo RAAM nine years later and his finishing time set a record for the 60-and-over age group that still stands.

Today Boethling is a compact, powerfully built 64-year-old with a balding head and a round, youthful face. He's a self-described "lifelong adventurer," filling his leisure hours with skiing, mountaineering, river-running, and cycling. In quieter moments he's an avid reader, music lover, and a wine connoisseur. Boethling is one of those guys who excels at just about everything he does, and he does a lot of things. He's smart as can be, and since he's been a business executive for decades, he has gravitas. People respect him, and as a result he's built a talented team to shepherd RAAM forward. Every so often, in the middle of saying something important, Boethling will flash his goofy sense of humor. After beating cancer, he is most of all a man who wants to enjoy life.

Before Boethling took control of RAAM, the race had been run out of a shoe box. Most of the know-how was in the heads of its previous owners, two ultracyclists who ran the event like a hobby. He knew he had a major project on his hands, and he expected it would take a couple of years to put RAAM on the right path. He was one of the few people on the planet who had the time, motivation, and expertise to get the job done.

Boethling had been the CEO of a small company before he bought the race, but RAAM gradually took over his workdays. It was no longer his avocation; promoting the race became his personal crusade. The strength of the 2009 field was proof that Boethling was headed in the right direction. "This is the deepest solo field in years—maybe ever," he remarked. "The men's field, the women's field, everyone. It's going to be an exciting race."

RAAM insiders like Boethling typically divide the solo field into three groups: the rookies (men and women), race veterans (men and women), and the race favorites (all European men in 2009). Each group experiences the race in vastly different ways.

The Rookies

There's no clear road map for how a solo racer should prepare for his first RAAM. First-time marathoners or aspiring Ironman triathletes have access to a vast cottage industry of how-to books and coaching programs. But once an endurance race moves from "long" to "ultra-long," participants enter a realm where advice is hard to come by and often contradictory. In addition, RAAM presents a spectacular number of challenges that a rookie racer must master quickly. Finances, crew recruitment, training regimens, equipment selection, logistics—any of these factors can bring the whole enterprise crashing down before it even begins. "I spent hours on the phone with the old timers, trying to learn everything I could about the race," explained Ben Popp, one of 2009's most fastidious rookies.

Of course, training for RAAM is the biggest hurdle. In the Tour de France, a racer is practically assured a top spot on the leader board if he can achieve a power-to-weight ratio of 6.7 watts per kilo. Only a handful of race favorites manage to do this, but since power-to-weight is such an important determinant, everybody tries. After months of training, a Tour de France racer will starve himself in the days before the race in order to goose his ratio as close as possible to the magic 6.7 threshold. When a bike racer drops a few pounds right before a big event it's called "stepping out on the razor." As he balances on a razor's edge between glory and catastrophe, his emaciated, finely tuned body becomes so vulnerable to infection that he avoids shaking hands, presses elevator buttons with his elbows, and lets others turn door knobs for him.

Things aren't nearly as clear-cut in RAAM. An eye-popping power-to-weight ratio is nice to have, but it's insufficient to ensure success. ProTour cyclists train for the Tour de France with scientific precision, but preparing for RAAM is more like a medical experiment gone wild.

Then there's the race itself, an ordeal that is impossible to simulate during training. Most obviously, it's impossible to prepare oneself for racing 3,000 miles practically nonstop without actually doing it. RAAM contestants rarely go longer than 700 miles at a time in training, and some struggle to fit in one 500-mile training ride prior to their first race (about 36 hours of nonstop cycling). The shock of racing beyond even two days is impossible to describe to somebody who hasn't experienced it.

Most rookies arrive at the starting line having already raced RAAM on a two- or four-person team. But racing RAAM solo is an entirely different beast. Even two-man RAAM pales in comparison. Rookie Kevin Kaiser, a low-key pharmacist from Georgia, had done RAAM as part of a two-man team in 2008, when he and his partner became the first ever to go the entire distance on fixed-gear bikes—machines where the pedals are directly connected to the rear axle and rotate at the same speed, without the capacity to shift gears or coast. Even hard-core cyclists have a difficult time comprehending this immensely difficult feat.

Despite his prior triumph, Kaiser explained that, "Two-man RAAM was all about having fun. Even getting the crew together was a breeze, because you have two sets of friends to draw from." Then he paused and lowered his voice. "I'm usually optimistic, but lately I'm more scared of solo RAAM than anything else," he said. "Scared about biting off more than I can chew. This race frightens me, it really does."

Like many other elite cyclists, Kaiser does not stand out in a crowd. The slender 41-year-old is of average height and build, and when you meet him he doesn't blaze with energy like some of the other competitors. Kaiser is a reserved, taciturn man who lets his cycling accomplishments speak for themselves. Chit-chat doesn't come naturally, and he prefers answering questions in short, declarative sentences. For him, admitting to feeling afraid was a big deal.

As a rookie, Kaiser brought an enormous amount of ultracycling experience to his solo debut. The year before his fixed-gear attempt, he had taken part in a RAAM simulation tour led by two RAAM pioneers from the 1980s, cycling across the U.S. in 17 days (he would need to go almost twice as fast during the actual race). Previously, Kaiser had completed the 744-mile Paris-Brest-Paris ride, as well its equally long cousin, Boston-Montreal-Boston.

And that wasn't all. Kaiser is a dedicated student of RAAM who had pored over every aspect of race strategy before his solo debut. He knew the race's history better than most, and he had studied the field more carefully than anyone else.

But all his experience and planning didn't ward off the feeling of dread as race day grew near. When I asked Kaiser a few weeks before the race what he feared most about his solo debut, a look of concern swept across his otherwise placid face. Kaiser knew his strengths and weaknesses, and cycling in desert heat was definitely a weakness. "Falling apart 200 miles into the ride," he whispered as his brown eyes opened wide. "You know, many great athletes have done it. If I blow up in the desert it might psychologically kill me."

Kaiser was one of 14 first-timers in this year's race. He would be racing for rookie of the year honors, hoping to be the first of the bunch to cross the line in Annapolis.

Like Kaiser, Ben Popp was another American who had prepared meticulously for his rookie attempt. But that's where the similarities end. Popp is an affable, 35-year-old stay-at-home dad and part-time athletic coach who grew up in Minnesota competing as a Nordic skier. He has the small, slender body of a cyclist who excels at climbing. When this enthusiastic, loquacious man speaks, the words gush in three directions at once before settling on the point he's making.

When he wasn't cycling or caring for his twin toddlers, Popp burned off what remained of his abundant energy by hashing out his RAAM race plan. He was determined not to leave anything to chance.

Popp has always been an exacting person. For example, Popp explains that before he goes to bed, he likes to set the table for the twins' breakfast in a particular way: their cereal bowls go here, their cups go there, and so on. On nights when he's busy, his wife Megan sets the table instead. This usually drives Popp around the bend; she never seems to get the table organized the way he likes it.

Popp is even more finicky about his bicycles, dialing in his equipment with the precision of a diamond cutter: seat height, stem length, saddle angle, cleat position, wheel selection, gearing ratios—he sweats every detail. He approached his RAAM preparation with this same care, and like Kaiser, Popp became an avid student of the race.

In his early twenties, Popp crewed for his father-in-law Bob Mackie when Mackie raced two-man RAAM. Popp also sought out ultracycling legends Lon Haldeman and Allen Larsen for their advice on how to survive the event, keeping them on the phone for hours. Also like Kaiser, Popp had raced twice on a two-man team himself, and he had digested and analyzed every aspect of the race. But unlike Kaiser, because of all his planning, Popp arrived in Oceanside feeling confident that his race plan was bulletproof.

Very few rookies make a solo attempt without having raced RAAM as part of a team. This year, young Austrian phenom Christoph Strasser was attempting this audacious feat. Although just 26, Strasser was already a formidable ultradistance cyclist, and he had trained his sights on solo RAAM longer than any other rookie. "RAAM has been on my mind since I was 15," he said. "But it wasn't until I won the ultracycling world championship in 2007 that I realized maybe RAAM was a possibility for me. Before that, my attitude was, 'Do the best you can and have fun.'"

After winning the world championship, Strasser dedicated himself to training for RAAM. But it never felt like work to him. "I don't feel I sacrifice much of anything in pursuing this sport," he told me a week before the race as we sat in a ramshackle restaurant on a dusty desert road near his training camp in Borrego Springs. "My life and my sport are integrated. I might not be able to party with my friends 11 months of the year, but since I don't drink anyway, this isn't a big loss for me." Strasser is a passionate man who craves love and friendship, but he doesn't give himself much space for frivolous socializing.

Like Strasser, the South African über-athlete Michele Santilhano was one of a handful of rookies who had never raced two-person RAAM before. She had competed on a four-person team the prior year, but sharing the load with three others is a far cry from what she was up against now. And while rookie Strasser had already notched a big ultracycling win, Santilhano's ultracycling credentials didn't place her at the pinnacle of the sport. She knew she was facing the biggest challenge of her storied athletic career. Thanks to her ultradistance running and swimming successes, she knew she had the mental toughness to persevere. She had cemented her reputation for grit when she swam the English Channel in a raging storm, struggling for 19 hours and feeling so nauseated she was able to consume only mint tea and bananas for fuel.

But her cycling endurance was untested at anything close to this distance. She felt unsure and tentative throughout her RAAM training. Like Kaiser, this race scared her. Her confidence shaken and distrustful of her intuition, she lacked the self-assurance to manage her own training program and develop her own race plan.

Santilhano suffered from attention deficit hyperactivity disorder as a child, which destroyed her self-esteem and isolated her socially. She felt lost and suicidal during her teenage years. At 17 she stumbled into adventure racing, and to this day she credits sports with saving her life. She thinks all the training and racing somehow resets her brain chemistry, flooding her system with endorphins that squelch the dark feelings lurking below the surface.

You can still see some of her youthful troubles in Santilhano today. Sometimes she seems tentative and maddeningly self-critical, and other times you can sense her deep strength. Santilhano is a contemplative, philosophical person. When she has something important to say, she speaks slowly and seriously with long pauses between words, as if she were having a debate with herself before selecting the perfect ones.

She might have been tentative about RAAM, but as a Baptist, she knew she could always pray for salvation if she got in trouble on the road. Santilhano believes that through her passion for sport, she is able to express her love for God. She hoped this "fire deep inside me" would carry her through.

The Veterans

The veterans all had one thing on their minds: how to improve on their previous RAAM results. Everybody who returns to the race is driven by this compulsion. In 2009 there were 14 returning veterans in the field of 28 soloists, most of them Europeans. American veteran Janet Christiansen was back for her second consecutive year. In fact, she was the only one in the women's field who had raced solo RAAM before. Because of her experience in 2008, she had more to prove than most returning veterans.

Christiansen is a gangly, fair-skinned, 48-year-old software engineer who has that slightly frumpy, nerdy look that screams "techie" from a mile away. But this hard-core endurance athlete doesn't sit at a computer terminal 80 hours a week. Christiansen was a bike racer in the 1980s and become a podium-finishing Ironman triathlete in the 1990s, developing a reputation for prodigious physical stamina and toughness. Her ultracycling résumé is filled with impressive results, including first- and second-place finishes in several 500-mile races, such as the Furnace Creek 508 where she once placed third overall, beating all but two of the men. She also garnered a first-place finish in the Hoodoo 500 (where she raced unsupported), and after that she helped set a course record for a two-woman RAAM team.

I had trouble getting a read on Christiansen when I first met her. With a clever, sarcastic sense of humor, it's hard to tell if she's making a serious point or trying to pull your leg. Once she grows comfortable with you, Christiansen's goofy sense of humor is easier to gauge. This is a woman who loves Broadway show tunes and movie scores, and who, in her solo RAAM debut, donned cycling shoes with red sequins in Kansas, paying homage to *The Wizard of Oz* even in the throes of the race.

After her sense of humor, the second thing I noticed about Christiansen was how serious she is about her sport. As an engineer, she brings a fact-based, analytical approach to ultracycling, always tinkering and musing about how to make her performance a tiny bit better. But this didn't help her in the 2008 RAAM.

In spite of her *Wizard of Oz* high jinks, Christiansen suffered a tragic DNF, dropping out almost within sight of the finish line after having raced her heart out for 2,750 miles. As an experienced endurance athlete, Christiansen knew from the beginning she was in trouble. She had arrived in Oceanside that year overtrained and burned out. As the starting gun went off, she was already thinking, *Boy, my legs are dead.*

With only 250 miles left, Christiansen could almost smell the Atlantic Ocean after 12 days of punishing racing. But every inch of her journey had been torture, and she was a broken woman. She had abandoned her sense of humor hundreds of miles earlier. That first RAAM bid had ripped her asunder. "I just got to that point—you couldn't tell me, 'C'mon Janet, get back on your bike and keep going,'" she told me. "One of the crew said, 'I can't bear to watch this anymore,' and just gave me a big hug, and at that moment my spirits just—that was it, it was over." Within hours of quitting the race, even in the depths of her misery, Christiansen knew she would return.

Christiansen changed it up preparing for the 2009 race. Physically, she cut down her training mileage; mentally, she learned to control her negative thoughts when something started hurting. "This year, I began my toughest training rides thinking about all the things that were going well, all the things that were good," she said. "Then when one or two things started going wrong—a pain here or there—I reminded myself about the good things."

But the most important change she made was to commit to having more fun during the race, and that went for everybody. She worked to find crew members who could be as silly, wacky, and witty as she was. She was happy with the composition of her crew. This year Christiansen wanted to cycle across the country on the power of laughter.

The Race Favorites

The race favorites in 2009 were all Europeans, and they were all men. No woman was expected to crack the top five or even top 10 finishers, nor were any Americans expected to finish on the podium. The six European favorites all knew one another and had raced each other in the past. There were four German-speakers in the bunch: three Austrians (young Strasser, bad boy Preihs, and determined Gulewicz) and one Swiss (the cool-headed Wyss). After that came the two Slovenians: defending champion Robič and the doting dad Baloh.

Hailing from a tiny country with a population about equal to Houston or Paris, Robič and Baloh had known each other longer than anybody else in the field. Slovenia is a sports-crazed nation of 2 million inhabitants that has spawned more than its fair share of elite cyclists since it won independence from a disintegrating Yugoslavia in 1991. Ultracycling is modestly popular in Slovenia—where it is covered alongside other more traditional sports by mainstream media outlets—and it generates justifiable national pride. Robič was a bona fide celebrity and national hero back home. He was crowned Slovenian of the Year in 2004, catapulting both himself and his sport into mainstream consciousness there, as well as in neighboring countries like Austria. Baloh lives in Robič's shadow, but even he attracts Slovenian media attention and local sponsors.

Though they're fierce rivals on the road, the two men have been friends for almost 20 years. Their relationship is an intriguing one; they admire each other immensely, but their personalities couldn't be more different. Baloh is a full-time civil servant and devoted father of three known for his consistency, humility, and equipoise under pressure. Robič was a loving father as well, but that's where the similarities end. Robič lived on the edge, always pushing his personal limits and thriving on the drama that ensues. Fiery and intense, he clearly enjoyed dramatizing the already dramatic highlights and low points in his life.

Baloh had beaten Robič in a head-to-head race years ago, but it was Robič who appeared on television that evening, a more telegenic and compelling figure. Baloh sometimes feels exasperated by how much harder he works to attract attention and sponsorships, and he's quick to point out that Robič doesn't have a "day job" like he does—Robič is employed by the army as a full-time athlete. But always the gentleman, Baloh doesn't let this affect their friendship.

As an example of their significant bond, Baloh told me a story about the unwitting role Robič played in helping him break the 24-hour world outdoor track record, a revered ultracycling achievement that landed Baloh in *Guinness World Records* and ranks as his proudest athletic accomplishment.

Baloh was going strong and on record pace after 18 hours on the track that evening in 2006, but then he hit a rough patch that slowed him down and threatened to derail his effort. A short while later, Baloh looked up from the head-down crouch of his time-trial position and noticed that Robič had strolled onto the track's infield to watch the final few hours of his friend's attempt. Baloh was cheered by his presence, and he credits Robič with helping him increase his pace for those final, crucial hours. With 30 minutes to go before his 24 hours expired, Baloh smashed through the previous distance record. He wound up covering a staggering 553 miles, a new high-water mark for ultradistance cycling. "What lifted me up was Jure's acknowledgement of my…my…greatness," Baloh admitted, pausing briefly before this humble man could squeeze out that final word.

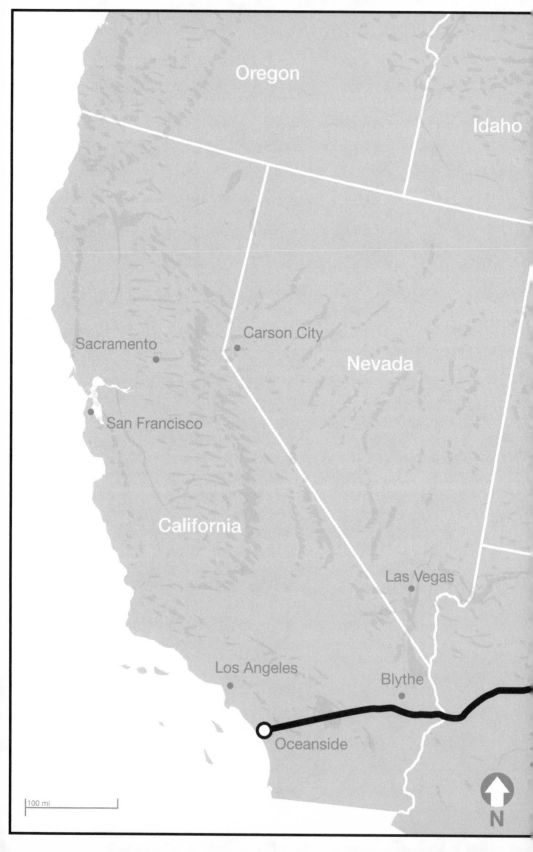

4

Day One: Rolling

Oceanside Pier, June 16 and 17, 12:00 PM Pacific Time

There were actually two starting days for RAAM soloists. The four solo women set off from the Oceanside Pier at noon on June 16. As the men's field assembled at the starting line on June 17, the women were already 350 miles down the road in Congress, Arizona, having raced all night through the desert and then well into the next day.[*]

About an hour before the start of the women's race, the racers' support vehicles delivered them to the staging area. A small crowd of well-wishers, crew members, and race personnel milled about hoping to get in a quick word of encouragement. Each woman sat astride her bicycle in a different part of the staging area, surrounded by crew members and fans. RAAM media staffers buzzed about, pointing their microphones and video cameras, asking each racer that same question they'd ask the men the next day: "How are you feeling?" Two other RAAM representatives were there: Fred Boethling, the dapper and low-key president, and Jake Zhrmal, the all-important race director. Zhrmal's anxious, the-world-is-on-my-shoulders look gave people comfort that every detail of this complicated race was under control.

These officials greeted each racer and then clambered onto a stage positioned in front of the starting line banners. They both dispensed some

---

[*] The women's field and the men over 60 started 24 hours ahead of the rest of the solo men's field and had an extra 21 hours to officially complete the race. This way, everybody would reach the finish line around the same time, since the women and older men would merge with the men's field as the race progressed.

pleasantries, and then the women's field was introduced. As each racer's name was called, she rolled up to the starting line, stopped, and stared straight ahead, lost in thought.

For several years in a row the female division had boasted only one or two starters, so 2009 was a bumper crop. The race organizers hoped that a few of them would finish officially. It had been a while since any woman had.

THE LAST OFFICIAL FEMALE FINISHER had been elite triathlete turned ultracyclist Shanna Armstrong back in 2006. The next year all five female starters DNF'd, and in 2008 two more did. One problem was that the women simply missed the time cutoffs, which are only 7 percent longer than the men's. Any woman crossing after that is officially disqualified.

Women used to regularly place in the top 10 overall, and years ago some even cracked the top five. Nobody had a good explanation for why things had changed. Perhaps it was because the early women pioneers weren't mentoring the next generation of female ultracyclists well enough; only 26 women have ever finished the race, and few of the early ones remain involved in the sport.

The golden age for the women was 1985 to 1997, when Susan Nortorangelo, Shelby Hayden-Clifton, Elaine Mariolle, Seana Hogan, and Muffy Ritz finished in the top five overall. Hogan twice accomplished this feat. With six victories (compared to Robič's four), she's recognized as the greatest female RAAM champion ever. Her women's finishing record of nine days, four hours, and 32 minutes still stands today. That mark would have won the event outright eight times in the race's history.

In 1993, Hogan set out to beat the men—all of them—and she did just that. She came across the line first on the road, though she and the rest of the women had started well before the men. If they'd started at the same time, Hogan would have still placed third, just ahead of another woman who was only an hour back, former Olympian Muffy Ritz, a legend in her own right. In 1997, Hogan was promised a $25,000 prize if she beat all the men. She led that race for the first 1,200 miles, eventually finishing third overall. "I have no mechanism to pee from the bike," she said. "Thus, I lose four minutes each time I have to go, which is quite often." Despite being slowed by nature breaks, the amazing Seana Hogan had given the men a run for their money.

JANET CHRISTIANSEN KNEW THIS HISTORY WELL. Poised at the starting line, the veteran seemed relaxed, confident, and even a bit feisty. She chose to shade her eyes with a pair of bright-pink cycling glasses, as if to announce she expected to be the center of attention.

Thanks to her sparkling athletic résumé, many insiders picked the South African Michele Santilhano to win the women's race even though she was racing solo RAAM for the first time. But as she approached the starting line, Santilhano looked edgy. She simply wasn't sure she had her nutrition nailed down, her sleep plan dialed in, and the crew dynamics sorted out. And she was worried about making the cutoff times that had bedeviled so many women over the years.

The two remaining women were also race rookies. There was Ann Wooldridge, a 50-year-old Briton aiming to be the oldest woman ever to finish. Like Christiansen, Wooldridge was a veteran ultracyclist with many ultracycling victories, including a course record for the Sebring 24-hour race that has stood for years.

Wooldridge also looked nervous at the starting line. She was scowling, keeping to herself, and avoiding eye contact. Was that just her way of psyching herself up? Only time would tell.

The fourth woman was the enigmatic Daniela Genovesi, a 41-year-old Brazilian personal trainer with an unusual athletic bio for RAAM: she was a jiujitsu world champion. She had done some multiday mountain bike races, but the mother of three was untested as an ultracyclist, so nobody really knew what she had in her.

Still, Genovesi seemed well-financed, sporting a large crew and a fleet of fancy support vehicles plastered with dozens of splashy sponsors' logos. At the starting line, this petite, vivacious woman who didn't speak much English simply flashed her million-dollar smile at everyone as though she didn't have a care in the world.

Once these four women had arrived at the starting line, someone sang the national anthem, then the small crowd counted down in unison. An air horn sounded. Within seconds they had disappeared from sight, and it was once again quiet enough to hear the waves crashing against the pilings of the pier a stone's throw away.

RACERS DREAD THE FIRST DAY OF RAAM more than any other. The Sonoran Desert, like its cousin the Mojave to the north, is one of Mother Nature's cruelest and most feared environments. This first part of the course is a death zone. The scorching heat, desiccating air, and windswept sand produce a discouraging number of DNFs, even among race favorites. So in these first few hours the racers try to find their rhythms, reminding themselves not to go out too fast and not to be carried away by the rush of adrenaline they feel.

The first hours also offer an early gauge of how well crews are working with their riders, as well as a test of crew camaraderie. Problems crop up quickly, and they compound if they aren't solved: missed turns, poor communication, dehydration, heat stroke, and digestive problems all show up early. The racers know that how they respond to these Day One challenges can make or break their race. "We were all nervous, especially our navigator," one crew chief explained. "But by the end of each shift, everybody's confidence really improved."

Within the first hour the women were climbing away from the ocean and over the coastal range. In this short time the temperature had already risen 20 degrees. By late afternoon they dropped down the eastern side of the coastal mountains through the "glass elevator," a dizzying, winding, 4,000-foot plunge into the low deserts of Southern California.

If you've never been on a sheer mountain face thousands of feet above the desert floor, it's a breathtaking sight. The mountains that run along the western flanks of the Sonoran and Mojave Deserts offer plenty of picturesque perches like this. Standing high above ground, you're surrounded by pine trees, chirping birds, and cool breezes. But when you look down at the floor, all you see is a featureless, barren wasteland stretching as far as the eye can see, crisscrossed by a few perfectly straight, desolate roads that look like tiny, white filaments.

As the women descended the glass elevator onto one of these roads, the bone-dry heat hit them like a blast furnace. Suddenly it was well over 100 degrees and the air seemed like it was on fire.

Thanks to a steady, favorable tailwind spiriting them along, so far there hadn't been any catastrophes. The women were settling in and trying to keep cool as they glided past cacti, tumbleweed, and ocotillo on their dusty route across the desert floor. They had covered nearly 150 miles by sunset, and the turquoise waters of the Pacific but a distant memory.

THE NEXT DAY, IT WAS THE MEN'S TURN. Half an hour before the start, they were all in the staging area, each surrounded by his fans. The biggest throng was mighty Robič's. Some of the lesser-known racers had only a few crew members with them to murmur encouragement during the final moments.

After the six European favorites, the rest of the men's field was about evenly split between first-timers and those who'd raced as soloists before. A few were making their third bids, and these stalwarts had set aggressive goals for themselves. Jim Rees was one of them.

Rees is a suave 46-year-old motivational speaker who lives an hour north of London. He doesn't have a lot of formal education, but you'd never know it: Rees is widely read and deeply thoughtful. The most urbane racer in the field, Rees is always transformed by RAAM into a simpler, more primitive being. He had raced four-man RAAM in 2005 and made his first solo bid in 2007. That year he was plagued with hallucinations, digestive issues, and dehydration, but his greatest torture was his failing neck muscles. He rode for several agonizing days with his head lashed to a backpack-like brace; it was the only way he could hold his head up and see the road ahead of him. By the time he had reached the Appalachians, he could barely turn his pedals over. He was a zombie on a bike.

With less than 200 miles to go in his solo RAAM debut, Rees' crew tried letting him down gently. He wasn't going to make the time cutoff; his pace had slowed too much. This news came as a shock to Rees. "I was absolutely *gutted* when my crew didn't think I could finish," he said. "I couldn't believe they had given up on me like that. Obviously they didn't know me well enough." In an instant, he was wide awake and newly motivated. To his crew's amazement, he found untapped reservoirs of energy and upped his speed for the final 200 miles by an additional six miles per hour—an almost unfathomable acceleration that he sustained for more than 15 hours.

He beat the 288-hour time cutoff with less than an hour to spare.

Knowing he could do better, Rees came back the following year confident he would break the British record. This time he brought a chiropractor along for his neck, closely monitored his electrolyte intake, and kept his time "fiddling around off the bike" to a minimum. He managed to shave almost a full day off his previous year's time, coming over the line ahead of the previous British record. The problem was there was another British man racing that year—a rookie named Mark Pattinson—who came from nowhere to finish second, more than a day and a half ahead of Rees, who still placed a respectable ninth.

Rees was determined to push himself even harder the third time around, now chasing Pattinson's time. But how? He had executed his race plan well the previous year, so where could he pick up the day and a half he needed? Rees came up with the obvious answer—he had to become a faster bike racer. So he hit the gym, dropped some weight, and reduced his training mileage but upped the intensity. "No garbage miles. No through-the-night rides. Only high-quality riding this year," he explained.

As Rees waited for the countdown on a sunny day in Oceanside, he knew he had it in him to race much faster. He also knew that this time, everything had to go perfectly for him to achieve his elusive goal. He hoped his green crew was ready for the challenges ahead.

THE START OF THE MEN'S RACE WAS DIFFERENT FROM THE WOMEN'S. Each man went off individually, one per minute, like a Tour de France time trial. A racer was introduced, and the crowd counted down from 10 as he glided down a ramp and disappeared. So, as they traveled across the continent, each racer carried with him a slightly different starting time.

Nobody paid attention to this detail because by the time riders had raced 3,000 miles, time differences on the road were expected to swamp the time differences at the start. But this year, small technicalities like this one would take on huge importance.

The men dread the first 24 hours as much as the women do, but they face an additional challenge that the women don't: controlling their egos. The men have historically had a harder time pacing themselves through the death zone. Many of them—especially the favorites—begin racing each other hard as soon as the gun sounds.

The Slovenian Jure Robič followed a game plan designed to minimize the risk of blowing up in the death zone, and much of the men's field sought to emulate it. The idea was to ride straight through the first night without sleeping to take advantage of cooler nighttime temperatures. Most racers are too wired to sleep on the first night even if they wanted to. Robič's goal was to race *without stopping* for about 600 miles before taking a much-needed first sleep break around Flagstaff, Arizona, after almost 30 hours in the saddle. (In 2003 a racer named Mark Patten made it almost halfway across the country before taking his first sleep break, but he soon collapsed and didn't finish the race.)

Going without sleep on the first night isn't a big concern. Most ultracyclists enjoy night riding, and some even crave it. They say that something magical happens when the sun goes down and they start riding the "tunnel of light."

Physically, the tunnel of light is the narrow beam cast about 30 feet down the road by spotlights affixed to the front bumper of a rider's follow-vehicle and to his bicycle, angled so that the racer can make out the road surface directly in front of him.

Metaphorically, the tunnel of light is a serene place where the racer feels his entire universe consists only of himself, his bicycle, and his friends in the vehicle behind him.

At night, the riding seems easier. The still of the night offers a calming, soothing respite. The air is cool and sweet. The roads seem better; rough spots that bother racers in the daytime are passed over unnoticed.

To slip along some country road, riding along a bright beam of light that bores its way into the wall of darkness ahead, to listen to the call of owls and the eerie sounds of natural surroundings—this is to feel again the thrills of childhood, when anything seems possible.

THE RACE WAS ON, with all 28 solo racers on the road. Their progress was measured through a series of 53 time stations spaced every 40 to 80 miles throughout the prescribed route from west to east (that's about two and a half to five hours of racing). Time stations are invisible spots along the road, usually situated at a shopping mall parking lot or gas station—convenient to food, facilities, and a pay phone. When a racer reaches a time station he isn't required to stop, but within five minutes the racer's crew must call race headquarters to report the precise time they crossed this invisible line, no matter what time of day or night.

Sometimes, time stations are attended by local cycling enthusiasts who offer the racers a well-deserved greeting and maybe some food or drink. Other times, race officials lurk nearby, enforcing call-in rules. But mostly nobody's there to greet the racers, and there's nothing for them to see.

Once a racer's time station report comes into race headquarters, it's quickly posted to the official RAAM website. Even for the racers and crews out on the course, everybody follows the race time station by time station on the web or by real-time GPS tracking. The racers are too spread out to do it any other way.

Time Station #2 (TS2) was located in a supermarket parking lot on Main Street in Brawley, California, the third-largest town in agricultural Imperial County, situated less than 25 miles from the Mexican border. Brawley is home of the Cattle Call Parade and Rodeo, and there are many more heads of cattle than people living there. Good thing, because it regularly hits 110 degrees in the summer.

Like the women the day before, the men enjoyed favorable tailwinds that pushed them through the desert on their first day. By dusk, the leaders had passed through TS2 and, as expected, the European favorites were out in front.

The young Austrian Strasser blew through first, with the calm and composed Wyss a few minutes back and the dangerous Robič trailing Wyss by only a minute, keeping him in sight. Tweety Bird Baloh wasn't far behind. Austrian powerhouse Gulewicz and tattooed Preihs were right there, too. It wasn't easy going for these European favorites. They were thankful for the wind-aided push, but it was a raunchy 97 degrees as the mean-looking Sonoran Desert sun disappeared over the horizon at TS2.

The favorites started racing each other as soon as the gun went off, averaging 21 miles per hour for the first 143 miles through mountainous terrain and blistering temperatures. Even this early in the race, they couldn't afford to hold anything back.

An American had also started well. At TS2, Christopher Gottwald was a surprising second. Gottwald was a wild card in the race. Similar to his predecessor, the cocky Tour de France racer Jonathan Boyer, this 38-year-old airline pilot came from a road racing background but had a slim-to-nonexistent ultracycling résumé. Gottwald wasn't an acclaimed road cyclist like Boyer and Spilauer had been, never making it past one of Colavita's regional teams, and that was back in the 1990s. Still, road racers had proven their mettle in RAAM before, and here Gottwald was, playing with the big boys.

Farther back in the pack, some racers were already struggling. Even though he was holding back in the death zone, Kevin Kaiser was feeling the effects of the merciless desert heat. Struggling to keep his emotions in check, Kaiser was falling to pieces on the inside. After all that training and planning, his race was already in jeopardy. Near TS3 in Blythe, California, 233 miles into the race in the middle of the first night of racing, Kaiser was having a hard time keeping food down. He stopped a few times, vomited, rested a bit, and carried on at a much slower pace while his concerned crew tried its best to keep his spirits up. He knew the desert would be a killer, and here he was, melting down just like his worst nightmares. Kaiser kept pedaling along in silence, trying not to think about the prospects of an early DNF.

Tony O'Keeffe was also in trouble. A 47-year-old lieutenant colonel in the Canadian Armed Forces, O'Keeffe is all about showing people what is possible. His friends describe him as the most inspirational man they've ever met. O'Keeffe is tall, broad-shouldered, and handsome, and his eyes sparkle and dart around when he talks to you, hinting at the energy bubbling inside. But now, O'Keeffe's eyes were dark pools of foreboding.

As director of cadets at the Royal Military College in Ontario, Canada, O'Keeffe leads Canada's best and brightest. He inspires them, too. He finished solo RAAM in his first try in 2006 after a sensational career as an Ironman and Ultraman triathlete. The Canadian superman was elected to the Canadian Military Sports Hall of Fame while still serving—the only active member of the armed forces ever given this honor. After all his successes, he wasn't accustomed to feeling so weak while racing.

O'Keeffe approached the desert with a lot of confidence for someone who lived and trained north of the border in temperate Ontario. This confidence was surprising, because in his 2006 race O'Keeffe had narrowly avoided catastrophe. That year, his inexperienced crew was mistakenly operating under triathlon rules, which meant no touching their racer and no helping except for handing him water bottles. But RAAM rules aren't as strict. Other RAAM crews worked to keep their riders cool by spraying them with water, draping them with cool towels and ice packs, feeding them popsicles, whatever it took. That year, O'Keeffe got nothing from his crew except severe heat stroke.

This year, O'Keeffe's all-military crew was on it, pulling out all the stops to keep him from overheating. Unfortunately, their efforts had little effect. During the night his buddy and paramedic Dan Bodden administered O'Keeffe's first intravenous saline drip and hoped for the best. O'Keeffe's mental toughness kept him in the game when his body wouldn't. Quitting just wasn't an option.

When he gets in trouble during a race, O'Keeffe repeats an affirmation in his head that goes something like this: *This is going to pass. The legs are going to come around. You've tried to kill them before and you can't.* After enduring a brutal first night, by the end of Day One O'Keeffe's mantra was playing on a continuous loop.* At midnight it was still over 90 degrees, and he was the 15th man on the road.

The desert was also pulverizing Patrick Autissier (Awe-TISS-ee-ay). Autissier is a handsome, blue-eyed 47-year-old French medical researcher who now lives in Boston. His easygoing, kind-hearted personality might be confusing until one notices how intensely his eyes sparkle with energy and zeal. This man is as driven as the others, and his motivating force is curiosity.

Like Rees, Autissier was back for his third race. He knew what to expect and his training had gone well. Autissier is a cerebral man, so his mind was going a mile a minute trying to diagnose what was wrong with him. As he struggled along, he felt deeply grateful for the support he was getting from his crew. Autissier was doing RAAM on a shoestring budget compared to the rest of the field. Team Autissier didn't have a motor home;

---

* Throughout this book, "Day One," "Day Two," and so on begin and end at midnight local time, not on 24-hour intervals from the start of the race at noon PDT. Accordingly, Day One ends 12 hours into the race, at midnight on June 17 for the men, and at midnight on June 16 for the women.

they fielded only two vans. Their transcontinental journey wouldn't be nearly as comfortable as the others', and that weighed heavily on him.

Autissier is one of those big-brained thinkers who might forget he turned the stove on because he's distracted by some aspect of his research. Even during RAAM, he couldn't put his scientific curiosity to rest. He planned on using his body as an immunology experiment during the race, drawing blood periodically and mailing the specimens back to his Boston lab so his colleagues could assess how his immune system was holding up to the rigors of the race.

RAAM is largely a test of will, but willpower is mediated by the body. The struggle between willful minds and brutalized bodies is something that draws researchers each year to study how the racers cope. If a medical researcher proposed subjecting athletes to the conditions cyclists experience during RAAM, he wouldn't be able to get his proposal past his medical ethics department. But since race participants are competing of their own volition, RAAM is an ideal lab for studying the limits of body and mind.

So Autissier was keen to stop and draw blood during the race to help improve science's understanding. Of course, his research project could only last as long as he did. A few weeks before the race, Autissier had come down with the flu and hadn't been able to ride since. At the starting line he was unsure of what he had in his legs. As it turned out, not much.

As soon as the road started tipping up just 21 miles from Oceanside, he found he couldn't settle into a rhythm and plummeted to the very back of the pack. He was exhausted and sweating profusely, his core temperature was soaring, he couldn't keep food down, and he was starting to panic. I caught up with Autissier around this time and found him slumped in a lawn chair in the shade next to his follow-vehicle. I was reticent to approach because I didn't want him to waste energy talking, and I figured he wouldn't want anyone to see him in such bad shape. I was shocked that this mighty athlete had been beaten down so quickly, but then again, this was the desert. Autissier's crew chief Rob hoped that if he could just get his rider through the first 24 hours, everything would be okay.

MEANWHILE, A FEW HUNDRED MILES UP THE ROAD the women had all made it safely through the death zone. The night before, they'd flip-flopped positions based on when they took their first sleep breaks. All four teams were grateful that their first nights had gone so smoothly.

Cycling at night across the open vistas of the southwestern deserts is a uniquely disorienting experience. Since the roads are so straight and the sight distances so long, "You can see the flashing lights on the follow-vehicle of a rider who might be at least an hour ahead of you," writes RAAM star Danny Chew. "It can be very discouraging to see the lights of a far-off town in a valley, and then having it take you like three hours to get there."

As the men looked forward to the cooling respite of their first night in the desert, the women were on their second night, somewhere between TS6 and TS7, having climbed out of the Sonoran Desert and through Arizona's Weaver and Bradshaw mountain ranges. Their first full day of racing had been a tough test. The 100-degree heat was only part of the story. On Day Two, the body and mind begin to comprehend just what they're in for. The mind needs to exert its will on the body, but on Day Two the racer's mind becomes overwhelmed by the magnitude of the challenge ahead; the will fails at just the moment when the body begins protesting. The trick, of course, is to keep the mind strong when the body falters, and vice versa.

Even though South African über-athete Michele Santilhano was still anxious and unsure, her crew chief Adrienne was feeling good about her racer's second day. There had been some stomach issues, but they were working to fine-tune Santilhano's diet, and at that moment her racer was cruising at a steady 16 miles per hour along sweltering desert roads. "It's looking like the tortoise and the hares at this point," Adrienne reported that afternoon. "Michele just keeps it going and the other women rest more and then charge ahead."

As their second night fell, the women were descending the eastern flanks of the Arizona range on their way to Cottonwood, almost 450 miles into the race. They rode through the quaint, historic copper mining town of Jerome in darkness. Nestled in the mountains at 5,200 feet, Jerome was once called the wickedest town in the West. Now this funky tourist destination is part artist colony, part hippie hangout. Too bad the women weren't able to stop there for a quick chai tea or tofu burger.

Christiansen, the lanky American with the sarcastic wit, was still leading the women's race around midnight, pulling ahead of the second-place Genovesi, the vivacious Brazilian with enough energy to light up a bulb from a distance. Christiansen was two hours ahead of her previous year's pace. *What a nice turnaround from last year*, she thought. Earlier in the day she had laid siege to Arizona's 1,800-foot Yarnell Grade, climbing powerfully under a cloudless sky in 105-degree heat. When she reached the top she paused briefly, wiped her brow, and with hands on her hips, deadpanned to her crew, "I hear there's a climb somewhere around here, right?"

Despite how well she had handled the Arizona mountains, two things weighed on Christiansen's mind. First, she had to grudgingly accept that Genovesi was the real deal. Christiansen was starting to build a gap on the unknown Brazilian, but Genovesi had already proven that she could gut it out in murderous conditions.

The second thing on Christiansen's mind was her growing discomfort. By her second nightfall on the road, only 36 hours into her race, she was already feeling the dreaded and unmistakable early signs of saddle sores. This was a worrisome development, because chafing problems usually develop later, the cumulative result of making hundreds of thousands of pedal revolutions while sitting hunched over on a bicycle seat for days at a time.

Saddle sores can appear on the crotch, the genitals, the butt, and the groin. They're made worse by dampness, and they fester and become oozing wounds even if a racer keeps himself spotlessly clean. Every ultracyclist suffers this fate; Christiansen was simply the first afflicted.

Because it was so early in the race, Christiansen and her experienced crew knew that something had to be wrong with her position on the bike, her saddle, her shorts—something. (It had been raining when they climbed up to TS6 in Prescott, Arizona. Could that have been the culprit?) They also knew they had to be quick with their diagnosis. There was no way anyone—even battle-hardened Christiansen—could withstand riding another 2,500 miles in this condition.

AS THE FIRST DAY CLOSED ON THE MEN'S RACE, cool-headed Wyss and maniacal Robič were tied on the road after 12 hours of racing, with each cyclist keeping the other in his sights. Robič's countryman Baloh, young Strasser, and Canadian Peter Oyler were closely bunched only a few miles back. These race leaders were feeling almost giddy thanks to the tailwinds pushing them along.

Gottwald, the American bike racer turned airline pilot who'd been in second place earlier on Day One, was now nowhere to be seen. Unlike the others, he had taken a big, long sleep break that first night, letting most of the field slip past him as he lay comfortably in his air conditioned motor home parked along a forlorn, dusty road somewhere in the California desert. Right now nobody wondered what he was up to because nobody expected him to do much. But Gottwald had a secret plan that would reveal itself much later in the race. He slept soundly now, confident his plan would lead him to glory down the road.

5

Day Two: Digging In

Bradshaw Mountains and the Painted Desert, June 18

As orange wisps painted the edges of the cloudless eastern sky at dawn on Day Two, the leading men prepared to scale the 1,800-foot Yarnell Grade. They pushed over the Bradshaw Mountains and into Arizona's High Desert up a seven-mile climb that reached a demanding 8 percent in spots. The terrain looked like the surface of the moon—a barren, treeless wasteland strewn with boulders the size of refrigerators. Not the kind of road anyone would want their car to overheat on; there's no wireless coverage, water, or shade, and nothing lives there except sagebrush and ocotillo.

The leaders still hadn't slept yet, now 18 hours from Oceanside. They'd battled each other for 350 miles through the cruelest conditions Mother Nature could conjure up. In the southwestern deserts in late June, it's miserable enough just walking from an air conditioned car to the safety of an air conditioned supermarket. But these men weren't ambling across a parking lot; they had been pushing themselves along at 20 miles per hour since noon the day before over mountains and through desolate, godforsaken stretches of land, turning themselves inside out to gain just a minute or two on their opponents.

As they hit the Yarnell Grade, defending champion Jure Robič, known for his ferocious drive that pushed him to the brink of madness during races, was in the lead, 20 minutes up on fellow Slovenian Marko Baloh. Rookie Christoph Strasser, golden boy of the field, was keeping Baloh in his sights two minutes back. But because of their staggered start, Strasser had begun racing 20 minutes before Baloh, so the gap was actually wider than it appeared on the road.

Dani Wyss was the only race favorite who had stopped for a bona fide break overnight, so he had fallen off the pace of the leading group. Still, this cunning tactician was feeling calm and confident.

Robič always set a ferocious pace, and this year was no exception. Wyss was the only one who had managed to stay with the rampaging Slovenian early in the race. Robič's potent legs propelled him over the coastal range, but his glazed expression gave nothing away. This was his seventh trip through the desert death zone and Robič knew what the desert heat could do. He kept within himself. He hoped others would try matching his pace. *I'll show them,* he thought. *They'll melt down trying to stay with me.*

Wyss knew what Robič was up to but felt confident he could stick with him. It had been three years since Wyss had won RAAM in his rookie debut, and he was much stronger and smarter now. *Robič hates being chased,* Wyss thought. *Got to send him a signal and get into his head early.*

Robič and Wyss raced neck and neck for more than 12 hours straight, grinding up and over the coastal range, plunging down the glass elevator to the scorching desert floor by late afternoon, and then plowing along desert roads, past sand dunes and miles of nothingness shimmering in the heat.

Balanced over the jagged horizon behind them, the ruthless sun had finally shown mercy and slipped out of sight by the time the two men reached TS2 in Brawley, almost eight hours and 150 miles into the race.

After they had passed through Brawley, Robič's pace and the stifling, arid heat became too much for Wyss. With Robič gobbling up the pavement just ahead of him, Wyss grew dizzy and nauseated during the night. He jumped off his bike and vomited. Then, he calmly climbed back on his bike and kept going, determined to keep pace. He managed to hang on for a while longer, but in the middle of the night things fell apart. He dismounted his bike and began stumbling around in the darkness on the soft shoulder of a ramrod-straight desert road 350 miles from Oceanside with the world spinning around him. He had made an uncharacteristic miscalculation. He had taken Robič's bait, gone out too fast, and now he was paying the price.

Trailing him in their follow-vehicle with their warning lights flashing, Wyss' crew mates quickly recognized how serious the situation was and yanked their racer off the course. When an athlete produces more heat than his environment can absorb, he risks heat stroke, a potentially life-threatening condition where one's organs can begin cooking themselves inside the body. The organs can shut down if this continues long enough, resulting in coma and even death. Wyss' crew had to get their racer's core temperature down quickly, and the fastest way was to have him stop cycling and rest in air conditioned comfort. Wyss didn't put up a fight.

Wyss felt so destroyed he almost quit the race right there. Even the most committed cyclist would consider a 350-mile nonstop ride in conditions like this to be a career capstone. But for one of the top ultradistance racers on the planet, quitting after 350 miles on the first night of the most important race on the calendar would be a disaster, especially for someone like Wyss. His sponsors had spent serious money shipping a large crew and mountains of gear from Switzerland to California. As he lay there with ice packs around his neck and his legs propped up above his head, he looked deep inside himself. *Should have known better,* he thought. *I need to race my smartest race ever. No more mistakes from this point on.*

Wyss was lucky. He had made an uncharacteristic tactical blunder trying to match Robič's early pace, but after a two-hour cooldown along the road outside of Blythe, his head stopped spinning. Before dawn he got back on his bike, drew a long breath of parched desert air, and pushed off again, determined to chase Robič down. Before his meltdown, Wyss had been tied with Robič at the head of the field. As the leaders approached the Yarnell Grade at dawn, Wyss trailed by two hours. It was the last time Wyss and Robič would be so far apart.

AS FOR THE WOMEN WHO HAD BEGUN THEIR RACE A DAY BEFORE THE MEN, they rode through Monument Valley, Utah, grateful that the desert tailwinds had pushed them fast enough to arrive before dark. They had been racing for about 50 hours and had traveled almost 650 miles. Monument Valley's towering outcroppings have been photographed countless times, but this day would have been a photographer's worst nightmare, as a raging dust storm had covered the valley in a haze. Fierce winds whipped up the red dust into small tornadoes that spun crazily for a few moments and then vanished.

As they pushed through stiff headwinds, the women struggled to keep their bikes vertical and their eyes and noses clear of sand. Race leader Janet Christiansen was fulfilling her promise to rely on the power of laughter, raising her voice over the din and putting her sarcastic sense of humor on display. "You can't stand up in this wind without being blown all over and getting pounded. It's just part of the relentless torture-charm of the desert," she said. The previous year Christiansen had lost her resolve and was forced to quit 250 miles from Annapolis. As she battled the winds this year, she merely chuckled at the slow headway she was making.

Christiansen passed through Monument Valley and by midnight on her third night she was still on her bike, less than 100 miles up the road from the leading men and holding a 90-minute edge over Daniela Genovesi, her mysterious Brazilian rival. The two other women in the race were both faltering: the scowling Briton Ann Wooldridge was in third over three hours back, and South African über-athlete Michele Santilhano had fallen to fourth, a dispiriting six hours in arrears. Santilhano, an experienced endurance athlete, mountaineer, and adventurer, had somehow left her mojo back in Oceanside, and she was being brutalized in her solo RAAM debut.

Santilhano put on a brave face in the waning hours of June 18, straining to show her crew she was still on form, but she was having big problems. For one, she and her crew were quarreling over what she should be eating and drinking, and in spite of her prodigious athletic résumé, she didn't have the confidence to take charge. "I'm bad at decision making," Santilhano admitted to me before the race. This was now coming back to bite her.

She was also stymied by pain in her right quad muscle that made every pedal revolution excruciating, so she was in no mood to argue with her crew. "Pain is communication. Pain is like clay," she explained. "You can do so much with it. There's good pain and bad pain. Bad pain needs to be dealt with." This was bad pain.

Santilhano grimaced with the effort of each pedal stroke and her progress slowed. Santilhano works as a nurse in a pediatric oncology ward south of San Francisco. To keep himself going, she began thinking about her patients and the courage they mustered. "Their bravery has so much to teach us. My kids help me look for the gift in each moment—to cycle with gratitude," she said. She knew her troubles paled in comparison to what her kids went through every day.

As a bright crescent moon rose over Monument Valley, everyone on Team Santilhano hoped that the dawn would bring new life to their brave racer.

WHILE SANTILHANO STRUGGLED, AN AMERICAN NAMED SCOTT LUIKART had already withdrawn from the race after he blew out his calf muscle, sending him and his bike to the ground. This first DNF reminded everyone about the perils of the first few days of RAAM. Luikart had initially planned on competing as a two-man team with his brother, but soon afterward his brother was diagnosed with Parkinson's disease. Luikart had decided to carry on and do RAAM as a soloist with his brother accompanying him as his crew chief. Luikart had dedicated the race to his stricken brother. Now they were both headed home.

The French research scientist Patrick Autissier didn't have to be reminded of the cruelty of this race. Nor did Kevin Kaiser, the shy pharmacist from Georgia. Both men were in even worse shape than Santilhano. As midnight drew near, Autissier was crumbling. A few hours earlier his crew chief Rob had pulled him off the course after 30 hours and 400 miles of disappointing racing. He booked a seedy hotel room near Prescott, Arizona, so that Autissier could cool off and take a nap.

Once inside, Autissier turned up the air conditioning as high as it would go and collapsed into bed. *At last,* he thought. *I just need to close my eyes and everything will be better again.* It was so hot outside that his small hotel room never really cooled down. As soon as his head hit the pillow, everything started spinning and he felt queasy. Autissier was tormented by how things were going. Determined to outsmart his problems, he lay there ruminating about what he could do to conjure more power from his legs.

Too agitated to rest, Autissier reminded himself how imperative it is to minimize wasted time off the bike during RAAM. He got up, alerted his crew, and headed back outside with a grim look on his face. Even though it was before dawn, as soon as he opened the door he felt a blast of appallingly hot air. Once his follow-vehicle was ready with its amber lights blinking and its spotlight blazing the path forward, he got back on his bike for a long, hot climb through the red rocks of Sedona and up to Flagstaff.

As Autissier started pedaling he had to work hard to beat back the feeling of dread. It was a lonesome few hours. The stillness of the early morning suffocated him as he cycled through forests devoid of any signs of civilization. All he heard was his own breathing and the sound of his follow-vehicle's engine. There were few crickets or birds to serenade him along the Arizona plateau. He was miserable. He didn't want to stop, afraid that if he did the stillness might be too much to bear. But his condition forced him to stop every hour or so for a brief respite before slogging on.

Kaiser was even farther behind, trailing a hapless Autissier by more than an hour and at risk of missing the first time cutoff up the road in Taos, New Mexico. If that happened his race would be over no matter how badly he wanted to continue. RAAM meant everything to this cycling fanatic. It defined and animated his life more than his job as a pharmacist ever could. He couldn't imagine how he would cope if he was forced to withdraw, but he was so shattered he began entertaining the thought.

"At that point I almost wanted to quit, but I didn't let on to my crew," he said later. "In the desert I felt like my chest was caving in and I was sick to my stomach a lot. I was getting more and more frustrated with myself." Kaiser had heat exhaustion, and since he was nauseated and couldn't eat he was growing weaker by the hour. His teammates hovered around him whenever he stopped for a break, but there wasn't a lot they could do. They'd pull out a lawn chair and Kaiser would slump into it, hanging his head dejectedly and not talking much.

As these struggling riders passed through sacred Hopi and Navajo lands, they came close to Spider Rock, a spectacular 800-foot-tall red sandstone monolith. As legend has it, Spider Rock is home to Spider Woman, one of the most revered of the Navajo deities. The Navajo believe that Spider Woman possesses powers to save lives and help people overcome grave challenges. Had they been aware of her at the time, Santilhano, Kaiser, and Autissier might have taken a short detour to beg Spider Woman for salvation.

THOUGH IT WAS STILL EARLY IN THE RACE, Jure Robič was in the lead and attacking the course with such viciousness it was hard to resist jumping to the conclusion that he was going to win his record fifth RAAM title. He was just too fast, too strong, and too determined. It hadn't always been this way.

Robič might be the world's most fearsome ultradistance cyclist, but he is also a man who has known desperation. Robič's biography is similar to that of many elite cyclists, from Tour de France legend Lance Armstrong on down. He had an absent father and a hardscrabble upbringing, and he'd been forced to fight for everything he got. On this day, he was still tapping into the aggression of a betrayed, wounded child to fuel his incomparable drive to win.

In his youth, Robič's younger brother Saso—a world champion junior alpine skier—received all the attention. One day when Robič was 11, his mother was driving the two of them home from one of Saso's races when Robič spotted two cyclists careening down the mountainside in front of their car. Growing up in a rural Slovenian village, he'd never seen such a sight.

Robič was mesmerized by the spectacle of the two cyclists weaving through tight mountain hairpins and going so fast his mother's car couldn't keep up. From that point on, all Robič wanted to do was ride a bike. He begged his mother for one, and she told him he had to get perfect grades first. He did exactly that and was rewarded with his first rickety, steel-framed bike. It was stolen a few months later, and Robič was devastated. He had to work that summer and beg his father for a loan in order to buy a replacement.

That's how Robič acquired his first real racing bike, a sparkly gold Motobecane. "I thought it was the best bike in the world—it looked great, and that motivated me to train really, really hard," he remembered.

What an understatement.

Robič started climbing mountains alone on his bike at the age of 12, thinking he was the only Slovene cyclist in the world. He rode throughout the countryside by himself for two years before finally encountering another serious cyclist his age who sported a snappy team jersey. Robič went wild when he saw that jersey, and soon he joined the team.

It wasn't easy becoming a state-supported athlete in former communist Yugoslavia. At 17 he was forced to move to Novo Mesto, a nearby village, to join the only competitive cycling team around, living in spartan barracks shared with migrant workers twice his age. Robič quickly discovered that the head coach was already grooming a local kid who lived in town named Sandy Popich, so Robič would have to be second in line. Robič didn't feel he was in any position to complain. He was grateful for any opportunity. At least he was racing his bike.

Robič soon began winning races, and even though the coach quietly acknowledged he had more talent than Popich, Popich remained the team leader. Robič eventually quit in frustration to join another squad, and his success continued.

Cycling became Robič's life. It gave him a glimpse of the world outside his tiny Slovenian village. It helped him prove his worthiness and escape from behind his brother's shadow.

At the peak of his road racing career in 1992, he won the biggest stage race in the disintegrating nation of Yugoslavia, and at 27, he still harbored hopes of turning pro. Then he fell in love with a beautiful and successful Austrian businesswoman, who proceeded to belittle him for competing for so little money. "She earned 30 times my salary, and she made me feel like a fool for doing what I was doing. After all her criticism, I was mentally dead and lost the motivation to train," he said.

So Robič quit racing. He abruptly walked off the course to the amazement of his coach and team in the fifth stage of a multiday race. His girlfriend promised to help him find a well-paying job in Austria, but she never delivered. Robič fell into a deep depression when his love affair ended shortly afterward. Now he had no relationship, no cycling career, and no future.

He stopped eating, starving himself nearly to death, and retreated into his beloved Slovenian mountains, hiking in solitude for a month. When he came out of the woods he knew what he had to do. He borrowed money from his brother and bought a mountain bike. He loved racing bikes, and he'd show everyone just how much. He wasn't in it for the money; he simply wanted everybody to understand that racing was a worthy thing to do, and that he deserved their love and respect. He'd show them.

That epiphany got him back on the path he was destined for. He trained like a man possessed, joined a Dutch professional team, and won some races even though he was working full time for a bicycle distributor. He held this job for several years, but in 2001 enlisted in the Slovenian Army, hoping that a soldier's lifestyle would afford greater leeway for training and racing.

Robič had to be creative to maintain his racing fitness during boot camp. After being driven hard by his drill sergeant all day, he'd go on three-hour runs deep into the night, returning to the barracks as late as 4:00 in the morning. Robič continued his winning ways, even placing fourth in the Crocodile Trophy, a prestigious multiday mountain bike race in Australia.

On a lark one rainy day in late 2001, he headed out to see how far he could pedal in 24 hours, his first real encounter with ultradistance cycling. Never mind the cold, damp conditions; his timer told him he made it 498 miles, almost a world record. But he never checked the record books, so at the time he didn't know how close he had come (a few years later he would set the world record, covering 522 miles). Robič didn't test his physical limits for fame or glory. He did it because he loved to ride more than anything else, and he was curious to see how hard he could push himself. He sped along with such ferocity it seemed as if his life depended on it. He rode in complete anonymity along back roads in a small, rural nation for reasons even ardent cyclists have trouble fathoming.

Robič got his first real break about a year later, when a sergeant called him into his office. There he was told to report to the Slovenian Armed Forces Sports Squad starting in January 2003. Robič had been admitted to an elite club—a small group of athletes sponsored by the army to train full time and represent Slovenia in races around the world. It didn't mean a lot of money, but it was a dream come true: Robič was now a professional cyclist.

A few months later he was racing across the U.S. in his first RAAM bid.

ROBIČ'S PERFORMANCE IN THAT 2003 RACE earned him a reputation as a possessed and often frightening cyclist. In his RAAM debut Robič experienced the withering heat of the southwestern deserts for the first time. Temperatures hit 115 degrees. He couldn't believe the heat; he was told it would feel like an oven, but he never expected how suffocating the sensation would be. Every time he exhaled it felt as though he was expelling fire.

There were other reasons his 2003 race was a nightmare. Robič had arrived ill-prepared and on a shoestring budget, accompanied by his wife Petra, who doubled as a crew member to save money. The first problem was mechanical. Robič hadn't raised enough money to bring a bike mechanic, so when he broke his bottom bracket (the spindle that allows the cranks to spin freely), he had to use a spare bike that was too small.

He rode 600 miles on this too-small spare, hunched over and in increasing discomfort. Finally he stopped and threw the bike into the bushes, ready to quit. But his crew chief begged Robič not to give up. Somehow Robič pulled himself together. Luckily his countryman and friend Marko Baloh was also racing that year. Baloh's mechanic installed a new bottom bracket on Robič's primary bike, and Robič was back in the hunt.

But the bike was not correctly adjusted, so there was no respite for his aching back. His hands and fingers grew numb because of pressure on the nerves in his wrists. Even changing clothes became difficult. The cleats that affixed his feet to the pedals weren't positioned correctly, so Robič endured the searing pain of "hot foot," where the balls of a rider's feet feel like they're on fire because nerves between the toes become inflamed. In the heat, all these compounding physical problems resulted in such intense and unremitting agony that he had difficulty speaking or thinking.

On top of this witch's brew, Robič confronted the effects of severe sleep deprivation for the first time in his life, bringing about wave after wave of hallucinations so realistic he jumped off his bike to battle monsters he encountered deep into the night. Robič thought he saw the mujahideen, so his crew chief told Robič they were chasing him so he would keep moving. "You cannot imagine the hallucinations that first year; it was a nightmare," Robič told me, grimacing even years later.

To escape the waves of pain shooting through his feet, hands, muscles, and tendons, Robič's mind left his body and he raced along completely disoriented and not knowing where he was. Robič put it bluntly: "I suffered like Jesus Christ on the cross out there." About Robič's experience that year, journalist Daniel Coyle writes that, "He talks of incomprehensible suffering one moment and of dreamlike anesthesia the next. Perhaps the closer we get to its dual nature, the more elusive any single truth becomes, and the better we understand what Emily Dickinson meant when she wrote that 'pain has an element of blank.'"

Pain depersonalized Robič that year and nearly drove him mad. He cried, stomped around screaming, and lost all inhibitions. Petra hid in their motor home rather than watch her husband in such a state. Calling him an animal or a monster doesn't do justice to the power and irresistible dominance of unrelenting pain.

Robič's fear and desperation reached a crescendo late in the race, but not because of his physical discomfort or the hallucinations. What scared him most was his bestial behavior and the prospect of not winning. He passed the two-thirds mark at the Mississippi River solidly in third, seven hours behind the man in second, RAAM star Rob Kish, and a few hours ahead of another rookie, Marcel Knaus.

By the time they reached Ohio, Knaus was suddenly at his heels. When Robič stopped for a break in the middle of the night, Knaus passed him and decided to skip his own break to build a lead, but Robič jumped back on his bike just as Knaus flew by. Robič somehow summoned his reserves and thundered on through the night, and by 9:00 in the morning he'd pulled away from Knaus for good.

During Robič's final break, his masseur reminded him that only a strong 200-kilometer time trial separated the semi-conscious racer from Kish and a second-place finish. A delirious Robič set off, thinking he was in a road race back in Slovenia and mumbling something about riding from Ljubljana to Zagreb. His first RAAM had become a mosaic of mixed-up puzzle pieces that didn't all fit, but he didn't care. The only thought in his addled brain was *Catch Kish*. He no longer felt pain. Driven by a force even he couldn't understand, Robič slept only 30 minutes during the final 30 hours of his race.

"I was in a trance," he said. "I had so much pressure and responsibility. This was my job and the army was supporting me and I had to do well. I was trying to prove to everyone that I was not a bad guy. That I was a winner."

In hilly Pennsylvania with about seven hours of racing left, a possessed Robič blew by Kish, moving at such speed it seemed as if Kish were standing still. Robič finished second, bested only by Allen Larsen.

"It was a nightmare," Robič remembers. "I collapsed at the finish line."

Almost unbelievably, it took Robič no time at all to recover physically from his first RAAM, and he even won a one-day European road race less than a week afterward. But he was so mentally destroyed by the experience that it was six months before he had fully healed from the emotional trauma. Even his wife needed time to open up her heart to him again and forgive him for what he had become out there.

Robič returned the next year, still trying to prove his worth. His then-pregnant wife Petra stayed behind. He won that race and has been back every year since. After the birth of their son Nal, several years later he and Petra divorced. The loss of his marriage failed to dampen Robič's outbursts. In the years since, his incomparable drive to win has caused Robič to push himself to the brink of madness in each race. His mental breakdowns during RAAM have become legendary. People speak of his eruptions as though they'd seen something they weren't supposed to see—something primal and unsettling. One reason Robič wins RAAM over and over is that he sleeps less than almost all of his competitors, functioning on about eight hours of sleep over eight or so days of racing. Sleep deprivation beyond two days is known to produce hallucinations. It also reduces resistance to pain, makes people suggestible, and heightens their emotions. This contributes to Robič's wild temper swings.

Journalist Daniel Coyle describes the transformation Robič goes through during RAAM this way: "Around Day Two...his speech goes staccato. By Day Three, he's belligerent and sometimes paranoid. His short-term memory vanishes, and he weeps uncontrollably. The last days are marked by hallucinations: bears, wolves, and aliens prowl the roadside; asphalt cracks rearrange themselves into coded messages. Occasionally, Robič leaps from his bike to square off with shadowy figures that turn out to be mailboxes."

Now plying the backroads in his seventh straight RAAM, Robič remains a ferocious, obsessed racer, but he is as human as can be, driven by wounds and yearnings we can all relate to. He might exude the relaxed confidence of a Slovenian national hero, but he's quick to admit how much he suffers during RAAM and even how frightened he is of himself.

"I feel like if I go on, I will die," he said. "It is everything at the same moment, piled up over and over. Heat, muscles, bones. Nobody can understand. You cannot imagine it until you feel it."

Whatever he's talking about—the weather, the rivalries, or how much this race tortures him—he chooses his words for maximum effect. Robič is always working to stand out, to matter.

AFTER CRESTING THE YARNELL GRADE IN THE MORNING, the leading men passed through the Painted Desert, an arid expanse of badland hills, flat-topped mesas, and buttes. Normally these multicolored geological spectacles would capture one's attention. One can't help but marvel at the pastel colors of the sedimentary layers popping out of the austere landscape. These striking bands of color made the hills look like humongous layer cakes good enough to eat if only one had a fork the size of the Eiffel Tower.

But as the racers passed these scenic wonders, something else was on their minds. Getting through Day Two in the High Desert meant paying close attention to the cumulative effects of racing in the heat, especially as the climbs started kicking in. Gastrointestinal distress, dehydration, heat stroke; any of these could spell doom. In addition, the race leaders who had skipped sleep the first night were also starting to droop, so they had to decide when to take their first catnaps.

The leaders planned to push all the way up the long, oppressive climb at least to TS8 in Flagstaff, 500 miles into the race. Flagstaff sits at an altitude of 6,700 feet, and the next major climbs weren't until the Rockies. After Flagstaff, the leading men would descend the eastern slopes of the Arizona range and begin looking forward to one of the world's natural wonders—Monument Valley—as they entered Utah.

Racing nonstop all the way to Flagstaff is no mean feat. It's not just the 100-degree heat; it's also the desiccating air that sucks the moisture from one's mouth and eyeballs, the billowing dust that gets into every crevice, the desolate landscape, and the relentless, merciless climbing. With all the ups and downs, racers ascend well over 20,000 feet in the first 500 miles of RAAM, more than four miles straight up. That's higher than the elevation of the most advanced base camp used by Everest climbers. The final segment before the racers reached Flagstaff was rated as the toughest section on the course west of the Mississippi River.

Jure Robič was the first to reach TS8 in Flagstaff in midafternoon on Day Two, after 26 hours of racing with hardly a moment off the bike. In his first 500 miles, he had charged over the coastal range, sped through the furnace-like Low Desert, scaled the desolate Bradshaw Mountains, and crossed the broiling High Desert, all the while maintaining an average speed just shy of 20 miles per hour. That type of performance is enough to make the jaws of most cyclists hit the floor.

But he wasn't done yet. He zoomed right through Flagstaff and raced on for eight more hours before taking his first legitimate sleep break just past TS10 in dusty Kayenta, Arizona, an astounding 635 miles from Oceanside. By then he'd been racing for almost 34 hours. He was caked with dust, his eyes were so dry they stung, and his back and hands had been aching for hours. He couldn't wait to climb into his air conditioned motor home.

Robič had been on such a blistering pace he passed through Monument Valley after dark, unable to take in the scenery that in daylight would have provided the Slovenian with an enduring image of the American West. But then again, this RAAM veteran had probably seen more of America than most citizens, as he was riding across the country along 3,000 miles of backroads for the seventh year in a row.

Chasing Robič across Monument Valley was the youthful rookie Christoph Strasser, who was going all out in his first RAAM. Then came the savvy tactician Dani Wyss, tranquil as can be. After his scare the first night, Wyss now seemed to be riding effortlessly and in complete control. Wyss was happy *not* to be in the lead at this early juncture. He and his crew chief Christian Hoppe, a savvy tactician as well, agreed it was better to be the hunter than the hunted. Robič's countryman Marko Baloh rounded out this tightly bunched group of four.

Teams Wyss, Strasser, and Baloh all watched Robič closely, eager to see when he'd finally take his first sleep break. The race favorites all spied on each other, sending crew vehicles back and forth to get reports on their rivals. In the 1990s, RAAM great and 19-time finisher Rob Kish had even lashed a scooter to the back of his motor home expressly for this purpose.

Wyss, Strasser, and Baloh planned on dismounting their bikes only after Robič did. For these favorites, breaks only lasted an hour or two, just enough time to get a massage, change clothes, and close their eyes for a power nap—hopefully long enough to go through one REM cycle of deep sleep. Getting through a REM cycle is so important that a racer usually enlists one of his crew members to watch his eyes flutter with the unmistakable sign of REM sleep before being awakened.

Once Strasser's crewmates saw that Robič was finally off the road, they gave their weary racer about an hour to get closer to Robič's position near TS10, then pulled him off the course. Everyone on Team Strasser was exhausted but grateful that their young charge was almost through the death zone and holding up well. His pre-race training camp appeared to be paying off. Team Baloh followed suit, positioning its motor home near Strasser's.

Wyss, ever the cunning race strategist, had a different plan. By midnight he had already erased 30 minutes from Robič's two-hour lead. He was steadily closing and feeling much better than he had the previous night. After learning that the champion was asleep, Wyss rode on for a few hours longer, eventually passing Robič's motor home and erasing his two-hour deficit. Wyss took his first break about 40 miles farther on, at the other side of Monument Valley, after 38 hours of nonstop racing. Wyss knew that once Robič awoke he'd be surprised that Wyss had raced so far beyond his position. Of course, Robič would retake the lead while Wyss was napping, but Wyss was shrewdly sending a signal that Robič had a fight on his hands.

Their epic battle was just beginning.

6

Day Three: Surprise!

Monument Valley approaching the Rockies, June 19

After completing the agonizing task of rousing their aching bodies and returning to their bikes, most racers savor the early morning hours more than any other time of day. Refreshed from their rest breaks they drink in the sweetness of the dawn. The roads are quieter at sunrise, the air is easier to breathe, and anything seems possible.

The early morning of Day Three was particularly agreeable for the leaders of the men's race. Their second dawn came as they plied the cattle roads just past Monument Valley. Thanks to the reddish-pink dust still suspended in the air from the windstorm the day before, the warm hues of early morning were even more alluring here on the openness of Utah's High Deserts.

The leaders knew that on this day they would meet the fearsome Rockies head-on. Barren, pastel-colored deserts would become verdant pine forests and wild meadows. The gruesome heat of the first few days would give way to frigid alpine passes. Concerns about heat stroke would shift to worries about oxygen deficit at elevations surpassing 10,000 feet.

Out on the road, reigning champion Jure Robič was surprised by a sneak attack. His wily Swiss adversary Dani Wyss had delayed his sleep break and passed him while Robič napped. Wyss even briefly led the race through Mexican Hat at the far end of Monument Valley around 4:00 in the morning. When Wyss finally stopped for a well-deserved rest, Robič was just getting back in the saddle and he quickly reclaimed the top spot. In fact, this morning Robič even passed faltering Michele Santilhano, who had started with the rest of the women's field one day before the men.

As the leaders reached the westernmost flanks of the Rockies around noon, Robič was an hour and a half ahead of Wyss. His Slovenian countryman Marko Baloh and Austrian rookie Christoph Strasser were essentially tied another hour behind Wyss. After them, there was a gap of four hours to Gerhard Gulewicz, another formidable Austrian and the fifth man on the road. Even this far back, Gulewicz was still a threat. After all, he was racing with a chip on his shoulder after crashing out of the race the previous year while in second place. The only real surprise among the leading men was the absence of Franz Preihs, the third Austrian among the race favorites. He was struggling with knee problems and had been mired in the middle of the pack since Oceanside.

THERE WERE PLENTY OF SURPRISES FARTHER BACK IN THE FIELD. Take the affable, stay-at-home dad Ben Popp. A full 10 hours behind Robič, the RAAM rookie was able to enjoy the sights of Monument Valley in broad daylight. As dawn broke on Day Two, Popp was tied with Michael Cook as the leading male rookie on the road. Punching well above his weight, Popp remembers thinking, *We did it—now we're safe!* once he'd completed his perilous Low Desert crossing and reached Monument Valley. He might have been far behind the leaders, but Popp was still a surprising seventh. He had enjoyed a solid three hours of sleep in Flagstaff overnight (two REM cycles!), and he greeted the day brimming with confidence. Popp's careful planning was paying off, and so was the secret weapon he brought with him to boost his odds of making it through the desert death zone.

Popp's prized possession was a fancy cooling vest he wore when the temperature soared, the only racer in the field who sported this particular piece of gear. Filled with frozen chemical packs, these vests moderate a racer's core temperature. Athletes typically use them for pre-cooling right before a race. It turns out that only 25 percent of the energy that is generated during exercise goes into work, with the remaining 75 percent transforming into heat that needs to be dissipated. Since the vest acts like a big heat sink, it can greatly improve performance. If one's core overheats, then the circulatory system has to work to carry that heat to the skin's surface—where the air rushing over one's body can dissipate it—instead of working to provide oxygen to the muscles. Once one's core temperature reaches 102 degrees, power output drops precipitously and heat stroke can result. In the end, heat stroke is caused not so much by dehydration but rather by the rate at which the athlete produces heat and the capacity of his environment to absorb that heat.

Dehydration is also a fearsome problem in the desert, as it leads to reduced blood volume, spiking one's heart rate—not helpful for a cyclist already coping with fatigue. So in addition to all manner of cooling techniques, it's standard practice for RAAM racers to push intravenous fluids into their veins during rest breaks. Most racers bring along a nurse, doctor, or paramedic to administer IVs. True to form, Popp was on this, too. His crew included two medical doctors: his wife Megan and his father-in-law Bob.

In spite of Popp's careful planning and early confidence, Day Three didn't go well for him. He began feeling pain in his Achilles tendon and patella, signs of early tendonitis. Popp enjoyed the picturesque beauty around him, but for the first time he was wilting in the heat of the day. His pace slowed. Still, he kept a wary eye on the leader board, trying to protect his position on the road. But RAAM has a way of challenging racers in ways they don't expect. Passing through Monument Valley this morning, the swirling dust had irritated Popp's eyes. Rubbing them later in the afternoon, he scratched his cornea. In agony, he taped one eye shut around 8:00 PM, just in time to hit the heart of the Colorado Rockies like a blind man in the dark.

THERE WERE A FEW SURPRISES FOR JIM REES, TOO. Rees, the erudite British veteran, had passed through Monument Valley three hours behind Popp in the middle of a sweltering summer afternoon in the Navajo Nation. For Rees, reaching Monument Valley in daylight was a special moment. For one thing, it meant he was making pretty good time. For another, passing through sacred Navajo lands inspired Rees. His mostly

British crew was thunderstruck by the dramatic, otherworldly outcroppings on either side of the ramrod-straight road that ran along the undulating valley floor. "See, now you know why I didn't want to sleep last night! I wanted you to see this during daylight," Rees exclaimed with glee.

The first surprise for Rees was that, even in the summertime heat, he had crossed the valley comfortably and still on British-record pace. Like Popp, Rees had a secret weapon that was working well to help him hold up in the heat. He had wrapped his arms and torso with white bandages drenched in a special evaporative cooling liquid, and they provided instant relief. Even though he looked like a mummy, he was surprisingly comfortable.

Rees was racing solo RAAM for the third year in a row. That in itself is a big accomplishment for a European who faces the added challenge of just getting to Oceanside. But Rees makes most things look easy.

Rees is one of the most generous guys you will ever meet. When I first introduced myself, he immediately invited me to stay with him and his family north of London. Upon my arrival, the ever-casual Rees stepped out to greet me wearing nothing but a bath towel, having just finished his après-ride shower. The first thing I noticed was how his clean, smartly-shaven head gleamed in the morning sun. Once I had spent a few hours with him, I was struck by his strong self-identity and how deeply and honestly Rees has examined his motivations and behavior toward others. This would both haunt and help him during this year's race.

Upon entering Rees' home a month before the race, I felt a buzz of energy. On this Saturday morning Rees was in the midst of polishing a motivational speech he was giving later in the day, fielding a call from his daughter who needed comforting after a failed relationship, tracking down RAAM crew members whom we intended to meet for dinner, trying to find his cell phone, and helping his wife select a paint color for their foyer walls. All at the same time. I marveled at how calmly he dealt with the mayhem.

Like RAAM star Wolfgang Fasching before him, Rees is a keynote speaker and executive coach in his day job. Rees excels at what he does because he's a serious student of ideas and human behavior, using his knowledge to forge new ground at the convergence of business, consciousness, and compassion. But his real passion is to "inspire children to believe in their own greatness and change limiting beliefs about what is possible." A father of six, Rees founded a charitable organization called Team Inspiration to do just that. In his speaking and writing he uses RAAM to demonstrate what is possible when a "normal guy" like him chooses to embrace a positive and determined mind-set.

At first glance Rees doesn't seem anything like Slovenian cycling legend Jure Robič, but they do share more than a little in common. Rees also had a tough childhood—probably tougher than Robič's. His single mom gave him up for adoption when he was 18 months old after he was beaten by the woman who babysat him. His adoptive dad was "an aggressive, cantankerous fellow" who caused Rees' adoptive mother to flee the family several times, abandoning him along with his terrified siblings. There was drinking and even some abuse in the troubled Rees household. Finally Rees had had enough; he quit school at 15 and shortly afterward decided it was time to leave home.

Rees' hard-luck story doesn't end there, but he believes that his difficult childhood and strained relationship with his father gave him the grit to take on RAAM. "My dad was a bully, and I guess I'm still trying to prove I can accomplish big things," he explained. He moved to the United Kingdom and married young. Like Robič, Rees' first wife tore into him about how much time he spent competing in Ironman triathlons, so he quit racing. As Rees put it, "I lost myself, lost my identity, and started sleepwalking through my life." Also like Robič, Rees' first marriage didn't last.

REES' MUMMY WRAPPINGS WERE HELPING HIM beat the heat, but all wasn't well on Team Inspiration during the afternoon of Day Three. For one thing, the loudspeakers on his follow-vehicle weren't working, and his earpiece was proving too uncomfortable to wear. This meant it was impossible to communicate with Rees unless his crew pulled the follow-vehicle alongside him and rolled down the window. They couldn't keep this up for long because the follow-vehicle—which normally crawls behind the racer staying way over on the shoulder and out of traffic—would block the road. Even worse, fatigued crew members have been known to run into their own riders. As a result Rees was all but isolated and he was unable to take his mind off the heat by listening to music through his balky loudspeakers or earpiece.

Rees was also having vivid hallucinations. In his solitude, riding along hot, hazy, featureless roads, Rees' sleep-deprived mind began to float away. Without aural or visual stimulation or distractions from his crew, he created an alternative reality to fill the void. Every time his crew mates thought his mind was wandering too far astray, they'd briefly pull alongside him and bring him back.

At one point Rees thought he saw cyclists riding nearby yelling at him to turn left. But there wasn't any left turn he could make, and he grew frustrated. He saw pandas in the road, so he waved cheerily at them. He saw a panther leap out of a hole in the asphalt and lunge at him, teeth bared, and he recoiled in horror.

Then there were the spats with his crew. Crews support their rider by rotating on and off duty every eight to 12 hours in teams of three or four, and each shift is led by a crew chief. When Chief Phil's shift was on duty, they counted every calorie and only permitted Rees healthy foods. Chief Martyn's shift, on the other hand, let Rees eat whatever appealed to him at the moment. This created tension between the two shifts, with Rees stuck in the middle. Then Rees began having problems with Lindsey, who was responsible for monitoring his intake of food and drink. Rees felt she was adhering to a predetermined nutritional protocol without regard for how Rees was actually feeling day by day, hour by hour. For instance, Rees might insist that he be given more electrolytes because he was seeing some peripheral edema—a condition often caused by an electrolyte imbalance or muscle breakdown—and Lindsey would argue that he was getting all the electrolytes he needed.

Nevertheless, Rees was still managing to stay on his race plan and targeted pace. As he approached Monument Valley, he was able to share his optimism with fellow Brit Richard Newey, another RAAM soloist who had caught up to him on the road. Rees knew Newey well, as he raced the previous year on a team backed by Rees' Team Inspiration charity. In fact, on Day Three Rees had a lot of company, riding this stretch of road within sight of both Newey and Brazilian veteran Claudio Clarindo. So during this portion of his journey, Rees wasn't missing his music. For the time being, he had all the stimulation he needed.

THE SURPRISES DIDN'T END THERE. Up the road, Michele Santilhano, the contemplative South African, was struggling through her fourth day of racing. RAAM insiders had expected more from this accomplished ultradistance racer, mountaineer, and adventurer.

Santilhano is one of those people who can vividly recount the best and worst days of her life. Her best day was one of the last she spent with her mother. At the time, Santilhano was in her early twenties and still living in South Africa. Her mom had moved back to her native England after losing her husband, so Santilhano didn't see her much anymore. On the spur of the moment, Santilhano convinced her mom to join her in Norway for a weekend of hiking and skiing—two things her mother hadn't done since before her children were born.

They borrowed some skis and found their way to the slopes. Santilhano will never forget the look on her mother's face when her mom stood on the top of the ski run ready to take off. "She looked so excited and free, like a little kid. It was a very special, beautiful moment," Santilhano remembered. "It was one of the best moments in my life—a precious gift." Her mother passed away soon afterward.

The worst day of Santilhano's life came many years later, at an elevation of 23,700 feet on the slopes of Mount Everest. Santilhano was making the concluding climb of her Seven Summits bid, and only Everest remained to be conquered. She and her team made it all the way to Camp Three, where they prepared their final push to the "death zone" beyond Camp Four, and then onto the summit. It's called the death zone because there isn't enough air to sustain life at that altitude. Up there, a climber's heart rate spikes and his breathing quickens because his lungs can't pull in sufficient oxygen, so even a fit climber can become exhausted, and every step requires a mighty effort. If a climber's supplementary oxygen runs out, he could easily die. A climber can also succumb to frostbite, hurricane-force winds, and death by falling. If he's seriously injured in the death zone, his teammates probably won't be able to help him down. More than 150 bodies have never been recovered from these heights.

As Santilhano trudged along after Camp Three, her teammates watched her carefully. She had taken a nasty fall earlier, which made them wary. Eventually her team concluded that Santilhano was a weak link. On the way to Camp Four, just below the Hillary Step, her team leader became convinced Santilhano wasn't capable of summiting. "There was a lot of negative energy on Everest," Santilhano explained. "I respond well when people believe in me. When they're willing to take a risk and be optimistic with me. I achieve far more this way. But this team just didn't want me to summit."

Santilhano turned around and started back down the mountain in a fog of despair. "I was devastated," she said. "The guilt, the blame, all the time and money spent. This is a ghost that will haunt me forever. It's like a broken bone; it's never the same again. This is how I feel about Everest: a deep scar that will never ever heal. I'm petrified that RAAM could be another Everest. I don't know how I'd cope with this."

Sure enough, as Santilhano began her rendezvous with the Rockies, she was having flashbacks of her Everest experience. Santilhano's balky quad muscle was so traumatized by now that she could barely turn her pedals over. The previous night had been a long, difficult experience for everyone on Santilhano's crew. In a nod to her South African roots, she called her team "the Shongololo Express" after a grand, refurbished rail line that traverses seven countries on the southern African continent. Right now, the Shongololo Express was in need of a fresh tank of diesel fuel.

Santilhano was desperately trying to find her mojo. She took a long rest after crossing Monument Valley in the dark, booking a room in a cheap motel so she could take a shower after cycling all day in 100-degree heat. Her crew tried its best to deal with the injury, but strangely, Santilhano didn't have a physical or massage therapist on her crew. Desperate for a solution, her crew chief Adrienne eventually tracked one down by phone and got some long-distance advice about how to treat Santilhano's problem.

Santilhano had promised herself that when the going got tough, she would try to "find the gift in each moment." In her nursing job, Santilhano learned coping skills from the terminally ill kids she cared for. One thing her young patients taught her was that if you didn't have the will to fight, you didn't stand a chance.

To stave off the Everest flashbacks and calm her panic, Santilhano recited her mantra over and over again: *Every day, in every way, I'm getting stronger and faster.* She thought a lot about her kids back at the hospital and about how bravely they faced their battles. She also gained strength from knowing that she had dedicated her ride to raising awareness of the scourge of child sex trafficking. There were so many reasons to keep going. Finally, when all else failed, she prayed, relying on her strong faith to see her through.

As Santilhano attacked the unending climbs up the western flanks of the Rockies, her inflamed leg muscles slowly came around and she was able to apply a bit more power to the pedals. Each pedal stroke still hurt, but now she was managing a steady slog upward as she left Utah and entered Colorado.

The Shongololo Express crawled into Cortez, Colorado, around midday, on its way into the heart of the Rockies. Santilhano was about 770 miles into her ride, closing in on the first time cutoff in Taos, New Mexico, 275 miles farther on. By now the desolate, dusty desert terrain had given way to green pine forests, and she found new energy in the crisp mountain air she pulled into her lungs with every breath. I caught up with Santilhano at about this point in the race and jogged alongside her for a few hundred yards up a steep grade. In the thin air her breathing was labored. Still, she forced a strained smile. "I'm trying," she said in a hoarse voice. "I'm feeling better today, but this is hard."

By then her crew chief was really worried. Santilhano had lost a lot of time. She'd covered 350 miles in her first 24 hours of racing, but managed only 200 miles during the third day as she hit Durango, Colorado, and winded her way over the 8,500-foot San Juan Skyway. All that climbing meant Santilhano's pace was down to around 10 miles per hour, and the math was starting to work against her.

As dusk fell, Santilhano had a little over 20 hours to make it another 200 miles to Taos. But it had been quite a while since she'd had a break, and she was tired—bone tired. She couldn't get all the way through the mountains without another rest stop. As her fourth day on the road came to a close, Santilhano reached down as deeply as she'd ever done before. Deeper than during her 135-mile running races. Deeper than in her quintuple Ironman. Even deeper than during her Channel swim—the one that took her 19 hours in frigid waters and choppy seas.

The Everest flashbacks kept coming as darkness fell. Santilhano just pedaled on.

7

Crew Control

June 19, still back in Arizona

Spirit guides are entities who help and lead you on your physical journey into spiritual awareness. During RAAM, a racer's crew members are his spirit guides, helping and leading him from one side of the continent to the other. They feed and hydrate their racer, motivate him, protect him, guide him down the course, and take care of his equipment and supplies.

After a few days of nonstop cycling, a racer's dependence on his crew mates is almost total. For this relationship to work, a racer has to trust them completely. One reason for Michele Santilhano's problems was that she had given her untested, unfamiliar crew loads of decision-making authority. By the time she realized they weren't all on the same page, it was too late to make needed changes.

Like Santilhano, defending champion Jure Robič gave his crew tremendous leeway. "By the third day, we are Jure's software," explained Lt. Miran Stanovnik, Robič's former crew chief. Journalist Daniel Coyle describes Robič's crew as his "second brain." Coyle explains that, "His system is straightforward. During the race, Robič's brain is allowed control over choice of music (usually a mix of traditional Slovene marches and Lenny Kravitz), food selection, and bathroom breaks. The second brain dictates everything else, including rest times, meal times, food amounts, and even average speed. Unless Robič asks, he is not informed of the remaining mileage or even how many days are left in the race." Stanovnik adds, "It is best if he has no idea. He rides—that is all."

Robič's is an extreme case, but a cyclist's crew can make or break his race. Every solo racer needs support around the clock. Crew members typically work in teams of three or four, rotating in eight- to 12-hour shifts. Shifts are long and stressful. Racers are often demanding and ornery, and crew members have long lists of responsibilities. The weather's always too hot, too cold, or too wet; the follow-vehicle is cramped and chaotic; cell phone coverage is spotty; and crews are almost as sleep-deprived as their racers. On top of all this, crew members often can't take the time to shower or call home for days. Emergencies come at crew members all the time: flat tires, navigational errors, equipment breakdowns, personality conflicts. It's remarkable that anyone volunteers for this duty.

Responsibilities for On-Duty RAAM Crew Members

Race and Equipment Management: Navigating the course, calling in time station splits, ensuring compliance with race rules, keeping track of competitors, monitoring pace against goals, interpreting race rules, maintaining bicycles and equipment, planning rest breaks.

Nutrition and Physical Safety: Driving slowly behind the rider to shield him from passing traffic, providing food and drink, monitoring nutritional and fluid intake, furnishing riding clothing, keeping the rider alert, addressing medical problems, providing massage and physical therapy, monitoring sleep breaks.

Mental Health: Motivating the rider, keeping friends and family updated, sharing messages received from the outside world with the racer, capturing photos and video.

Responsibilities for Off-Duty RAAM Crew Members

Race and Equipment Management: Analyzing weather forecasts, tracking competitors, planning rest stops, fixing broken gear, performing bike maintenance, keeping vehicles in working order, coordinating shift changes and breaks with the on-duty team, making hotel reservations for crew and racer.

Housekeeping: Buying supplies and food, keeping vehicles clean, washing clothes and water bottles, planning, and preparing meals.

Communications: Updating friends and family, coordinating crew shift changes and whereabouts.

If crew members are a racer's spirit guides, then crew chiefs are the high priests of RAAM. A racer's crew chief means everything to him. He's the racer's principal problem solver, guru, and cheerleader. Almost as much as the racer's legs, the decisions a crew chief makes determine the outcome. He has to be right *every* time; even a trifling detail like a missed sleep break, a disrespected crew member, or an inaccurate nutrition log can mushroom into a race-ending catastrophe.

One journalist describes ultradistance running races as "a binary equation made up of hundreds of yes/no questions. Eat now or wait? Bomb down this hill, or throttle back and save the quads for the flats? Find out what is itching in your sock, or push on? Extreme distance magnifies every problem. A blister becomes a blood-soaked sock; a declined PowerBar becomes a woozy inability to follow trail markers." The running race this journalist was writing about—the Leadville Trail 100—has a cutoff time of 30 hours, whereas RAAM's is almost *10 times* longer. Talk about magnifying every problem.

As the days tick by and their racers' cognitive capabilities decline, crew chiefs take over more and more decision-making responsibility from their racers—deciding when they should rest, what they should eat, and what clothes they should wear. Crew chiefs rearrange crew shifts when personality conflicts brew and direct the teams' responses to emergencies of all kinds. Over time, they develop reputations within the ultracycling community. The best ones are coveted by other ultracyclists intent on entering RAAM.

Bill Osborn is a case in point, back for his second tour as Janet Christiansen's crew chief. Osborn has raced bikes since he was a teenager, and his knees and elbows bear the scars of too many crashes to count. Like most crew chiefs, this friendly man with a soft-featured face is easygoing and enjoys a good laugh—even at his own expense, if necessary. He likes being helpful, and in an earlier age might have been described as a gentleman. An adventurer at heart, Osborn loves crewing, especially for the jaunty and fun-loving Christiansen. "She's always in a good mood, always ready with a silly, off-hand remark," he explained. "And her desire will always stick with me. She's become family."

Having learned from their mistakes the previous year, Osborn had carefully honed his strategy for getting Christiansen across the finish line this time. One part of the equation was ensuring that everybody on her crew had a good time during their trip across the country. This is no trifling matter. Conflicts inevitably flare up in the close, uncomfortable quarters of a race vehicle. If they're allowed to fester, this can spell disaster. Disrespected crew members have been known to walk off the course, bringing their racer's bid to an abrupt end. Even little spats among crew members can spill over and affect a racer's morale. Osborn was committed to making sure everybody had a blast as they spirited Christiansen along, and Christiansen was going to rely on her deliciously quirky sense of humor to keep things light. "You can't really be strong until you see the funny side of things" is one of her favorite aphorisms.

Christiansen and Osborn shared a similar problem-solving philosophy and approach to the race. Christiansen had completely absorbed herself in the sport of ultracycling. She had an encyclopedic understanding of the maladies that have plagued her over the years, from peripheral edema to saddle sores, dehydration to ulnar nerve compression in the wrist. When she explained how she planned on dealing with these issues, she was so intensely serious it was obvious there was nothing more important to her than getting it right.

Like Christiansen, Osborn has aquired such depth of knowledge that he can anticipate and counteract the myriad physical, mental, logistical, and mechanical problems that arise during RAAM. For example, he learned about circadian rhythms when he was in the military; as a result, he decided to schedule Christiansen's sleep breaks so that she arose just before dawn in order to preserve her circadian rhythms as much as possible.

Osborn had prepared binders for each crew's vehicle containing all the information they would need to do their jobs, down to a list of self-service laundries in each of the towns they would visit. Between them, Osborn and Christiansen had considered every contingency that they could imagine, and they were completely on the same page.

For the hesitant Santilhano, her relationship with her crew wasn't nearly as solid, and the first days of the race confirmed what she already knew—she needed her crew to trust her and believe in her. Without that, she was doomed.

SUPPORT CREWS MEAN A LOT TO THEIR RACERS, but they can't turn the pedals for them. As this year's race wore on through Day Three, some racers were so far gone that nothing their crews did seemed to help.

After being unable to sleep during his prior night's stop in Prescott, Patrick Autissier began the punishing predawn climb to Flagstaff a broken man. He could only manage a nine-mile-per-hour pace and had to take frequent rest breaks during his long slog. Crew chiefs Rob and Jerome didn't push him, however. These two had supported Autissier before, and they knew something was terribly wrong this time. "I knew he wasn't the same guy," said Jerome, a native of French Guadeloupe, in his heavily accented English. "It didn't make sense to put pressure on him," added Rob, a medical doctor who knew Autissier well. Neither Rob nor Jerome felt Autissier could hang on much longer.

During the night Autissier's wife Anne-Cecile had joined up with the crew, having just flown in from Boston. As soon as she saw her husband's state she also feared the worst, but kept a brave face.

Anne-Cecile's arrival gave Autissier a boost, but he was physically and mentally spent by the time he reached Flagstaff the next morning. He stopped, looked around at his crew with hollow eyes, and collapsed on a folding chair set up in the shade beside his follow-vehicle. Autissier called a team meeting and stated the obvious. "This isn't going the way I wanted," he said grimly. "I'm wasted. I have nothing left. I'm dead. I'm not going to finish the race." Finally he gave voice to what everybody was thinking. This unleashed the emotions that had been roiling inside him, and the tears finally came. "I cried more than I had in the last 20 years," Autissier said. "Anne-Cecile cried, too. I was so embarrassed for my crew and my wife."

Gently, Anne-Cecile, Rob, and Jerome helped Autissier inside their van, encouraging him to rest for a while before making a final decision. But just like the night before, Autissier was so anxious he couldn't close his eyes. Still, his sense of pride and responsibility for his loyal teammates didn't allow Autissier to give up just yet. He somehow remounted his bike and headed for the next time station in Tuba City, some 70 miles down the road.

IMAGINE DRIVING ACROSS THE UNITED STATES on a route that completely avoids interstate highways. You'd travel mostly on two-lane roads, and it would be a long, strenuous experience as you dodged farm vehicles, scooted around lumbering 18-wheelers, and paused at countless stop signs. In return, you'd experience the countryside intimately, passing through hundreds of small towns and watching the terrain gradually evolve across deserts, mountains, plains, foothills, and forests. These towns are an enduring feature of the RAAM experience, and Tuba City is a perfect example. This High Desert outpost of 8,000 sits just east of the Grand Canyon in Arizona's Painted Desert. The largest population center in Navajo Nation, Tuba City was named after Tuuvi, a Hopi headman.

Tenuously connected to the outside world by asphalt and power lines, telephones and radio waves, the RAAM route passes hundreds of small towns like Tuba City. Especially in the West and the Great Plains, communities like this one popped up to serve the burgeoning transcontinental railway system as depots for cattle, wheat, corn, produce, and minerals. These days they survive on the fringes, struggling to carve new roles for themselves and serving as living reminders of earlier, simpler times.

Patrick Autissier crawled to Tuba City on this day, taking almost seven hours to get there from Flagstaff, a 72-mile mostly downhill ride past elk warning signs and multicolored cliffs. This segment should have taken him a little over four and a half hours. It was a heartbreaking sight to watch this doomed man hunched over his bike, holding on for dear life. Later that afternoon, race headquarters received a call from Autissier's crew. He had officially abandoned the race, the second contestant to do so.

Low-key pharmacist Kevin Kaiser reached Flagstaff two and a half hours after Autissier, the second-to-last man on the road. By Flagstaff he was already 90 minutes off the pace he needed to maintain in order to beat the cutoff time that would be officially registered in Taos, another 550 miles farther on.

Earlier that morning Kaiser had decided to have a big, sit-down breakfast near Sedona, Arizona. At that point he had just about given up. The service had been slow in the crowded Sedona breakfast spot, but Kaiser didn't care because he didn't expect to get back on his bike after his meal.

He hadn't been able to digest much of anything since departing Oceanside, so Kaiser had completely exhausted his energy stores and felt he had nothing left in his legs. He hoped that devouring a huge omelet might somehow kick-start his stomach. During the previous night he finished a long, treacherous descent through the mountain village of Jerome, Arizona, and had taken an emotional phone call from his wife. He became teary-eyed during their conversation and promised her he was "doing the best I can."

It turns out that Kaiser had indeed ordered a magic omelet that morning. In RAAM, you never know when or how providence will shine down on you. No matter how strong you are, it always takes a bit of luck to finish the race. Kaiser's good-luck charm happened to be a plate of eggs. As soon as he finished it his digestive system kicked back on. Within no time he felt a surge of energy and knew he could race on.

Reaching Flagstaff around midday, Kaiser asked his crew to huddle around him. He was concerned they were too relaxed and not working efficiently as a team. Was it because they didn't sense enough desire in him? He needed them to see he still had a lot of fight. Normally mild-mannered, Kaiser made a passionate appeal. "Let's fight for every second! I want you to rally around me," he implored. "We can do it! It's time to get to work!" Kaiser was determined to pick up his pace or die trying. Kaiser's rallying cry in Flagstaff was out of character for such a reserved man. Maybe that's why it worked.

Kaiser had blown up racing in the desert before. During a 1,200-kilometer (744-mile) event in 2005, he melted down in the Mojave. It happened during a seven-mile climb in 105-degree heat when he simply lost his will to keep the pedals turning over. Sitting dazed and confused on the side of the road, he was about to quit when a couple of friends rode by. Somehow, he climbed back on his bike and into their slipstream. Kaiser had rediscovered his resolve.

The same thing was happening now in RAAM. Kaiser's speed inched up to an acceptable 16 miles per hour, and he passed through Monument Valley around midnight.

Up until this point, most meltdowns like Autissier's and Kaiser's had been happening further down the leader board. By the next day, this would change. The ravages of riding hundreds of miles in the blistering desert heat would soon take a brutal toll on the entire field, and nobody would be immune—not even the race leaders.

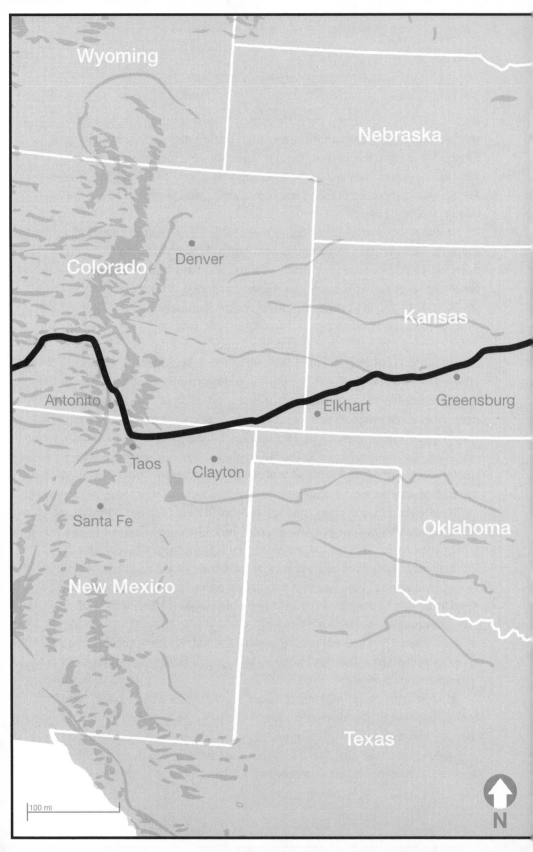

8

Days Four and Five: Extreme Extremes

Climbing the Colorado Rockies, June 19 and 20

Serious cyclists enjoy the simple pleasure of ascent. They lose themselves in trance-like rhythms during long climbs. *Breathe-pedal, breathe-pedal, breathe-pedal.* But at night, it's a different matter. Since they can't see the pitch of the road ahead, they're unable to judge how long a particular gradient will last or anticipate the shape of upcoming undulations. The only way they can measure their progress is by the passage of time, since the sweeping vistas are invisible after sundown.

Jure Robič was familiar with the rigors of nighttime climbing. He had ascended the Rockies in darkness for many years, and he was usually the first man over the top. It was hard being Jure Robič. The expectations, the scrutiny, and the knowledge that everybody was out to get him always weighed on his mind.

A few hours after crossing through Monument Valley, the leaders reached the westernmost flanks of the Rockies and the climbing began. As Robič began his assault on the evening of June 19, speculation had already started. *Team Robič looks vulnerable. He has a sore throat. His crew is making mistakes and costing him time.* Robič himself knew nothing of this chatter. Truth was, he did have a scratchy throat, but otherwise he was feeling strong. His coach insisted that Robič's mind was clear and his mood swings less severe than in previous years.

Still, halfway up the Rockies, Robič took a break just before starting his climb to the highest point on the race course. He clomped into his motor home and shut the door. I stood outside, swatting away mosquitoes on a chilly evening in the mountains, and waited to see how long he'd remain inside. Despite how close the race was, he stayed off the course for almost an hour. This unexpected break wasn't part of Robič's usual race plan. Also, earlier in the day, his sleep-deprived crew had made a wrong turn in Durango that cost Robič a few more precious minutes.

Back on the first night, his crew had made a more significant error that brought a 15-minute time penalty. The race route steers clear of interstate highways, but there were a few short stretches of unavoidable interstate travel. Racers aren't allowed to pass each other along the shoulders of these dangerous roads. Back in the California desert, the rampaging Slovenian had found himself behind a slower rider on Interstate 10. His crew thought they'd received a visual cue from a race official that it would be okay to make the pass, and they proceeded to do so. The official slapped a penalty on Robič a little while later, claiming he had never given such a signal. This official asserted he would never waive the interstate "no-pass" rule, even for the reigning champion.

Robič's crew members had begun grumbling about officiating even before the race began. In Oceanside waiting for the gun to go off, Robič had stepped off the stage and relieved himself behind the bandstand. A police officer spotted the act, and the RAAM organization gave Robič a 15-minute penalty for unsportsmanlike conduct. By the time Robič reached the Rockies, he was carrying 30 minutes of penalties, compared with none for the other race favorites.

To soothe his scratchy throat, Robič had started taking antibiotics before he began his final push over the Rockies, hoping to stave off more serious respiratory trouble. As Robič stepped from his motor home the evening of June 19 after his hour-long break, the moist mountain air soothed his aching throat and lungs.

Robič had a few other things on his mind other than his penalties and a sore throat. While he was in his motor home preparing to begin his push up to La Manga Pass, Wyss flew by and actually grabbed the lead. Robič considered himself to be the stronger climber, so he was sure he'd regain the top spot by the time he crested the Rockies late that night.

The Slovenian defender was supremely confident. After all, he'd won RAAM four times, more than any man ever had. Still, at about this point in the race, the first grimaces of discomfort began flashing across his face. It hurt a lot to compete in this race, even for Robič. So what motivated this man to come back year after year, knowing that he'd suffer so much and that a second-place finish would be considered a failure?

Robič had tried quitting his RAAM addiction a couple of times before. He declared the 2007 race would be his last, but after vanquishing the legendary Wolfgang Fasching in a tight battle he came back in 2008 and won going away. "For me it is not difficult to stay motivated for an event like RAAM because it is the greatest and toughest race in the world," he explained. Of his decision to return in 2009 for his seventh time, he said, "I will try to win again…because it is my lifestyle, my habit, and I see no reason to stop when I am at the top of my lifetime performance."

Robič had raced Wyss twice before. Their first matchup in 2006 didn't last long. An ambulance spirited Robič off the course early in the race near Pagosa Springs, Colorado, after he had spiked a fever and had trouble breathing. He had suffered a dangerous fluid build-up around his heart and lungs and did not finish—Robič's only RAAM DNF. Wyss went on to win the race in his rookie attempt. The next year Robič resumed his winning streak, besting the fourth-place Wyss by almost nine hours.

Now Robič was back again, ready to suffer to win the race he loved and that had become his obsession. As he rejoined his battle with Wyss that evening, Robič winced as he climbed onto his bike. It turns out he had one more problem—blossoming saddle sores. Robič's wounds would cause agonizing pain for days to come. But this champion had business to take care of—a rendezvous with the 10,250-foot La Manga Pass. So after his break he rode off determinedly in search of Wyss.

A few hours ahead of Wyss and Robič, the ever-cheerful Janet Christiansen was also about to crest the Rockies at La Manga Pass. She had begun her race a day before the men and by midmorning the following day they'd begin overtaking her. But for the time being, she was enjoying her faux battle with Robič and wanted to delay the inevitable as long she could. So far Christiansen had managed to stay a few hours ahead of her real rival, the spirited Brazilian Daniela Genovesi, so her mood was good despite the unending pain literally in her butt. "I'm having all kinds of fun with my saddle," she joked. "I've got my best minds on it!" The saddle sores she had been enduring for days now were getting worse, and everybody on her team was concerned.

Her crew chief Bill Osborn tried every trick in the book, from pieces of moleskin to antiseptic salve. Adding to her discomfort, Christiansen's tailbone was still deeply bruised from *the previous year's* race, so she was already using three neoprene saddle pads for extra cushioning. The pads helped the bruising, but worsened the rubbing. Christiansen reminded herself of the power of laughter and kept cracking jokes all the way up the Rockies. When her crew told her that Robič was gaining in the middle of the night, this spunky gal spun up her cadence and attacked the steep climb.

Starting from the spot where Robič took his unexpected break and got passed by Wyss, the route ascended about 2,000 feet to reach TS15 in Pagosa Springs, 30 miles away. From there the racers had 70 more miles before they finally crested La Manga Pass. But reaching the top through the peaks and valleys of the Rockies demanded another 6,000 feet or so of climbing. All told, the racers ascended roughly 9,000 feet in about 100 miles—equivalent to climbing up more than seven Empire State Buildings stacked on top of each other. Darkness had fallen, and at roughly 8,000 feet the temperature had dipped below 40 degrees. Robič was working so hard to catch Wyss that he didn't notice.

This mountainous stretch of Route 84 makes a brief excursion into New Mexico and then turns back into Colorado. Just before it does, it passes through TS16 in the tiny village of Chama, only 21 miles from La Manga Pass. By the time Robič arrived in Chama, he'd regained a slim seven-minute lead on Wyss, passing him on a twisty mountain road as these two athletes continued their epic battle.

ROBIČ CAME OVER LA MANGA PASS IN THE LEAD around midnight on June 19. I was up there waiting in the darkness, my driving partner Les Handy fast asleep in the back of our minivan. The pitch-black mountaintop was so still and quiet, I felt as though I was in an isolation chamber. Then the lights of Robič's follow-vehicle lit up the road in front of our position. Suddenly Robič appeared in view, illuminated from the spotlights behind. He coasted to a halt but didn't see our minivan parked only a few feet away.

If he had bothered to look up, Robič would have marveled at the black sky teeming with millions of bright stars. As he reached this high point he paused but remained straddling his bike as two crew members jumped out and ran over to him. Wordlessly they handed him a hat and some gloves for the long, cold descent. There was no time to celebrate, no whoops or high-fives. Nothing much to say, either—just work to do. Within seconds, Robič was off again, careening down the mountainside into the inky night.

As I settled down for a quick nap, I was surprised by a sudden commotion: it was Wyss, in hot pursuit only minutes off the pace. Robič hadn't managed to open up much of a gap on him during the climb, and Wyss didn't stop at the summit like Robič had. Within seconds it was quiet again.

As the field's strongest climber, Robič had anticipated building a decent lead through the Rockies. Instead he came through on antibiotics, carrying 30 minutes of penalties, and essentially tied on the road with a man who had won RAAM before. On top of that, Christoph Strasser and Marko Baloh were only a couple of hours back. Luckily for these leaders, the determined Austrian Gerhard Gulewicz was nowhere to be found.

Group psychology began affecting Robič's race. As with the other crews, Robič's was a tight-knit fellowship completely absorbed with the singular task of safely getting their racer over the line in the shortest possible time. To them, the outside world didn't exist; the only space that mattered was the 10-foot circle around their rider, and the only time that mattered was race time. The battle rhythm of a RAAM crew member is so demanding (especially for those working for the race favorites) that many of them suffer something akin to post-traumatic stress syndrome for days after the race ends.

Robič's crew faced additional pressure. Their actions were being closely scrutinized, and people were already chattering about their navigational error back in Durango. Plus, Robič's legendary mental breakdowns and emotional outbursts made crewing for him a stressful proposition. Slovenian Andrej Petrovic supported both Baloh and Robič in past races. "Marko is fun to crew for—he loves cycling even when he doesn't win," Andrej explained. "But Jure can get psycho out there."

Crew members were almost as sleep-deprived as their racer by this point, and their cognitive abilities were slipping just as precipitously.

Since sleep deprivation heightens emotions and encourages paranoia and suggestibility, crews often begin distrusting other teams and even the race organization itself as the competition grinds on. Some of Robič's crew members were convinced the RAAM organization was out to get them, and a feeling of victimhood began simmering on Team Robič. Besides, for these men it was easier to focus on the foibles of RAAM officials than their own mistakes.

It was only natural for Team Robič to turn their collective paranoia into a matter of patriotic pride. Coming from a small, rural nation that achieved independence only recently, these Slovenians lit a patriotic fire under their racer and derived great comfort from it. One of their favorite cheers during the race was, "For Jure! For Slovenia! For our team!" This cadre of soldiers was prepared to stick together and fight as if their lives depended on it, even if this meant facing down the RAAM organization itself.

ONCE ROBIČ CRESTED LA MANGA PASS he faced a dark and treacherous 2,500-foot descent featuring a four-mile stretch that plunged down at a murderous 7 percent gradient. Adding to the danger was a road surface slickened by a light mist. Robič had no choice but to continue with Wyss in hot pursuit; he couldn't afford to wait it out until dawn. Plummeting down a mountain at 35 to 40 miles per hour through tight switchbacks, on a wet road surface, and in the dark is the most terrifying sort of riding imaginable. Robič had to concentrate if he wanted to make it down safely.

The Robič-Wyss battle at the top of the Rockies wasn't the only one raging in the wee hours of June 20. Race headquarters fielded time station call-ins from at least 11 different racers in a three-hour stretch from 1:00 to 4:00 AM local time. In the middle of the night, in the middle of nowhere, the roads were crawling with cyclists illuminated by the bright lights of their follow-vehicles, somewhere in or near the Colorado Rockies on their way to Taos.

Four men were battling for leadership in the hours after midnight, separated by only a couple of hours after 60 hours of racing: Robič, Wyss,

Strasser, and Baloh. Gulewicz was in fifth, but this race favorite was more than eight hours behind.

Another battle raged in the middle of this night farther down the men's field, more than 150 miles behind the leaders. Back at TS13 in Cortez, Colorado, at least half a dozen men were tightly bunched within two and a half hours of each other. Some were riding in sight of each other in the darkness, their presence made visible only by the blinking amber lights of their follow-vehicles.

None of these men had any chance of finishing atop the podium in Annapolis, but each was committed to a personal goal so important that it compelled him to race deeply into the night. Only a handful of crew members working the graveyard shift were aware of what these men were putting themselves through.

The leader of the women's race was also on the road at this hour, still managing to maintain her positive attitude and to keep the jokes flowing. Janet Christiansen's sleep plan called for her to rest between about 3:00 and 6:00 in the morning, arising to greet the dawn. As she took her sleep break on June 20, she was unaware that Daniela Genovesi had been forced to take an even longer rest after being shattered by her climb over La Manga Pass. Genovesi would fall seven hours behind Christiansen by midmorning on this day.

Michele Santilhano was also racing through the night, still hoping to make up time after quelling her quad pain, but she was faltering and now trailed Christiansen by more than 11 hours. It wasn't looking good for Santilhano's Shongololo Express as they limped into Pagosa Springs after 3:00 in the morning on June 20. Completely spent, Santilhano hadn't slept in what felt like days. She had hoped that when her quad calmed down the day before she would be able to attack the Rockies with more vigor, but right now the mountains were winning. Nestled at 7,000 feet, the mountain community of Pagosa Springs is surrounded by the largest contiguous wilderness area in the U.S., but nobody on the Shongololo Express was in any mood to enjoy spectacular views of the San Juan Mountains. Besides, it was pitch black, so the only thing this strung-out, despondent bunch cared about was how far they were from Taos.

Santilhano normally maintained a gracious, even cheery demeanor during her races. The day before, her visage had begun cracking. She prayed, she repeated her mantra, and she thought about her kids back at the hospital. But as the race clock kept ticking closer to the Taos time cutoff, her predicament was looking more and more precarious.

To beat the time cutoff, the Shongololo Express had to make it to Taos four days and seven hours after starting in Oceanside. That meant they had to arrive by 8:00 PM local time today; Santilhano had 17 hours to race through 160 miles of mountainous terrain. But it was 3:00 in the morning, and right now she needed some sleep. She knew the clock wouldn't pause when she did. Still, even if she went down for two hours, she could make it to Taos in time if she averaged 11 miles per hour for the next 15 hours.

Unfortunately, it wasn't just the time cutoff that was jeopardizing her race. Santilhano's crew mates were totally dispirited. Not content to argue just with Santilhano, they were also arguing with each other and not working well as a team. They were having a wretched time, and as a result they were giving up on their rider. It wasn't an all-out mutiny, but Santilhano could sense that "they were ready to take RAAM away from me." The signals weren't subtle. "When I stopped earlier that afternoon in Durango, I asked for a snack and I had planned to eat while riding," Santilhano recalled. "But all of a sudden I was given a big plate of Chinese food, so I stood around eating it. Then later a crew member complained that all I wanted to do was waste time off the bike. I sensed they were out to get me at that point. They had given up."

From the moment the race had started, Santilhano said she never felt that her RAAM crew believed in her the way her stalwart English Channel crew had. Her current predicament reminded her more of her calamitous Everest experience than her triumphant Channel swim. "My RAAM crew didn't let me call the shots on nutrition, and we had a number of disagreements," she lamented. "There wasn't a single point of failure. It was my quad, the arguing and in-fighting within my crew, nutritional issues, and the way my crew was bossing me around."

In the still of the night, the Shongololo Express came to a shuddering stop. Santilhano felt she still had a fighting chance to reach Taos in time, but her crew chief Adrienne had seen enough. In fact, everyone on her crew was fed up, and that colored their assessment of the odds of success. Adrienne didn't think it made sense to continue, especially in light of how miserable everybody was.

RAAM was about to vanquish one the most accomplished ultradistance endurance athletes around. Just outside of Pagosa Springs, everybody on

Austrian Franz Preihs was making his second RAAM solo attempt in 2009. (Brendon Purdy)

Jim Rees, the affable father of six, was intent on breaking the British record for RAAM set by Mark Pattinson. (Brendon Purdy)

Two-time RAAM finisher Gerhard Gulewicz set a new world record for the crossing of Australia in 2007.
(Brendon Purdy)

Frenchman and medical researcher Patrick Autissier had two goals: to finish his second RAAM race and to measure its effects on the human body.

Despite his rookie status, Christoph Strasser was expected to finish in the top five.
(Brendon Purdy)

Dani Wyss was looking to win his second RAAM in 2009; in 2006, he became only the second man to claim victory in his rookie attempt. (Brendon Purdy)

Marko Baloh was counting on the presence of his family to keep him motivated during RAAM, but their presence concerned some of his crew mates.

Lt. Col. Tony O'Keeffe of the Canadian Army with his wife Jackie moments before the start of the race.

Although he is an experienced ultradistance cyclist, 2009 marked the solo debut for American Kevin Kaiser.

Kaiser's countryman, Ben Popp, was confident his advanced planning and experience as part of a two-man team had him well-prepared for his first solo race. (Brendon Purdy)

Brazil's Daniela Genovesi was one of only four women competing solo in RAAM in 2009. (Brendon Purdy)

After failing to finish once before, American Janet Christensen was determined to survive her second RAAM thanks to a positive attitude and tireless sense of humor.
(Brendon Purdy)

An accomplished triathlete, ultramarathon runner and swimmer, and mountaineer, South Africa's Michele Santilhano was nonetheless apprehensive about her first solo RAAM. (Brendon Purdy)

Slovenian Special Forces soldier Jure Robič entered the 2009 RAAM as a four-time champion and the odds-on favorite to win his unprecedented fifth title. (Brendon Purdy)

the Shongololo Express rested until dawn, slumped uncomfortably over car seats and not truly asleep, just waiting in a state of quietude while Adrienne called race headquarters with the news.

By the end of this day, three racers would withdraw, but it was this first casualty that caught everybody by surprise. Mighty Michele Santilhano— the woman who'd finished a half dozen ultramarathons, swum the English Channel, completed a quintuple Ironman, and *almost* summitted Everest— was done.

THIS WOULD BE A MEMORABLE DAY FOR ROOKIE CHRISTOPH STRASSER, TOO. Along with the rest of the leaders, the young charmer had laid claim to the Rockies the night before, reaching the top of La Manga Pass in the early morning hours. Reaching the summit had been an emotional moment for Strasser, and he teared up as his crew read him email messages from loved ones back home in Austria. *All I need is their love and support and I can do anything*, he thought. *Only positive thoughts now and I'll make it.*

Strasser was totally in his element in the Rockies; they reminded him of his training rides in the Austrian Alps. Once he had crested the pass, it was time for a sleep break. His last one had been way back in dusty Mexican Hat, Utah, more than 20 hours and 250 miles ago. He concluded it would be unsafe in his condition to launch into a long, dark, dangerous descent right now. Besides, the climb had been harder than he expected, and he needed to rest.

Anticipating Strasser's break, his mental coach Tomas prepared Strasser's food and arranged the bedcovers on the narrow bunk in the back of the motor home. As Strasser collapsed into his warm nest, Tomas whispered into his ear and gently stroked his forearm. "Now you will relax. You feel comfortable and warm and safe. Drift off to sleep. Sleep now, Christoph. Sleeeeeep," he soothed. Tomas used a shorthand form of hypnosis to calm Strasser down, and the young racer was out almost instantly.

Just before dawn on June 20, Strasser pulled his creaky body up from the bunk, ready to throw himself into the race once again. Bundled from head to toe, he stepped out into the predawn stillness anticipating a chilly descent down the verdant eastern flanks of the Rockies. It was a damp, gray morning, and as soon as Strasser built up some speed down the mountain his teeth started chattering. He couldn't shake the chill out of his bones, so Team Strasser decided to crank up the music and have some fun. "Everybody started singing, taking turns at the microphone so I could hear them through the loudspeakers," Strasser remembered later with a grin. "I was singing the loudest as we closed in on the Taos time station. Our team spirit was amazing. We grew so close to each other, we love each other like brothers now."

Their hearts might have been glowing, but the weather remained obstinately cold and dreary all morning. Then Strasser felt a sensation he had never felt before. The 26-year-old phenom had been holding his own against the best in the world, but now he had slipped into fourth place, passed by Baloh a few hours before Taos. And then...*boom.* It came on rapidly, a feeling of tightness in his chest. Before he knew it Strasser was having trouble drawing the mountain air into his lungs.

He put his head down and raced on, forcing his mind to go blank and covering the 80 miles to Taos by 11:00 AM. But nobody on Team Strasser was smiling as he glided to a stop at the Taos time station, which sat in front of an adobe-style hotel. As in Monument Valley, Strasser had no time to contemplate the Native American heritage surrounding him. Les Handy and I were waiting for Strasser after napping the previous night on the La Manga summit. He didn't seem relieved about reaching the one-third mark on his journey to Annapolis, and there were no celebratory hugs or high fives. Strasser looked haggard. He didn't even acknowledge the small crowd that had assembled; he huddled briefly with his crew in the light drizzle and then pushed off again along the misty mountain road, in fourth place and trailing Baloh by less than 10 minutes.

As Strasser was about to begin the steepest mountain climb of the entire race—a quad-busting two-mile ascent back up to 9,800 feet—the asthmatic wheeze in his lungs returned. He came around a bend and saw the road ahead shoot straight up at an alarming angle. It was Bobcat Pass. *Oh no*, he thought, *not now.* As he hit the climb he shifted into his lowest gear and tried to breathe, but the wheezing grew worse. His legs began protesting, so he rose out of the saddle and stood on his pedals to summon a little more power. His lungs were so clogged he could barely draw a breath, and he could hardly turn the pedals. He was just holding on.

Before long Strasser was hyperventilating in the thin mountain air, his lungs struggling to absorb the oxygen his aching muscles demanded. He felt faint and dizzy. His cycling glasses had fogged up, so his visibility was limited. Strasser grew disoriented, dispirited, and desperate. One thought repeated itself in his mind: *I will not stop*. He imagined himself smoothly cresting Bobcat Pass, and the visualization helped him hold it together.

The blonde Adonis who'd pranced around Oceanside just a few days before was now puffy-faced, glassy-eyed, and dazed. The transformation was shocking. Strasser's fluid grace had been replaced by a gasping, confused young man who suddenly felt very far from home. Watching their friend fight his way up Bobcat Pass, his crew fretted for the first time since California.

Coming after the extreme heat of the deserts, the extreme cold of the Rockies delivers a mighty shock to a racer's respiratory system. If the desert is a death zone, then the Rockies are a pneumonia ward for RAAM cyclists.

CLIMBING BOBCAT PASS, STRASSER RELIED ON THE POWER OF HIS THOUGHTS, not the might of his legs. When Strasser was a little boy, he figured out that thoughts were powerful things.

He remembers being scolded for never finishing what he started: puzzles, drawings, even television shows. The criticism made him feel bad—but not *that* bad. Young Strasser didn't see why grownups expected him to waste time finishing something once he'd already figured out the answer. In his mind, it was more important to move on to the next challenge. Introspective and already a deep thinker as a youngster, his ruminations gave him the confidence to take the road less traveled.

During his dreadful climb up Bobcat Pass, Strasser used mental techniques coach Tomas had taught him in order to tap into the power of his subconscious. "I program my subconscious with positive images and ideas, so that when I'm in trouble and can't remember why I'm doing the race, my unconscious mind comes to my rescue," he said. He takes his mental training as seriously as his physical conditioning.

Strasser summons his subconscious in peculiar ways. Back in the desert, he used peppermint oil to trick his brain into thinking he was cool. He rubbed the oil on his skin a lot during his pre-RAAM training rides, and each time he told himself, "Oh, this feels so cold," programming his subconscious to associate the peppermint scent with cooling. And when something hurt—his knees, his wrists, the balls of his feet—Strasser diverted attention away from the pain by focusing on, say, tapping his fingers on his handlebars, or wiggling his little toe in his shoe.

Psychologists have names for what Strasser was doing with his peppermint oils, his little toe, and his motivational imagery. Like other ultradistance racers, Strasser uses both cognitive distraction and dissociation to endure the endless discomfort that's so much a part of ultradistance racing. These techniques have been validated through scientific pain studies, many of which employ something called the cold-pressor test.

The test is pretty simple. A subject immerses his hand in ice water and leaves it there for as long as he can stand it. That length of time determines one's pain threshold, and most people can't last more than a minute. Studies have found that personality doesn't influence the amount of time someone can keep his hand immersed so much as one's ability to employ techniques like Strasser's. People with the lowest tolerance tend instead to "catastrophize" their pain by reacting with strong, negative emotions. Those people would yank their hands out of the ice water in under a minute, grimacing and shouting as if they'd lost it to the errant swing of an ax. People with the greatest tolerance use distraction and dissociation to remain calm. Such a person can last more than two minutes before calmly removing his hand.

Recent evidence from advanced brain imaging technologies like PET scans suggests two distinct pathways for how we perceive pain. The first sensory pathway registers the quality of the pain sensation (dull or sharp, for example). The second affective pathway, running through the brain's anterior cingulate cortex, registers how unpleasant the pain is and mediates how much suffering occurs. Those subjects who "catastrophized" the pain of the cold-pressor test might simply be genetically predisposed to have hypersensitive anterior cingulate cortices. But this genetic-biological model probably isn't the last word.

Our unconscious and subconscious minds also play crucial roles in our response to pain. Researchers have another model for understanding how the brain mediates the pain response, and it's helpful in understanding how ultradistance athletes endure their punishing races. Called the "gate control" model, it also goes beyond the simple view that the intensity of pain is directly linked to the messages sent by chemicals released by diseased or overstressed cells. The new thinking is that the mind isn't a passive actor; for example, it's a common experience for soldiers injured on the battlefield not to feel pain until the urgency is over.

Neuroscientist Patrick Wall evangelized this gate control thinking and coedited the definitive medical textbook on pain. He said, "The problem of pain used to be trivialized as a one-way system, but it is not so simple. As nerve impulses enter the spinal cord, the brain gives permission for the message to be sensed by saying, 'That's important' or 'I'm not interested in that.' The brain is a gate that decides whether the message is transmitted and the amplification it wants to apply."

Physiologist Timothy Noakes extended Wall's model to athletes. Noakes spent years debunking the notion that exercise performance is limited by metabolic changes in the muscles, with exercise terminating when our bodily systems are stressed beyond their capacities—the so-called "catastrophe" model of fatigue. He and others instead support a "central governor" model in which the central nervous system unconsciously adjusts effort based on factors such as past experience, immediate goals, conscious sensation of fatigue, current exertion level, and metabolic rate. In this model, fatigue isn't a physical event but rather a sensation that is the conscious manifestation of these subconscious processes. The revolutionary idea behind Noakes' research is that the fatigue is more like an emotion rather than a physical state.

This isn't so far-fetched. Recent research suggests that perception is much more than the sum of signals received by the brain. For example, people experiencing unpleasant sensations from missing limbs or other missing body parts now benefit from new therapies based on the premise that these phantom sensations are manufactured by a confused mind without any input from the nervous system. Today, amputees can get relief by creating a sensory illusion that the missing limb is still there. They do this by putting their remaining limb through a hole in a box with mirrored sides, so that looking down into the box, they see their arm's mirror image as if it were their missing limb. Once the individual perceives he has two limbs again, the phantom limb sensations immediately diminish or even disappear.

The theory is that when a limb is removed, the mind becomes confused because familiar nerve impulses simply vanish. So we unconsciously assume the limb is still there, but is paralyzed, clenched, or otherwise immobilized. Dr. Atul Gawande calls this the "best guess" theory of perception. He says that phantom limb syndrome is a stronger form of how you feel when your dentist numbs your gums and lip with Novocain; it feels as though you lip is swollen to twice its normal size, when in reality your brain isn't receiving any nerve impulses from your lip at all.

Here's another everyday example, courtesy of Dr. Gawande: "Contemplating what it's like to hold your finger in a flame won't make your finger hurt. But simply writing about a tick crawling up the nape of one's neck is enough to start my neck itching." So why does one thought cause an itch while another doesn't elicit an analogous response? PET scans show that when a nerve picks up an itch, it stimulates "the part of the cortex that tells you where on your body the sensation occurs; the region that governs your emotional responses, reflecting the disagreeable nature of itch; and the limbic and motor areas that process irresistible urges (such as the urge to use drugs among the addicted, or to overeat among the obese), reflecting the ferocious impulse to scratch." Divorced from actual stimuli, merely thinking about the tick can reflexively trigger these regions. Dr. Gawande explains that, "Itch, it turns out, is indeed inseparable from the desire to scratch."

So how we perceive the world—and how athletes perceive sensations like pain and fatigue—might not depend solely on nerve impulses and other physical inputs.

The central role our mind plays in our perceptions of pain and fatigue helps us see how athletic challenges one culture might consider murderous can be almost commonplace in another. Take the 55-mile Comrades Marathon that's been held in the South African province of KwaZulu-Natal annually since 1921. It's so much a part of the culture there that it draws 12,000 participants each year.

There is a similar tradition among the Mexican Tarahumara Indians, who have been running vast distances for generations. They'll chase deer, wild turkeys, and rabbits for days until the animals drop from exhaustion— the same persistence hunting approach that prehistoric humans likely depended on for survival before we invented weapons that work at a distance.

Because the Tarahumara live in rugged canyons where wagons and horses are impractical, foot travel is often the best option for getting from one village to another. But the Tarahumara don't stroll from place to place—they run. Men, women, and children, old and young alike—

everybody runs. The Tarahumara routinely run distances only covered by elite ultramarathoners while wearing only sandals, without aid stations or electrolyte drinks, up and down steep canyons, at elevation. Traveling from one village to another, a Tarahumara might run between 50 and 80 miles in a single day.

Perceptions about what is possible in RAAM have also evolved. The event was inaugurated in 1982 with four hardened cyclists, but now it's within the reach of athletes as young as 18 and as old as 62—even those who have lost the use of an arm or leg. The event hasn't changed, but our appreciation for what is possible has.

Obviously the mind is a powerful actor in our ability to persevere during arduous endurance races and other physical challenges. Even at the young age of 26, this is something Strasser knew well. While climbing Bobcat Pass, as he had done hundreds of times in training, Strasser conjured images of what it would feel like to cross the finish line in Annapolis. He imagined with great intricacy the sounds, smells, and sights of Annapolis Harbor: sailboats bobbing in the picturesque harbor, the fresh scent of salt air wafting off the water, seagulls squawking overhead. And when he felt woozy and faint, he concentrated on his left pinky instead. The power of the mind is what helped him carry on that fateful morning.

FOLLOWING THE LEADERS OF THE MEN'S RACE who had crested La Manga Pass in the middle of the night, fifth-place Gerhard Gulewicz— the Austrian who had crashed out of the 2008 race while second on the road—came through later that morning. Next came the top Canadian on the road, Peter Oyler. After them, eight men were tightly bunched within a few hours of each other, led by Spaniard Julian Garcia, who was back for his second time. Then came live-wire Ben Popp and the military officer Tony O'Keeffe, just 20 minutes apart. Five others rounded out the group, including Franz Preihs and British veteran Jim Rees.

These men were all on the La Manga Pass climb at the same time on this windy, wet afternoon with temperatures hovering in the low 50s.

Some racers climbing the Rockies on this day experienced their own private hell. But others exulted in a blustery afternoon that dazzled them with intermittent showers, fleeting rainbows, and puffy clouds that danced and skipped across the sky before a majestic mountain backdrop.

Rees was feeling spunky and in fine form during the long ascent. He had recently managed to speak with his wife Tracey in England for the first time since leaving Oceanside. "This massively motivated me," he recalled. His mates read encouraging emails from his friends over his now-functioning loudspeakers. "I was feeling so grateful for my young, rookie crew," he said. "They were trying so hard, and everything was going well.*" I can't believe it*, he thought. *I'm going to finally break the British record.*

During his climb up the San Juan Mountains, Rees was having a jolly time carrying on with his make-believe friend, Bruce, who lived on the face of one of his crew chiefs, Martyn. Upon their arrival in Oceanside, Martyn had stopped shaving and grew a long, bushy mustache that everyone welcomed as their new crew member. Bruce the Mustache was a real cut-up and had Rees in fits of laughter in Oceanside. Now Rees was making the same silly Bruce jokes over and over again, like a little kid.

Popp was also having the time of his life. He was in eighth place, helping to lead this pack of men up La Manga Pass, and he could barely believe his eyes. "The scenery looks fake! It can't be real," he exclaimed to anyone within earshot. His young buddies were blasting rock music and grooving along with him. Some of them scampered around the next switchback so they could cover the asphalt with chalked messages of encouragement before he rode by. One of their messages wasn't meant to be read: it was a drawing of a gigantic phallus, which had Popp climbing out of the saddle with a huge grin stuck to his face.

It's hard to understate the importance of getting raucous, enthusiastic encouragement from one's crew. When a racer's crew feels chirpy, so does the racer. When crew members feel beaten down, they sap a racer's energy. Everybody on duty this afternoon knew the climb up La Manga Pass would be tough, so they pulled out all the stops to help power their riders over the top.

Les and I stayed put on the mountain to watch this bunch push up to the summit. That afternoon we saw crew members don grass hula skirts and coconut bras and dance on the side of the road; a female crew member pull her shirt up to flash her male racer; and a few guys strip to their underwear and stand on top of their motor homes playing imaginary guitars while their charges flew by. It was pandemonium on this remote mountain road in the Middle of Nowhere, Colorado, and as usual, the outside world didn't have a clue.

After a grinning Popp crested the pass, O'Keeffe came next, only a few minutes behind. Both men were still on a 10-day pace, even though they'd managed "only" 250 miles in the previous 24 hours of mountainous riding. But they had each banked miles earlier during their wind-aided desert crossings, when both men had covered almost 400 miles during the first 24 hours of the race.

O'Keeffe hadn't seemed like much of a hardened military leader climbing the Rockies in the previous year's race. He had been miserable because he hadn't brought enough warm clothing to ward off the frigid temperatures. This time, once O'Keeffe hit the summit in a steady rain around 5:00 in the evening, his crew mates trotted over and bundled him in warm gloves, a hat, and whatever he needed for the chilly descent to come.

Preihs, the tattooed bad boy who had looked so intimidating at the starting line three days before, came over the top about 20 minutes later. Rees followed an hour and a half later, reaching La Manga Pass with his favorite music blaring. It was only 43 degrees now, but the sun was finally peeking out. In an impossibly green valley that was visible from the summit, the tall grasses were swaying in a stiff breeze as low-lying clouds raced across the late afternoon sky.

Many racers remembered that afternoon on the La Manga climb as a highlight of their race, and Rees was one of these. Mesmerized by the beauty of the Rockies and invigorated by the blustery weather, he felt deeply connected to nature and energized by its elemental power. The branches of the towering aspen trees were bending and swaying in the wind as if they were alive, and Rees felt their presence.

The Spaniard Julian Garcia led the pack earlier in the climb, but now he was the last one in this group to reach the top. He stopped abruptly a few hundred yards from the summit and called his motor home back to his position. The endless climbing, the thin mountain air, the chill, and the wind and rain were all too much for him to take. Headquarters received a call a short time later informing them that Garcia had withdrawn from the race.

RAAM was doing what it always does: dishing out extreme experiences—both good and bad—up and down the mountainside. They didn't know it yet, but as some of these racers screamed down the eastern flanks of the San Juan Mountains into the Conejos River Valley, it would soon be their turn to feel the wrath of RAAM.

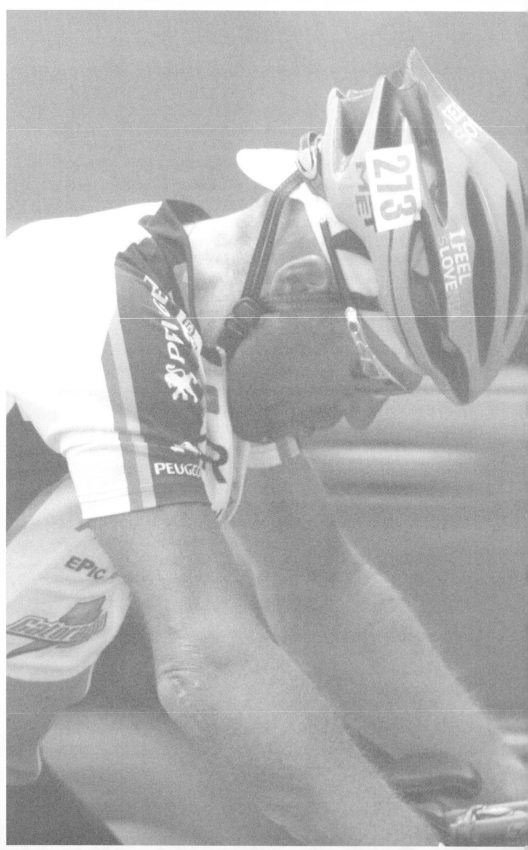

9

Day Five:
The Kansas Crucible

On the Kansas prairie, June 21

Back on Day Two, Franz Preihs' tattooed knee started killing him. The Austrian slipped down into the middle of the men's pack, all but ending his chance of a podium finish. Preihs had earned a reputation for being able to endure mind-boggling levels of pain; in the previous year's race, he refused to quit after crashing and breaking his collarbone. Following a detour to the local hospital, he returned to the race route and rode for days in this condition, never once entertaining the thought of quitting. He moved up the field late in the race and finished a hard-to-believe fourth. When ProTour racer Tyler Hamilton did the same thing in the 2003 Tour de France, his gritty performance made headlines around the world. When he broke a collarbone in the Giro d'Italia the year before, his pain was so intense he ground 11 teeth to the roots. Hamilton rode with a broken, bandaged collarbone for about five hours a day for almost three weeks straight during the Tour, while Preihs rode 20 hours a day or more for a solid week in RAAM the previous year. Who's tougher? Call it a tie.

Even though Preihs had given up hope of a podium finish because of his knee injury, this year the thought of quitting didn't enter the rugged Austrian's mind for a second. Then Preihs' painful knee began swelling up. Not a good sign with five days of cycling still ahead of him. He exhorted his legs to keep churning, but his pain only worsened. His physician Andrae used a gigantic syringe to drain bloody fluid from Preihs' ravaged knee. He just kept pedaling, trying to ignore what felt like a demon jabbing away at him with its diabolical pitchfork.

Perseverance is the molten core of this relentless race, and Preihs was living proof.

As an only child, Preihs was spoiled by his parents. They lavished positive reinforcement on him, and to this day he still craves encouragement when confronting big challenges. So when his knee started balking, he reached out to his wife Michaela in Austria, herself a long-distance cyclist. As he struggled along he took strength from Michaela's hopeful words, but she possessed no magic powers for warding off the demon's pitchfork.

Andrae had let Preihs know his knee could only be drained every eight hours, or else permanent damage might result. Like most of the cyclists who take on the challenge of RAAM, Preihs was capable of tuning out his body's distress signals. The flip side was he might ignore ominous danger signs. Andrae knew how Preihs' mind worked, so he was determined to put him on notice.

Preihs endured the terrible pain without complaint, somehow pushing up and over the Rockies late that night. Mired in the middle of the pack almost 20 hours behind the leader, he refused to use his knee as an excuse to let up. Words can't do justice to that kind of perseverance.

Andrae drained Preihs' knee the maximum three times on Day Four. It swelled up yet again, but Preihs kept pushing. "I just accept my suffering," he explained matter-of-factly. "It's just part of the sporting life." After cresting La Manga Pass practically on one leg, he rode through the dreary weather all the way to Taos, 1,044 miles into the race. In the end, it wasn't the pain that brought Preihs down; he could handle that. The problem was that his knee, swollen many times its normal size, finally locked up and refused to bend.

At midday on Day Five, RAAM finally felled one of the early favorites. The race's preeminent bad boy, Preihs didn't look very tough at that moment. With his minivan's sliding door open, he sat with his bad leg propped up, looking more like a forlorn puppy than a tattooed he-man. He felt greater remorse for his crew than for himself. Still, at his moment of capitulation, he stubbornly held on to one thought: *I can't wait to get back here next year.*

AROUND THIS TIME, THE THREE SURVIVING WOMEN had been racing practically nonstop for 110 hours—more than four and a half days. They had endured broiling deserts, climbed mountain ranges, breathed in the dust storms of Navajo Nation, then tackled the Rockies and rushed down its eastern flanks.

Through it all, Janet Christiansen—still powered by her quirky, sarcastic sense of humor—had covered 1,200 miles and was about to enter Kansas while holding a several-hour lead over the Brazilian Daniela Genovesi.

As dawn broke on Day Five, the men had been racing for almost 90 hours, and Jure Robič was still out in front after 1,400 miles. Crossing the plains of Kansas he held a two-hour lead on cool-headed Dani Wyss and was on pace to break the record for the fastest continental crossing in history. The men's field was stretched out over 450 miles by this point, from the leader Robič to last-place Herman Bachmann, a 50-year-old Swiss man who was still up in the high Rockies. Bachmann wouldn't make it to Robič's current position for a few days yet. With Preihs' withdrawal, the men's field was pared down to 20 racers, and two more would succumb later this day.

But the slowly dwindling field doesn't begin to convey the toll the race was taking. Besides the DNFs, consider how some of the other racers were feeling as dawn broke.

Janet Christiansen's voice was raspy and hoarse after enduring a raging dust storm in Utah, and her feet and legs were distended with the unmistakable signs of peripheral edema. Her saddle had rubbed her raw over three days ago, and each pedal stroke pulverized her pulpy, raw flesh even further.

Ben Popp's scratched cornea was much improved. He was currently the first American on the road, two and a half hours ahead of countryman Michael Cook. But now he had Achilles tendonitis. His physical therapist had bound his legs with Physio Tape to divert stress away from his barking tendons, but they still screamed with every turn of the pedals.

Like Christiansen, Robič was suffering from ghastly saddle sores. His butt and genitals were rubbed raw, but there wasn't anything he could do; he had to keep pedaling. Sleep deprivation was also playing with his emotions, and his famously volatile outbursts were beginning to rattle his crew.

Jim Rees was still clinging to his goal of a 10-day crossing, though he was starting to fall off the British-record pace. He was suffering wave upon wave of powerful, almost psychotic hallucinations. His support crew feared for his safety and was doing everything it could to keep him alert.

Sleep deprivation becomes a constant worry at this stage of the race. In 2004, TV viewers in Britain were given a firsthand look at the effects of this condition thanks to a reality show called *Shattered*. The program featured contestants who were asked to forgo sleep for seven days. Each day they were challenged to perform various tasks, and those who failed were eliminated from the competition.

First came deficits of concentration, such as the inability to do simple math problems. Those were followed by problems with coordination and fine motor control. (In fact, furniture on the set was constructed without hard edges, so that if a contestant fell he wouldn't be hurt.) Changes in behavior came next, as their heightened emotional states made contestants suspicious of one another, leading to frequent flare-ups.

As the days passed, delusions and hallucinations gripped all of them. One thought he was the prime minister of Australia, and another was convinced his clothes had been stolen. The show was canceled after the first season because viewers complained of its cruelty.

RAAM contestants would consider surviving *Shattered* to be child's play. After seven days, many racers aren't even out of Missouri.

AS THE CYCLISTS CONFRONT THE ROCKIES and melt in the sultry Kansas plains, their stories invariably become narratives about pain and suffering. Of all the entrants who didn't finish this race, about half withdrew during Days Four and Five. If a racer can survive the challenge of the Kansas prairie, the thinking goes, he has a good chance of making it all the way to Annapolis.

RAAM holds no monopoly as an arena for self-inflicted pain. Across cultures and throughout time, people have inflicted ritualistic pain in a religious context. Devotional acts of self-denial familiar to us—fasting and pilgrimages, for example—are mild reminders of other practices that go much further. The Plains Indians pierced their chests during four-day-long

Sun Dances, Hindu yogis still walk on red-hot coals, the Buddha meditated alone for years, and some Shiite Muslims whip themselves on the Day of Ashura. These are examples of ritual pain practices that serve to transform the consciousness and identity of the spiritual seeker.

Ritual pain plays a number of roles in religious contexts: as punishment to root out physical or sexual appetites, to achieve purity and self-mastery, as preparation for battle, and to expiate other people's sins. Shamans use painful rites and severe forms of self-denial to achieve transcendence and to commune with spirits. Practitioners of self-mortification claim it leads to euphoria and altered levels of consciousness (thanks to endorphins that are released during the pain response).

Freudian psychoanalysts believe self-inflicted pain is meant to appease the psychological struggle between the ego and superego. Other psychoanalysts think it's a way to affirm one's self-worth or identity. Some philosophers claim that pain is necessary for a beautiful world because complacent pleasure isn't satisfying. Various types of self-inflicted pain are quite literally aimed at beautification: extreme dieting, plastic surgery, and foot binding, for example.

As for self-inflicted pain outside of a religious context, some people make painful sacrifices such as fasting to draw attention to a cause. Others willfully seek out painful experiences that they can control in order to transcend their physical limitations and become more self-aware.

Self-inflicted pain for religious reasons often disturbs us, but in our modern culture, self-inflicted pain for sport is embraced and admired. Athletes who endure long and fiendishly difficult sporting challenges often point out that there is joy in mastering the pain.

As it turns out, suffering is a hallowed cultural value in the world of competitive cycling, probably more so than in any other sport. Cyclists equate suffering with excellence, and it's widely believed that those who can endure the most punishment will rise to the top of the heap. "I won because I suffered the most" is a familiar bike racer refrain. Another is "Once you learn how to suffer out there, you can do anything on a bike."

As Tour de France champion Lance Armstrong writes, "Cycling is so hard, the suffering is so intense, that it's absolutely cleansing. You can go out there with the weight of the world on your shoulders, and after a six-hour ride at a high pain threshold, you feel at peace. The pain is so deep and strong that a curtain descends over your brain. At least for a while you have a kind of hall pass, and don't have to brood on your problems; you can shut everything else out, because the effort and subsequent fatigue are absolute." As if any emphasis was needed, Armstrong goes on to say, "Once someone asked me what pleasure I took in riding for so long. 'Pleasure?' I said. 'I don't understand the question. I didn't do it for pleasure. I did it for pain.'"

Mountains are the ultimate proving ground in bike races, and many monstrous European passes have become famous because the Tour de France returns to them over and over again. The Tourmalet—lassoed by mist, 2,000 meters up in the Circle of Death. The dreaded Mont Ventoux—Domain of the Angels. Col du Galibier—the Giant of the Alps. Just uttering the names of these climbs stirs fear and excitement in a cyclist's heart. Every avid recreational cyclist dreams of conquering one of these celebrated European passes.

As English writer Graeme Fife explains, "The mountains are the extreme case, where you really find out about yourself, in the scary realms of physical and mental exertion to the limit. Even local folklore recognizes the weird forces at work on the cyclist chancing his fate against horrible gradients. Up here, they say, is where the black-hearted ogres of bad luck hang out…quick to pounce on any slippage in your resolve."

Unlike a ProTour cyclist who suffers for hours at a time climbing a mighty mountain pass or two, a RAAM contestant suffers for *days* at a time. Researchers have studied how cyclists cope with pain, and their findings are simultaneously obvious and yet impossible to follow. First, you have to believe that the perception of pain is a choice. You can "choose" to feel the pain at different intensities, knowing that if you're prepared and in control, you can tolerate it more easily. You need to remind yourself that pain on the bike is finite and temporary. You need to observe the pain, and then shift your attention to something more productive. You need to stay relaxed and confident, and accept your pain as simply part of the sport.

Every RAAM cyclist employs these strategies for coping with pain. Family man Marko Baloh's approach is workmanlike. "I try not to think about it," he says. "I just remind myself what my goal is." For Briton Jim Rees, pain is almost an intellectual challenge. "Suffering is my choice," he reasons. "So I don't feel victimized by it. If I'm miserable, I've got to remember I've chosen to do the race, and I've got to accept the gift of being uncomfortable.

"Let's say you have a goal of getting fit. This goal means you have to get up at 6:00 AM to get to the gym. When your alarm goes off your first thought is, *I'm tired*. Does this thought help you get out of bed? Of course not! All you do then is turn the alarm off and promise to start exercising tomorrow. Here's a better approach: since you know you're going to feel punky when the alarm goes off, just accept this feeling and ping out of bed. It's a very subtle process, and a lot of people don't get it. But you've got to reverse the 'feeling-thinking' process so it becomes an instinctive 'thinking-feeling' process."

Jure Robič's reaction to pain is to disassociate from it. "I know it is there because I feel it, but I don't pay attention to it. I sometimes see myself from the other view, looking down at me riding the bike," he explained to journalist Daniel Coyle.

Janet Christiansen admits she doesn't have a high tolerance for pain, especially when it comes to problems she can't find a solution for or make a sarcastic joke about. She uses her prodigious problem-solving skills to gain control over her pain, almost like she does in her day job as a computer engineer on the warpath against software bugs. "I spend at least half of my long training rides trying to figure out what techniques to use to lessen any pain I'm feeling. Relax when I get cramps in my shoulder blades, that sort of thing," she said. "None of us are out there to suffer. You have to figure out what's wrong and come up with a solution."

Gaining control means everything to Christiansen. And when she can't, it's quite possible she uses dissociation, too. After all, she describes herself in the third person when sharing race stories on her blog. Maybe this helps her erase the memories of pain and suffering. In these pieces, she calls herself "the Osprey," and the symbol she uses for Team Osprey is a picture of that majestic bird with its wings spread wide.

Echoing cycling legend Lance Armstrong's point of view, the inspirational Canadian Tony O'Keeffe explains that "pain is the goal." As a military man, he frames his approach as a warrior facing down an enemy. "I accept it. It's where I want to be. The key is not to get down on myself," he said.

Young Christoph Strasser takes a different approach that evokes the New Age spirituality of self-empowerment. "Don't use the word *pain* in your life," he stresses. "Leave the pain. Never think about what you don't want to happen, only what you *want* to happen—reaching the finish line, the top of the mountain." But when an injury does crop up, Strasser reacts just like the others. "You have to do something; gain control over the situation," he says. "You can't do this race without any pain, but you can use mental strength to keep your emotions in check."

DAY FIVE WAS ALSO FATHER'S DAY, so in spite of the toll the race was taking on them, a few doting dads made sure to connect with their kids from somewhere in rural Kansas. Ben Popp's twin boys were never far from his mind. Each day he taped up a new photo of them on the door of his motor home. He made sure to glance at it every time he climbed inside for a break. Each photo had a caption like "Keep Your Eyes on the Prize." As a stay-at-home dad, Popp missed his three-year-old twins and thought about them a lot, especially on this day.

From the moment the race started, Popp had cycled wearing a necklace made of stainless steel thumbprint impressions from the twins, to help him keep RAAM in proper perspective. The race wasn't the most important thing in the world to him; his children were. Popp's necklace bounced close to his heart as he pedaled, reminding him not to take too many chances and to return home safely. "The necklace symbolized the fact that I wasn't just some weird dude riding his bike all night long 'cause he didn't have anything better to do," he said. "The kids kept me within myself. Instead of destroying myself and taking all sorts of risks to pass the next guy on the road, I rode *my* race—a safe race."

Popp crossed from New Mexico into Kansas as night fell on Father's Day. His spirits were high because he'd just watched a video his wife made of their boys especially for the occasion. But the heavy, sticky Kansas air brought him back to the moment. Maybe because he was so energized by the gift of seeing his sons on video, Popp decided to beat the heat by forgoing any rest and riding through the night. Only time would tell if this was a wise move.

Marko Baloh was another dad who had surrounded himself with family during the race, in his case quite literally. His wife and ever-present crew member Irma was along for the ride, and this year he was also joined by his two eldest children, one nine and the other five. In previous years, he'd affixed photos of his kids to his handlebars, rotating them every 12 hours. This year he didn't have to.

Some race observers clucked disapprovingly about bringing kids along under such tough conditions, but for the Balohs, it was the most natural thing in the world. "Being away from them is really tough, so Irma and I just bring them with us," Baloh said. "I think a lot about my kids, especially when the going gets difficult. Without their encouragement I don't know what I'd do." His crew chief Andrej saw the tangible effects firsthand. "When his daughter yells 'Go, Daddy, go' over the PA system, Marko goes faster," he said.

Still, some of Baloh's crew members wondered whether having Irma and the kids along was really such a good idea. Robič kept winning because he became an animal on the bike, even scaring his ex-wife with his antics. If Baloh really wanted to reach that level, he'd keep the family at home and pour everything he had into the race, wouldn't he?

Young Christoph Strasser didn't have any kids. But on Father's Day, loved ones weren't far from his mind. After struggling up Bobcat Pass the previous afternoon, his crew mates knew Strasser needed a lift, so they read encouraging emails from friends over the loudspeakers. "That was a really an emotional moment for me," he told me later. Strasser spoke with his girlfriend several times during the night, and the tears flowed freely.

The day before, Strasser's physician had put him on antibiotics as soon as he began coughing, hoping to ward off the pneumonia that often fells riders once they reach Kansas. Sure enough, Strasser's breathing had started improving, but now that he had almost reached the grasslands, he had dropped six hours behind Robič. For the first time in days he began looking over his shoulder to see if anybody was challenging his fourth-place position.

Turns out, somebody was.

Strasser had been about six hours ahead of fifth-place Gerhard Gulewicz when he fell ill. His lead was down to two hours and change after Bobcat Pass. Sensing Strasser's weakness, Gulewicz rode like a man possessed, forgoing any rest on the fourth night in order to attack his Austrian countryman. He was trying to redeem himself after being forced to withdraw from the race the previous year, and he was mounting a fierce assault. He passed a sleeping Strasser in the wee hours of Day Five just before the Kansas border.

After Taos, the racers descend out of the Rockies. Leaving TS19 in the tiny mountain village of Eagle Nest, New Mexico, the elevation decreased gradually, but the scenery changed suddenly. Before they knew it, racers were lost in endless acres of neatly organized fields of wheat and corn, interrupted every so often by a grain elevator here, an agricultural depot there.

Strasser wasn't too disappointed about Gulewicz's pass because he was feeling much better after his sleep break. As he began his long journey through the heartland he hoped his breathing problems were behind him. Despite ceding his position to Gulewicz, he was really flying now. He recorded the fastest time split of the entire field coming out of the Rockies on a 90-mile stretch into Clayton, New Mexico, early that morning. He was the second-fastest racer on the next 80-mile segment into Elkhart, Kansas, averaging almost 21 miles per hour. Pretty good after almost four days of continuous racing.

But then it all went to hell for the second time. By midday the hacking cough was back, and this time it was worse. He and coach Tomas decided to back off the pace during this first blistering-hot afternoon of racing through the Kansas prairie. "I didn't expect the heat and humidity in Kansas," Strasser recalled. "It really hit me hard." He wasn't the only one. The newspaper headlines told the story:

"Heat Causing Pavement Buckling and Blowups," read *USA Today*.

"Major Heat Wave Set to Expand," reported AccuWeather.

"Heat Wave Continues to Bake Wichita," echoed the *Wichita Eagle*.

As Strasser and the rest of the leading men left the cold, wet Rockies, temperatures shot back up above 100 degrees. The appalling heat walloped their respiratory systems with a mighty blow. The air was also saturated with humidity, so on this day Strasser won a trifecta: it was hazy, hot, and humid—the kind of suffocating heat that traps most people inside air conditioned homes and offices.

Strasser wrapped ice socks around his neck and wrists and dabbed himself with his trusty peppermint oil. But the sweat still poured off his face as he crouched on his bike, trying to think positive thoughts.

He averaged a tad less than 18 miles per hour on the 82-mile segment into the town of Plains, arriving around 3:00 that afternoon. By then, the stultifying heat and humidity had taken their toll. Strasser's face, arms, and legs puffed up, and he started feeling fuzzy and confused. The raspy breathing continued, and his coughing became so violent he again struggled to breathe.

As the afternoon wore on, Strasser's pace slowed some more on the way to TS24 in Greensburg, Kansas, located in the heart of Tornado Alley. But he refused to quit. His crew watched in horror as this brave young man put his head down and gutted it out. Hacking all the way, he made it another 78 miles, struggling into TS24 by 9:00 that night. His friends ran over to steady him as he climbed awkwardly off his bike, turned around, and coughed up bloody sputum.

They helped him into the motor home, not sure what would happen next. They didn't have to wait long. Strasser soon spiked a 105-degree fever and started hallucinating. He passed out in the ambulance on the way to the hospital. In an instant, Strasser's race was over.

BY DAY FIVE, RAAM HAD BECOME A WAR OF ATTRITION for most of the surviving racers. But a few lucky ones were still feeling pretty darn good.

Way back in the field, American stage racer Christopher Gottwald was preparing to barrel his way out of the Rockies. Even though he was still way down the leader board, his race was going exactly as he had hoped. He was executing a race plan that had been perfected by other pro cyclists who came before him, including the brash American Jonathan Boyer and Austrian phenom Franz Spilauer. The idea was to get a lot more rest than the other racers but cycle much faster while on the bike, attacking late in the race after having banked more sleep than anyone else.

As for the easygoing pharmacist Kevin Kaiser, despite being brutalized by the desert heat it appeared he was going to make the time cutoff in Taos later in the day. He was now in the damp, cool mountains and hoped the worst was over. *I'm a new rider!* he thought to himself as he sped along.

At the front, Swiss threat Dani Wyss was still trailing Jure Robič by an hour or two. Observers admired Wyss' strategy of trying to stick close to Robič and unnerve him. At some point during the day, Robič's crew chief

Uroš Velepec admitted, "I'm surprised by how strong Dani is." Wyss' crew chief Christian Hoppe predicted his racer would make a move in the Appalachians a few days hence. "After the Mississippi, it's better for Dani, because he grew up in the mountains and he knows how to climb," Hoppe said. Of course, Velepec begged to differ. "Jure's the strongest climber," he declared. "He's stubborn, and he can endure pain and go without sleep better than anyone else. All of this is coming up in the next few days, so I'm not worried."

But Robič wasn't having a particularly enjoyable time in the sweltering flatlands; he preferred the undulating terrain of the temperate countryside. The RAAM route covered about 450 miles in Kansas alone, so Robič knew he'd have to slog through endless fields of corn for the next 30 hours or so.

Even with steady, favorable tailwinds, the conditions in Kansas were miserable for cycling, especially after almost four days and 1,300 miles in the saddle. Robič grew irritable in the heat, and because he was consuming so much fluid to keep cool, he began experiencing edema in his arms and legs. His crew members tried keeping Robič calm, and they worried that maybe, just maybe, Wyss' proximity was starting to get under the champion's skin.

In the High Deserts and Rockies, Wyss managed to slice in half the two-hour lead Robič had built during the first full day of racing. Just after midnight Wyss had actually passed a dozing Robič after TS22 in Elkhart. As he had done in Monument Valley, Wyss delayed his sleep break just long enough to fluster Robič with the pass, and then he went down for a rest, knowing that Robič would retake the lead once he awakened. The two men would continue to hopscotch through Kansas.

Robič was surprised that Wyss had made it through the Rockies so well. Wasn't Robič supposed to be the field's strongest climber? He knew he had to reverse Wyss' momentum, so the defending champion turned it up a notch in Kansas. By the time he and Wyss crossed into Missouri and reached the rolling, forested Ozarks, Robič's lead would swell again to a little over two hours.

As their battle raged, the buzz in the ultracycling world was that this was a race for the ages. One journalist blogged that, "For so long RAAM has given the impression that it isn't exciting because the riders aren't 200 yards apart, but now we're witnessing an epic battle unfold. A physical and mental battle of courage, strength, and cunning."

Robič took time for a little fun in the midst of his fight with Wyss. He always looked forward to reaching TS28 in Yates Center, Kansas, almost 1,700 miles into the race. For one thing, it was the second-to-last time station in Kansas. It was also the place where Robič enjoyed a strong dose of nationalistic pride, as each year a Slovenian family who lived nearby greeted him waving Slovenian flags and carrying-on like cheerleaders at a football game. This year Robič took time to pose for a few pictures with his Slovenian fans and then scurried down the ramrod-straight Kansas road and into the sweltering haze.

The day had slipped into that peaceful hour where the red sun flirts with the horizon but still burns hot enough to demoralize the most determined of racers. Robič hoped a thunderstorm would pop up to cool things off, but the towering cumulus clouds he spied in the distance didn't cooperate. It was still 85 degrees when darkness fell. Reflecting on his day, Robič concluded that things had gone decently enough. Not only had he been able to let off some steam with his Slovenian boosters, but his lead was growing again. His sore throat had not gotten worse, and before the next dawn he'd finally be out of Kansas, inching ever closer to his rendezvous with the Appalachians where he'd finally—*finally!*—crush his pesky and tenacious rival.

On this day when suffering had become so much a part of the story, both Robič and Wyss knew their epic battle promised more suffering in the days ahead, and they braced for what was to come.

10

Days Six and Seven: Collapse and Resurrection

Still in Kansas, June 22 and 23

Marko Baloh shook himself awake before dawn on Day Six after a quick nap on the side of the road near El Dorado, Kansas. He had managed about two hours of sleep in the back of his motor home starting around 3:00 AM—his reward for having covered about 400 miles speeding out of the Rockies and onto the sweltering Kansas flatlands. Baloh was having the time of his life. This was where he belonged. This was what he was meant to do.

As he wandered to the front of the motor home, his wife Irma was already awake and pecking away at her laptop, feeding news to her husband's fans back home. She glanced at him and her eyes sparkled even though the dawn had not yet risen. She was in her element, too. The kids were still asleep nearby, and their presence gave Baloh courage. Surrounded by family he felt complete and grateful. Plus, he had been holding onto third place for quite a while now, and the lung he had damaged in the 2003 race wasn't a factor this year.

Sure, he had endured 100 hours and 1,600 miles of racing and everything ached. Before his break he had taken an inventory: edema in his legs, a bruised palm, saddle sores that would not heal, a blackened toenail, and numb hands because of nerve compression in his wrists. But pain and discomfort were just part of the territory. He noted the sensations and then turned his attention to the task at hand.

Each time a racer like Baloh stops for a sleep break it becomes harder for him to get moving again. Stiff muscles take longer to loosen up as the days go by, and bone-crushing fatigue makes it tough to wake up. Once he accomplishes the wretched task of pulling himself out of bed, he must leave the warmth and camaraderie of the motor home. At this moment the racer is often overcome by loneliness and self-pity as he clomps over to his bicycle and rides off by himself, knowing he must race for 20 hours or longer before he can shut his eyes again.

These feelings don't last long. The early morning is a busy time once a racer remounts his bike and gets rolling. The routine involves brushing one's teeth, applying sunscreen, having breakfast, evaluating the terrain and weather report, and discussing race tactics—all done while riding a bike.

After willing himself up from the cramped cot in the back of his motor home and giving his dozing kids a wistful glance, it was time for Baloh to get to work. His morning crew warned him he needed to get going in a hurry if he wanted to preserve his once-comfortable third-place position: one of the most fearsome ultracyclists in the world was suddenly nipping at his heels. The previous night, Gerhard Gulewicz, the Austrian powerhouse with a chip on his shoulder, had erased what had earlier been a three-hour deficit, taking everybody on Team Baloh by surprise this morning. His tactic? Not sleeping. Gulewicz had started out conservatively but now he was storming the field and forgoing any rest. He was still stinging from his forced withdrawal the previous year after he crashed while in second place. He knew he had it in him to win the race, and now he was making his move. He could sleep once the race was over.

Baloh had chosen the race moniker Tweety Bird carefully. A normally good natured and happy-go-lucky cartoon character, Tweety Bird attacks with a vengeance when threatened. Now, RAAM's Tweety Bird had a decision to make. Would he permit himself to continue enjoying this fetching family experience, or would he unleash his animal spirits and react with the fury necessary to beat back Gulewicz's equally furious charge? Baloh's up-and-down cycling career offered clues about why this decision was such a vexing one for him.

BALOH BOASTS A STORIED ULTRACYCLING RÉSUMÉ, one featuring too many wins and podium finishes to mention. He's considered one of the best ultra racers in the world, but he's also known crushing disappointment.

In the early 1990s he made the Slovenian national team and was poised to go to the 1994 Olympics in the team time trial. But cash-strapped Slovenia withdrew from the event two weeks before the games, dashing young Baloh's hopes for Olympic fame. "This was one of the worst moments of my cycling career," he remembered. There was more disappointment to come.

Years later, after Baloh had established his reputation as a top ultracyclist, he was poised again for glory. This time he pinned his hopes on the 24-hour world championship in Iowa. Being a devoted family man, Baloh enjoys having their company at big races. That year he had convinced his parents to travel with him to the U.S. The Balohs were due to depart Ljubljana on September 12, 2001. On September 11, a friend called while he was packing and told him to turn on the television. The World Trade Center towers had just been attacked, and he was going nowhere.

He's known both triumph and tragedy at RAAM, too. Baloh was in the best shape of his life and had hopes of a high finish in his 2003 rookie attempt. But after riding near the front for more than five days, he was startled by chest pain and soon had trouble breathing. His crew encouraged him to keep his pace up, and Baloh dutifully followed orders. "They thought it was a muscle pull, or else that I was just faking it to get a rest," he said. But Baloh was in agony even as he tried to hide it. At the next time station hours later, another racer's trainer checked him out and said it was nothing serious. So Baloh got back on his bike, trying to ignore the sensation that his chest was being ripped open. He quickly slipped to seventh place. Finally unable to continue, he glided to a stop only 400 miles from the finish line—a one-day ride away. This time, a medical doctor from a different team examined Baloh, who was now crumpled up and no longer able to hide his distress. "You need to call an ambulance now," he barked with a worried look on his face. "This is serious—*go!*"

After 2,550 miles of racing, Baloh was rushed to a West Virginia hospital. He had gotten so far he could practically smell the Atlantic Ocean. A few hours later he was diagnosed with a life-threatening pulmonary embolism. He had raced so hard he practically destroyed his lung. The doctors told him if he had kept going much longer the clot could have traveled to his heart and stopped it. This DNF was devastating, and even today Baloh gets misty-eyed recalling the scene. Later that year part of his damaged lung was surgically removed. It was the low point of his career, and he felt lost during the many months he spent recovering. "I hoped I could come back from this, but I wasn't sure," he said.

But you can't keep Tweety Bird down. Two years later he returned to RAAM intent on winning. That year Baloh was a crowd favorite thanks to his remarkable comeback and winning personality. Baloh is so admired that Allen Larsen, the 2003 RAAM champion, had agreed to join Baloh's crew in a show of respect. RAAM insiders knew that Baloh could—no, *should*—win the race, and people like Larsen wanted to help.

Baloh raced in second place all the way through the Rockies, hoping his time had finally come. A lifelong asthmatic, he started having trouble breathing, this time in Kansas, after about four days of racing. He quickly slipped from second to fifth. Larsen and the rest of the crew tried to keep him going, but after his previous problems everybody on Team Baloh was skittish. Baloh managed to stay near the front of the field despite his raspy breathing, but then the unthinkable occurred: he spiked a fever. The crew couldn't afford to take any chances this time. He was again yanked off the course by ambulance and admitted to the hospital with pneumonia later that day. Baloh had managed to hold off most of the field while riding on one lung, but his second RAAM bid had been dashed just like the first.

Larsen wept for him at the hospital—coincidentally the same one Baloh had visited two years prior. This former champion knew how heavily another DNF would weigh on the Slovenian ultracycling great.

"This second DNF was much harder on me," Baloh remembered. "I had such a strong year in 2004, and it was like déjà vu. I even saw the same emergency room doctor who had treated me during my first hospital visit. With Allen Larsen there it was very emotional. I thought I was washed up."

Baloh refused to give up on RAAM and returned the following year, placing sixth in 2006. With 200 kilometers to go Baloh cried like a baby when he realized he'd finally be an official RAAM finisher. Still, he felt strangely empty afterward. He knew he could do better.

IN 2009, BALOH WAS STILL GOING STRONG ON DAY FIVE, cruising through the sun-baked plains of Kansas in third place and having fun with his kids on their great adventure across the continent. But even when a racer is healthy, every day is a tough day in the saddle during RAAM. When I caught up to him on the road that day, he was in no mood to talk. Every ounce of energy he had in him was going into his pedals. "The heat was terrible," he remembered later. "I got sick of drinking Ensure and started having cold shakes from McDonald's, and that really helped." Fueled by milk shakes, Tweety Bird flew as if on massive wings. He gobbled up the road, covering the 80-mile segment into Plains on Day Five faster than anybody else in the field.

By the morning of Day Six, a determined and combative Baloh wasn't happy to see his position challenged by the pesky Gulewicz. His kids helped fuel his ardor by cheering him on over the PA system. He was working furiously to stay ahead of his charging Austrian foe, but Gulewicz continued closing throughout a morning of desperate racing along the sultry flatlands.

The two world-renowned racers were like ghosts on the open road, their titanic battle all but invisible to local townsfolk who happened to spy them on their bikes. Occasionally someone out doing an errand would notice one of the tricked-out follow-vehicles plastered with sponsors' logos and pull alongside to ask what was going on. Few realized that two of the best ultracyclists in the world were battling in the most demanding race their sport had to offer, a showdown that was playing out in their neighborhoods, across their schoolyards, and right past their front lawns.

"Marko, stick with me, let's go get them!" a wired, raspy-voiced Gulewicz implored as he pulled alongside Baloh, hoping they could use each other as rabbits and work together to catch the race-leading Wyss and Robič.

"Ride your own race, Marko!" Baloh heard his crew chief Andrej warn in his earpiece. Baloh tried accelerating to keep up with Gulewicz, but was unable to match his speed. "I had a bad day," he remembered sullenly. Gulewicz overtook Baloh and claimed third place around noon on Day Six. Reeling in Baloh required Gulewicz to race without sleeping for two days straight; as a result, he had crossed Kansas faster than everyone except Robič.

Baloh stayed tantalizingly close to Gulewicz through the rest of the afternoon and into the night, fighting to keep pace through endless miles of cornfields and past countless grain silos. He managed to limit the damage, but couldn't summon the power necessary to close the gap that had by then opened up to an hour. Privately he questioned whether he had it in him. This thought had also crossed his crew members' minds, but they dared not voice their concerns.

"After Gulewicz passed me, I slowed down," Baloh explained laconically. "I just couldn't keep up." Actually, with his wife and kids there with him, it was a lot more complicated than that. But in their sleep-deprived states, nobody on Team Baloh was in a position to undertake a cogent psychological assessment of their racer's predicament.

In reality, Gulewicz's pass brought Baloh face-to-face with his one psychological vulnerability: he had never been able to reconcile his desire to enjoy his family during RAAM with his hunger to win the race. Who was he: a family man prepared to simply do his best, or a road warrior hell-bent on eviscerating the competition? He wanted desperately to win the race or at least finish on the podium, but he was unsure how much he was willing to sacrifice to achieve his goal.

Baloh's crew cranked up the music while his wife Irma and his masseur Matic tried their best to motivate him—Irma mostly with sharp words, and Matic with happy talk. Neither of them managed to inspire Baloh to increase his pace. RAAM had laid bare Baloh's one weakness, and as a result this ultracycling great began to crumble.

Baloh is not an easy man to rattle. Under most circumstances, he wears a placid, contented expression while on the bike, with the faintest hint of a permanent smile etched into the corners of his mouth. His long legs might churn the pedals and sweat might drip from his brow, but as long as he's riding, he's in heaven. He loves cycling so fiercely that when he forgoes a training ride, his blog entry makes it sound like he's having a nervous breakdown.

Baloh adores playing with his kids after work, so to fit in his weekday training miles he'll head out on a midnight cycling jaunt, return home for a short nap, then get up and go to work. He'll happily ride through frightful weather, and when a winter blizzard makes that impossible, he'll jump on his indoor trainer and go for six, eight, or even 10 hours at a time. Sometimes a long training ride doesn't satisfy Baloh's obsession, so afterward he'll watch old videos of races from years past.

Normally an even-tempered racer, losing third place had completely demoralized him. He had owned third since Strasser dropped out on Day Five and had already allowed himself to visualize finishing on the podium in Annapolis. Equally galling to Baloh was *where* Gulewicz had managed to slip past him. Baloh was supposed to be the best in the world at the ultradistance time trial, yet Gulewicz had caught him on the flats of Kansas—prime time-trialing territory.

Time-trialing is a cycling specialty—just you alone on a long, flat road racing against the clock. Doing this well requires special equipment, focused training, raw power, and perfect technique. In a sense the entire RAAM route is one gargantuan time trial; just like a traditional time trial, RAAM is a solo race against the clock where you can't ride in packs or draft other racers. But specialized time-trial techniques are only effective in a few relatively flat regions, like the deserts of California and Arizona, and right here on the flat Kansas prairie, where Gulewicz had smoked Baloh.

In the mountains, the most important predictor of performance is a rider's power-to-weight ratio. Since a cyclist has to overcome gravity when the road slants up, the best ProTour climbers are small and light and would have trouble tipping the scale at 140 pounds soaking wet. Time-trial specialists don't have to worry about gravity because their races take place on relatively even terrain, so what matters to them is raw power, not power-to-weight ratios. The key metric is how many watts they can generate and for how long. Experts in the time trial are big and strong, with tree trunks for legs. They can weigh 200 pounds or more and they put out enormous amounts of power.

Another important factor in a time trial is wind resistance. Up to 75 percent of the power a cyclist generates is wasted by pushing against the wind, and the faster he goes the more wind resistance he faces. When a cyclist races in a time trial, he needs to be as aerodynamic as possible because he can't hide from the wind by drafting a fellow racer. The cyclist's chest presents the biggest cross-section, so the best way to cheat the wind is to crouch down in a tucked position.

Specialized time-trial bikes are rakish-looking machines with bladed tubing that sheds air like an airfoil. They're fitted with aerobars in front so a racer can rest his forearms on padded surfaces with his hands pointing forward. Sitting on a bike this way, with his handlebars far below the height of his saddle, a racer's back is parallel to the ground and he has to crane his neck to look forward. Even though this position puts extra strain on his neck and back, he's nearly as aerodynamic as an arrow, ready to pierce the wind.

This is precisely the type of machine Baloh rode when he set the 24-hour world outdoor track record in 2006—the bid that his friend and countryman Jure Robič came to watch. Baloh hangs the framed *Guinness World Records* plaque he earned that day in the most prominent spot in his home in Ljubljana.

During RAAM, Baloh always rode his specialized time-trial bike once he was safely out of the Rockies, and this year was no exception. This was the bike he had been riding when Gulewicz passed him.

The racers had passed through seven time stations in their 450-mile trip through Kansas. It took the leaders a little over 24 hours to get through this seemingly never-ending state. Robič blitzed Kansas faster than anyone else. Gulewicz took about an hour longer. A calm and unruffled Wyss zoomed through with the third-fastest time. Baloh came next, but there was a big time gap between him and the other three. All told, Baloh lost more than four hours to Gulewicz in Kansas. There would be no glory on the prairie for the legendary time-trial racer this year.

Now racing in fourth, Baloh reached Missouri by afternoon. The Kansas cornfields had given way to rolling, forested hills. It looked more like Slovenia here than anything he'd seen so far, and the graceful trees and their welcome shade comforted him. He enjoyed a spectacular sunset over the Ozarks that evening, but all was not well. As the sun painted the sky reds and oranges, Baloh was instead headed to a dark and dreary place called mental collapse. He was grumpy, he badly wanted a shower, and he was now a couple of hours behind Gulewicz.

But Baloh wasn't the only one who had lost his resolve on the sweltering, windswept prairie.

EARLIER IN THE RACE THE DESERTS HAD CHEWED HIM UP and spit him out a dehydrated mess, but on Day Five Lt. Col. O'Keeffe, whose exploits were an inspiration to all the cadets back home, had sprung back to life in the Rockies. Still, coming into Taos soaked and freezing a few nights before, even O'Keeffe's motivation had been flagging. *Oh man, this sucks*, he remembers thinking. *I never want to do this again.* This decorated triathlete and leader among men was beginning to falter.

"Remember what brought you here, Tony," barked his crew mate Randy over the loudspeakers. "C'mon Tony, this is the fight you've been looking for!" These words were exactly what O'Keeffe needed to hear, and the crisis passed.

"We crossed the Continental Divide, and now all water runs into the Atlantic Ocean," a crew mate trumpeted once O'Keeffe crested the Rockies. In celebration, O'Keeffe slurped down some barley soup his wife Jackie handed him after his chilly descent.

Once he made it over the Rockies, O'Keeffe sprang back to life and became his normal, awe-inspiring self. He notched the fourth-fastest time split of the entire field on a downhill section into TS22 in western Kansas.

He had passed a few riders to claim sixth place by the time he slid onto the Great Plains the day before. With a healthy, hydrated, and hungry rider on its hands, O'Keeffe's all-military crew had finally been able to lock into a smooth battle rhythm. "We've gotten into a real good routine," a crew member chirped. "This is one of the coolest things I've ever done!"

Up before dawn on Day Six after a sleep break near Plains, now 1,400 miles from Oceanside, O'Keeffe's neck started feeling achy, but he dismissed the sensation and kept pushing. Heck, he was still on a 10-day pace.

Unfortunately, O'Keeffe was about to experience the most bizarre byproduct of competing in RAAM: the sudden loss of strength in the muscles holding up the head. It comes on abruptly and without warning.

The human head weighs between eight to 10 pounds. When a cyclist is hunched over his bike, his neck muscles experience something akin to holding a 10-pound free weight with a bent arm. Try this the next time you're at the gym and then consider what it must feel like to cycle that way for days at a time.

O'Keeffe's neck failed at exactly the halfway point in the race. After 120 hours of racing—five straight days and nights—his head fell forward in an instant. He coasted his bike to a stop and stood with his head hanging, chin on chest, peering down at his dusty cycling cleats.

It's almost inconceivable that a grown man—a superman like O'Keeffe, no less—could be incapable of holding up his own head. O'Keeffe, a venerated military leader and fearsome athlete, was suddenly as helpless as a newborn infant. He was horrified. His follow-vehicle pulled over and two crew mates jumped out, staring in disbelief. The only way he could look straight ahead was to arch backward and angle his eyes upward, like a gymnast starting a backflip.

Uncharacteristically, O'Keeffe was at a loss for words. *This is crazy; this never should have happened to me*, he thought. During his training leading up to RAAM, he had draped heavy weights from his neck during rides to strengthen it. O'Keeffe's neck was as strong as Hercules', but it didn't make a difference.

Standing on the side of the road, O'Keeffe even tried holding his head up with his own arms, placing his hands under his chin. But as a grizzled ultracyclist, he knew his neck muscles wouldn't regain their strength after a few minutes of chin-holding. It was time to retreat to the motor home so he and his wife Jackie could figure out what to do next. One of his waiting crew mates thought O'Keeffe's lolling head reminded him of what a bag looks like when you sling it over your shoulder. It made him uncomfortable to see his friend in such condition.

The victim of the first documented instance of sudden neck failure was Michael Shermer, who experienced this horror in the second edition of the race back in 1983. The syndrome is now called "Shermer's Neck" in homage to his struggles that year. His woes began in Illinois, when his head started feeling heavy and the back of his neck became increasingly sore. He described it as "a quick meltdown." Suddenly Shermer's head dropped, making it impossible for him to look up. Cradling his chin in the palm of one hand with his elbow on the padding of his aerobars, he supported his head well enough to finish the race that year. Despite excruciating pain during the event, his neck was back to normal within two days.

Everybody has his own ideas about how to prevent Shermer's Neck. O'Keeffe had relied on strength training. Jim Rees brought a chiropractor along. Others use trigger point massage focused on offending muscle groups like the sternocleidomastoids, scalenes, and trapezius.

Shermer's Neck sufferers have been known to rig up all manner of odd-looking braces so they can keep racing. Some fashion chin pedestals using posts that stick up about two feet from the handlebars, while others use simple neck collars. A few racers have lashed their heads to backpack-like scaffolds made of PVC piping, which look like ungainly splints. All these contraptions are maddeningly uncomfortable for a perspiring athlete in constant motion. Most racers drop out of the race shortly after their neck muscles fail.

Strangely, unlike almost all the other racers, O'Keeffe hadn't brought a neck brace with him this year. What to do now? Jackie was certain they could jury-rig something to relieve his muscles for a short while, giving them time to recover.

O'Keeffe didn't have to deliberate very long. "In my 2006 race, I had some come-to-Jesus moments, but for me quitting isn't an option," he explained. "It's just not something I will ever think about. I'm okay coming in dead last, but I'm *not* okay with not finishing what I started." Jackie designed a makeshift brace that O'Keeffe secured with bungee cords. Then he got back on his bike.

He made it through TS25 in Pratt by midmorning, ghastly looking brace and all. He even laid down the sixth-fastest time split on this short, 30-mile segment. Then he hit heavy traffic through suburban Wichita. Because the brace immobilized O'Keeffe's head and reduced his peripheral vision, it was a nerve-racking experience for the rider and his crew.

Unfortunately, he never saw them coming—railroad tracks, every cyclist's curse and dangerous things to roll over on a skinny-tired bicycle. If a cyclist doesn't hit them perpendicular, he's bound to go down. Most cyclists just get off and walk. O'Keeffe didn't have a chance because this particular set of tracks ran diagonally across the road; since he couldn't see straight down, he didn't know he needed to turn his handlebars to take them at a right angle.

His tumble painted O'Keeffe's flesh with patches of bright-red road rash, but physically he was capable of getting back on his bike, so that's what he did. A chagrined, braced, and bandaged-up O'Keeffe limped through the rest of the sweltering 77-mile stage into Maize, Kansas. He removed the brace and his head again flopped around like a rag doll's. There had been no improvement.

He was alone in the motor home with Jackie. "I feel like I'm putting other people in danger; I can't see a thing out there," he confided in a weary, halting voice.

"Okay, why don't you just take a rest and we'll think about it later?" she offered gently.

An hour later, O'Keeffe motioned his crew members toward the motor home. He had decided to withdraw from the race for safety reasons. He told his buddies he was thinking of them, not himself. He thought it would be too taxing for them to spirit him safely to Annapolis in his condition.

"Boys, I think it's the right thing to do," he offered. They were all in a circle now holding onto each other's shoulders, and there wasn't a dry eye among this group of hardened soldiers. "You're right, Tony. We're with you," one said. Another teammate recalled that, "It was the best example of leadership I've ever seen in a sporting context."

RAAM had felled another proud warrior, reducing him to tears as it always does at the moment of surrender.

CANADIAN SOLDIER TONY O'KEEFFE WAS NOW ON HIS WAY HOME to Ontario, but farther back in the field, some racers had found new life after faltering earlier.

Reversals of fortune are the mother's milk of this race. Fans might watch a racer's demise with ghoulish fascination as it plays out over hours and days, but when a racer who's been written off suddenly storms through the field, now that's a story worth celebrating.

Everybody was buzzing about Gerhard Gulewicz's spectacular charge, but Gulewicz was, well, *Guelwicz;* one of the top ultracyclists alive, racing with a chip on his shoulder, no less. Another competitor making noise well off everyone's radar screen was taciturn small-town pharmacist Kevin Kaiser.

Kaiser had been pulverized by the desert heat during the first few days of racing, but he had squeaked safely past the Taos time cutoff after he devoured that magic omelet back in Sedona that rejuvenated his stomach and his legs.

After Taos, he coasted down the eastern slopes of the Rockies and stopped for a sleep break just before the first time station in Kansas. By the time dawn broke on Day Six, he'd decided to make an audacious bid to attack the field from his lowly position as second-to-last man on the road, fully 500 miles behind the race leaders. He had passed two competitors by midmorning and thought, *Okay, now I'm back in this thing.* Kaiser had stormed like a banshee into 12th place as the sun set over the Kansas cornfields on Day Six, settling in just behind his American rival, the secretive former stage racer Christopher Gottwald.

Kaiser continued charging up the field on Day Seven, passing fellow cyclists left and right. He even clocked the fastest time split of the entire field into Fort Scott, the last time station in Kansas. Thanks to a few DNFs ahead of him, by midnight he was in sixth place, challenging Gottwald as the leading rookie on the road.

How is it possible for a broken, vanquished athlete like Kaiser to move toward the front of the field after more than five days of lethargic racing? A reversal this dramatic almost never happens, even in a 5K foot race or a high school basketball game, let alone after *five days*. What magic trick did Kaiser perform back there in Taos? Not even Kaiser had a good answer for that. "When I got close to the pack of riders who were bunched up together, I just decided that I'd be the rider who would break free," he offered in typically understated fashion.

It was hard to square Kaiser's dramatic charge with his personality off the bike. Soft-spoken and mild-mannered, on "dry land" Kaiser is so reserved he seems appears anxious. Lined up on stage along with the 27 other starters at a pre-race party the night before the race began, he looked uncomfortable, like he didn't belong.

But on the bike Kaiser tapped into a wellspring of ferocity that came from—who knows where? This unassuming man was a beast at heart.

KAISER WAS AT A LOSS TO EXPLAIN HOW HE HAD MANAGED TO FIND NEW LIFE and charge up the field. Baloh was having an equally difficult time admitting why he had been unable to fend off Gulewicz's attack and hold on to third place. Instead of looking within himself at his contradictory motivations—family man or ferocious competitor?—he appealed to his crew members for help.

Kaiser and Baloh couldn't explain their reversals of fortune. But O'Keeffe offered some clues about why he had lost his resolve in Kansas.

O'Keeffe had never been forced to drop out of an endurance race before. He had succeeded at RAAM once already; finished second in the Ultraman world championships four times; and successfully completed more than 20 "regular" Ironman distance races, including four Ironman World Championships in Hawaii, where he garnered first place in the military division.

He had accomplished all this while raising two kids, getting a master's degree, serving two tours of duty in Saudi Arabia, and spending time in Bosnia at NATO headquarters.

O'Keeffe credits his success in endurance sports to one thing—his mental strength. "I don't get down on myself easily, and I won't quit," he said. "If a DNF ever does happen it will either be because I've been hit by a car or the police are taking me off the course in handcuffs."

But on this day in Kansas, O'Keeffe did something he said he would never do. He could have raced on with the jury-rigged brace while his crew mates fashioned something more permanent. Others have, but he chose not to.

In the months preceding RAAM, O'Keeffe had a disagreement with his wife Jackie about whether to bring a proper neck brace.

"You'd better think about Shermer's Neck," Jackie warned.

"I know what I need to know," replied O'Keeffe.

"So we'll bring a brace?" she offered.

"There's no way I'm going to show up wearing one of those things!" O'Keeffe snapped. "If I bring it, I'll be tempted to use it."

O'Keeffe pointed to the story of his father's death in explaining his decision not to bring a brace. A few years prior, his dad had been diagnosed with terminal cancer and given only a short while to live. Friends and family encouraged the elder O'Keeffe to make the most of the time he had left by seeing the world.

As his father was considering whether he had the strength to travel, a hospital bed was delivered to his home, just in case. O'Keeffe remembers being horrified when he spied the bed in his father's living room.

"Dad, *don't!* Don't get into that bed because you won't get out!" the younger O'Keeffe begged his dad.

"It was a foregone conclusion," he recalls. "Once Dad had climbed into that bed, he died two weeks later. That was my mental image of the neck brace. That's why I didn't bring one with me, and that's why I could never wear one."

O'Keeffe insisted he had decided to withdraw from the race out of concern for his crew's safety. He maintained it would have been too challenging for them to look after him with a brace on. But plenty of other crews had managed to keep their braced-up racers safe over the years. O'Keeffe's reasons were probably more complicated. More than likely, he couldn't race with a brace because it conjured painful images of his father dying in the hospital bed installed in his living room.

RAAM had done it again, as it had with Baloh a few hours earlier. This tough soldier had one, tiny vulnerability; one possible psychological weakness—O'Keeffe's memory of what had precipitated his father's demise. RAAM found the chink in this soldier's otherwise impenetrable mental armor, and sadly enough, his race was over.

11

Day Seven: A Race for the Ages

Illinois and Indiana, June 23

RAAM veterans like to say the race doesn't really start until the Mississippi River, two-thirds of the way from Oceanside to Annapolis. Around midnight at the beginning of Day Seven, Jure Robič and Dani Wyss were the first to cross this grand river. After 130 hours of continuous racing they had covered 2,059 miles and were separated by just 12, a difference of six-tenths of 1 percent. This minuscule gap equates to 250 yards in a 26.2-mile marathon. Only by this point, they had both been racing *65 times longer* than it takes an experienced runner to finish a marathon. Robič was leading by a hair, but Wyss was laying down the performance of his life. Even in the rolling hills of the Ozarks, the four-time champion Robič hadn't been able shake him.

By this point, the war Robič and Wyss were engaged in was as much a psychological war as it was a physical one. Their battle shares similarities with the legendary 1974 heavyweight championship fight between Muhammad Ali and George Foreman, known as "The Rumble in the Jungle." Through the first seven rounds Ali covered up, leaned against the ropes, and took hundreds of shots that landed mostly on his arms and sides. He made little attempt to fight back. Nobody knew what to make of it. Was Ali so out of shape he couldn't throw a single punch? Turns out he was waiting for Foreman to exhaust himself physically and mentally. Ali came alive in the eighth round and glided around the ring like a break-dancer on speed, startling a weary Foreman with a devastating combination and knocking him out. Ali's "rope-a-dope" strategy proved to be a brilliant ploy.

Was the savvy Wyss playing rope-a-dope with Robič? As they entered the final third of the race, the psychological advantage was indeed swinging Wyss' way. Ask any track and field runner or endurance athlete and he'll tell you it's better to be in second place, just off the leader's shoulder, entering the homestretch. Better to be the hunter than the hunted.

Meanwhile, on Robič's race blog his crew exhorted the champion's fans to "Help him in his quest with your posts on our guest book. Overload our server! Show him your hearts! Let Jure be your hero in this great race!"

Endurance athletes say that the longer the race, the more mental strength matters. If so, this contest must have scored some sort of record for psychological warfare set in an athletic context.

Robič was no fool, and he knew Wyss held very good cards. But Robič had devoted a lot of attention to his psychological preparation this year, engaging mental coaches to help him dampen the wild emotional swings he usually experienced during RAAM. So he wasn't struggling like he did when another racer was nipping at his heels back in 2004.

Robič had earned a reputation for becoming unnerved when a rival was close to him on the road. After finishing second as a race rookie in 2003, Robič went on to win RAAM in 2004, 2005, 2007, and 2008. In all but one of those victories, he crossed the country in less than nine days, a feat matched by only a handful of ultracyclists. His 2004 and 2007 races were especially close. In 2004, Robič was being pursued by a determined American racer named Mike Trevino. By the fourth night in Kansas, Trevino had actually reeled Robič in, but the Slovenian regained the lead for good the next day. Robič's crew later accused Trevino of cheating in order to close the gap.

The RAAM rule book is more than 30 pages long, covering everything from the traffic laws cyclists must obey to when and how follow-vehicles should trail their riders to protect them from passing traffic. The race organization fields a squadron of officials who patrol the course day and night and assess time penalties for infractions, but officials can't be everywhere along the 3,000-mile route. Robič never took his accusations further in 2004 because he won the race handily, beating Trevino by 11 hours.

In 2007, Robič's margin of victory over RAAM great Wolfgang Fasching was just four hours after 211 hours of racing—a difference of less than 2 percent. Afterward Robič told reporters that, "RAAM is not a bike race. This is a war."

This year the contest was even tighter. Robič was still clear-headed enough to know that he needed to channel the pressure being exerted by Wyss in a positive direction. Instead of becoming unnerved, it was time to tap into the fear of the hunted to summon a final surge of power.

But Robič was Wyss' prey, so the first thing he had to do was forgive himself for feeling afraid. This wasn't the first time RAAM had struck fear in Robič's heart. His nightmarish 2003 debut was as terrifying for him as it was for his crew and his then-wife Petra. That year his greatest fear was his own bestial behavior and his overwhelming conviction that if he failed to finish at or near the top, he would be seen as a worthless failure. All of these roiling feelings were magnified by severe sleep deprivation, which destroyed his coping mechanisms and fanned his paranoia.

Now in his seventh RAAM bid, Robič was still trying to prove himself, desperate to summon a similar level of ferocity. Robič knew there was still a lot of racing ahead and anything could happen—accident, injury, mental collapse, crew mutinies, navigational errors—so he had been trying to build a lead on Wyss for a solid week. Now time was running out.

Endurance athletes who push their bodies for days on end enter a realm where science has not tread, so in the homestretch the prospect of physical or mental catastrophe is ever present. As race veterans, Robič and Wyss were prepared to endure the final throes of RAAM. They feared this day but they also craved it. Still, they both questioned whether their training regimens had prepared them for what the final 36 hours had in store—a 500-mile-long, wheel-to-wheel duel coming after seven days and nights of nonstop racing.

THE QUESTION OF HOW TO PREPARE FOR RAAM is an interesting one. Some racers log 25,000 miles in a year, others fewer than 10,000. Some racers cycle 48 or 72 hours straight in training, while others avoid even a single through-the-night effort. Some racers affix fancy power meters to their bikes and follow strict workout regimens, whereas others just go out and experience the joy of covering vast distances on a bicycle.

Then there are the odd, poorly understood conditions that strike RAAM participants, like peripheral edema, Shermer's Neck, and pulmonary edema. How can a RAAM contestant prepare for these? Everybody has a different theory, and the experts—if you can find any—are equally split.

Take sleep deprivation. Some ultracyclists believe it is possible to condition themselves to withstand the effects of forgoing sleep for over a week, while others say that's nonsense. But how do these others explain racers like Robič and Rees? Both of these veterans undertake sleep deprivation training and each has earned a reputation for managing to sleep less than their rivals during RAAM—about an hour a day. After experiencing terrifying hallucinations in his 2003 RAAM debut, Robič trained for sleep deprivation by staying awake for 48 hours straight while riding 10-hour shifts once every month. Others follow similar approaches.

While racers may debate about whether one can train for sleep deprivation, at least it is a well-understood phenomenon. Other RAAM maladies, not so much. Acute, exercise-induced pulmonary edema is one of those strange afflictions that befalls RAAM participants and is found almost nowhere else. Pulmonary symptoms usually start in the Rockies and come to a head in the Plains, at which point racers are often whisked to the hospital by ambulance suffering from pneumonia, pulmonary edema, or even pulmonary embolisms.

"Severe pulmonary edema is exceedingly rare, although very mild edema—not enough to cause symptoms—may occur more frequently," according to Susan R. Hopkins, a professor at the University of California, San Diego. "Only a few cases of severe edema causing fluid in the airways have been cited in the literature."

The first sympton of the condition is shortness of breath; riders then develop a severe cough, their skin turns blue for lack of oxygen, and they begin to sweat profusely. Finally they cough violently and start expelling pink, frothy sputum. Dr. Hopkins told me this has to do with "increases in pulmonary arterial pressure, eventually resulting in alveolar flooding." The condition is hastened by electrolyte imbalance, excessive sodium intake, and exercising at high altitudes—the former two factors being things the cyclist can control, and the latter being something he cannot.

As with Shermer's Neck, science cannot yet explain why some athletes experience pulmonary edema while others do not. Dr. Hopkins recently had a public debate with another scientist about how widespread this condition is and what can be done to prevent it. The hope is that future RAAM contestants may at some point have better prophylactic approaches.

CONSIDERING ALL THE CHALLENGES THAT MIGHT PRESENT THEMSELVES, Robič and Wyss both hoped these last few days would bring no nasty surprises. Since Robič had much more RAAM experience than Wyss, he was confident that if anything went amiss Wyss would be the victim, not him.

Deep down they both wanted a fair race to the finish. So did the worldwide ultracycling community. RAAM fans sat glued to their computer screens around the world and followed the drama with bug-eyed wonderment. As one of Robič's crew members put it, "This is a dream scenario for RAAM followers, fans, and spectators. The old king defending his crown against a new challenger." Then he declared defiantly, "Everybody's talking about cracks in the armor and seeds of doubt—that's all fairy tale nonsense." But during RAAM every day is full of surprises, most of them nasty.

Wyss' goal on Day Six was to close the two-hour gap to Robič before they reached the Mississippi River. He was feeling strong, his mind was clear, and he was executing his race plan perfectly; tactics, strategy, nutrition, sleep—everything was unfolding with Swiss precision. Tactically, Wyss preferred to remain in second place while keeping Robič's lead small enough that the defending champion would know he was lurking.

Wyss pushed hard all day and managed to shave more than an hour from Robič's lead in the 150-mile stretch before they crossed the Clark Bridge spanning the Mississippi just north of St. Louis—Robič just before midnight, and Wyss just after. This was a lot of time to shave off in such a short stretch. Wyss knew that he had gotten Robič's attention.

Both men went down for the briefest of power naps a short time after crossing the river, with each team watching the other to gauge how long a break they could afford. To recover from his desperate push, Wyss needed a slightly longer rest in the wee hours of Day Seven, so Robič's lead edged back up to about 90 minutes early that morning. Then came

Surprise No. 1: Team Wyss made a navigational error in the late morning somewhere in southern Illinois just before crossing into Indiana. Here the RAAM route roughly paralleled Interstate 70, about 20 miles south. There were only seven turns to make on the 75-mile stretch between TS36 in Effingham, Illinois, and TS37, just over the border in Sullivan, Indiana. Somehow, Wyss' tired and harried crew missed one of them. They caught their error quickly, and as the RAAM rule book dictated, returned to the spot where they had gone astray and carried on racing.

This mistake cost Wyss maybe 15 minutes, possibly less. Team Wyss took it all in stride. There was no rancor, and everybody was still smiling and staying positive. By the time Wyss reached TS37, his deficit had widened to one hour and 45 minutes.

Surprise No. 2 wasn't so easily dismissed. It occurred later that afternoon less than 100 miles from where Wyss went astray. The RAAM course followed State Route 46 through a good portion of southern Indiana, but in order to avoid racing through Bloomington's downtown business district, it circled around this city of 70,000 before rejoining Route 46 on the eastern side of the city. It was during these maneuvers that Team Robič made a critical error.

A full-time navigator sits in each racer's follow-vehicle, right next to the crew chief who usually doubles as the driver. The navigator's job is to follow instructions in the route guide, relaying roadside hazards, terrain, and turns to his racer via the crew chief, who works the microphone. Each segment of the course occupies at least two pages in the guide: one with a map and elevation profile, and the other with navigation instructions listed by mile marker. The crucial 65-mile segment into TS38 in Bloomington had 24 separate navigation steps. For instance, here was one turn 51.4 miles into segment 38:

> *51.4 LEFT Traffic Light: S Curry Pike. Just before you get to Wal-Mart on SR 45.*

Instructions like this seem straightforward to follow, but sitting in a steamy, slow-moving car for days on end, with little sleep and no creature comforts, navigators struggle to stay focused on where they are, and mistakes come easily. This year's route guide was well over 100 pages long and contained hundreds of navigation steps and turns. Miss one and you're lost. The navigator's job is tedious and needs to be error-free, but it never is. Most racers get lost at least once during RAAM and usually shrug it off. But in a race this close, any mistake could spell disaster.

It turned out that Robič's navigator wasn't following his route guide this afternoon. Instead he was relying on a dash-mounted GPS unit programmed with the RAAM route. After all, it's easier to let the GPS tell you when to turn rather than trying to correlate a vehicle's odometer with instructions listed in the route guide. But the RAAM organization doesn't guarantee the accuracy of the GPS data it makes available to racers as a courtesy. As a result they strongly advise navigators work from the written instructions in the route guide. The navigator's first mistake was failing to double-check each GPS-commanded turn against the written instructions. But Team Robič made another more inexplicable error: before the race they had loaded their GPS device with the *previous year's* route file by accident. As it turned out, the two routes differed only slightly, but one of the differences was right here, near Bloomington. The 2008 route took racers through streets jammed with traffic lights and vehicles, so the 2009 route designer led the racers down quieter roads instead (this new routing was also six miles shorter).

Team Robič was unaware of their errant ways as they watched the champion snake around stopped cars and slow down at traffic lights through the center of Bloomington. Finally, the navigator realized they were off course.

Instead of returning as required to the spot where they had initially lost the route, Team Robič decided to press on, hoping not to get penalized. After all, they reasoned, the route Robič took was longer and more difficult than the official one, so in a sense they had already penalized themselves. Even if they did receive a 30-minute penalty, it would have taken them more than 30 minutes to backtrack. They decided it was better to just keep going.

When RAAM officials discovered that Team Robič hadn't backtracked, they hit him with a 30-minute penalty, the maximum allowed. He received no mercy even though his error had already cost him valuable time. Since he had followed the wrong route through Bloomington, it took Robič 43 minutes longer than Wyss to travel the 65 miles between TS37 and TS38.

The result was disastrous for Robič—including the hefty penalty, he had relinquished 73 minutes to his rival.

By evening on Day Seven, Robič was carrying an hour of penalties and his lead on the road had shrunk to less than that. For the first time, he was officially trailing Wyss. Even worse, the hot-headed Robič was infuriated about the navigation mistake. He gave his crew a piece of his mind, ranting and stomping around like the Robič of old. He was even more upset with RAAM officials. All told, they'd already slapped him with an hour of penalties for technical infractions and crew mistakes having nothing to do with how he was actually racing his bike. Wyss didn't have a single penalty yet. *What a way to treat a champion,* he thought to himself. *Where's the respect?*

Team Robič was convinced the RAAM organization was biased in favor of his Swiss challenger. The team had picked up a scent of favoritism in off-the-record comments a member of RAAM's media crew had made to Robič during their roadside encounters before and during the race. "I felt he didn't want me to be the winner," Robič said. "Bad for business for me to win again and again." Robič claimed other media staffers confided that their colleague had openly encouraged Wyss with comments like, "Jure's dead, he's looking really bad! You can beat him!"

In their sleep-deprived states, everyone on Team Robič was cranky and paranoid. Around this time, some of Robič's crew members began watching their archrival, hoping to capture Wyss breaking a rule on video and offer race officials all the evidence they'd need to finally hit him with some penalties. Recognizing that officials can't be everywhere, the race rules permit a racer to offer evidence that another contestant had committed an infraction. But the RAAM organization never envisioned one racer monitoring his rival so closely.

Only time would tell if Team Robič would be able to catch Wyss in the act and how the race organization might respond if presented with such evidence. This incredibily close race was now getting ugly.

AFTER PASSING THAT TROUBLESOME TIME STATION in Bloomington, Robič held a 55-minute lead on Wyss on the road, excluding penalty time. Robič and Wyss battled through the evening and deep into the night, crossing from Indiana into Ohio after midnight on Day Eight. They passed three time stations during this segment, stretching 163 miles all the way to Blanchester, Ohio, arriving there early the next morning after a brief, carefully coordinated rest break.

Each time Robič went through a time station that night, his crew gave him more bad news. Wyss had picked up 22 minutes on the segment just after Bloomington and kept closing all night. By the time they hit Blanchester at daybreak on Day Eight, Wyss finally laid eyes on his prey, spotting the back of Robič's follow-vehicle just up the road. With these two men now in sight of each other after 2,500 miles on the road, the tension in each man's follow-vehicle became unbearable. These two men were beyond exhaustion. How could they possibly ride neck and neck like this for the next 500 miles? It was anybody's race, and both teams understood that, 36 hours down the road, there would only be one champion.

12

What Fingerprint Do You Want to Leave?

Jefferson City, Missouri, June 24, 2:30 AM

It might come as a surprise that most RAAM participants don't see themselves as particularly gifted athletes. A great many of them failed at their sport of choice and took up cycling as a second or even third option. As a kid, Canadian Tony O'Keeffe gave up on hockey and started running competitively, then caught the multisport bug and went on to light the triathlon world on fire. Turns out the longer the race, the better he did, so it was only a matter of time before he stumbled into ultradistance cycling. "There's no genetic gift here, it's just hard work," he said of his formidable athletic accomplishments.

American pharmacist Kevin Kaiser played tennis in high school but he was "just an average hack." After washing out on the court, he became inactive and unfit in his twenties. He discovered ultracycling in his thirties and transformed himself into a monster on the bike. "You don't need a lot of innate talent to be a great cyclist, you just have to work hard," he said modestly.

There has recently been a flurry of provocative work on the question of whether exceptional performers are actually imbued with natural-born talent. Take Mozart, for example, a child-prodigy composer and musician. Surely his gifts must have been a result of a divine spark. Journalist Geoff Colvin disputes this notion. He writes that Mozart's early compositions were mostly copied from others, and his own musicianship would not rank him among the best modern child performers. His genius took years to blossom and was mostly the result of hard work, Colvin says.

Pop-sociologist Malcolm Gladwell attributes exceptional performance to practice, timing, circumstance, upbringing, culture, and opportunity. He claims that the most successful among us in all fields of human endeavor—musicians, athletes, mathematicians, business tycoons—weren't born with natural talent. Instead, they had the right upbringing and a supportive culture, and through untold hours of hard work and a few lucky breaks, they went on to achieve great things.

What Mozart had, Colvin says, was an ambitious father who initiated a strict training program when Mozart was a young boy, thousands of hours of focused practice, early successes that reinforced his resolve and self-worth, and strong support inside and outside the home. Colvin says that long hours of focused practice is "the factor that seems to explain the most about great performance."

Others argue that simply toiling away to hone a set of skills won't get you very far if you lack the divine spark that comes from an innate gift. So what is natural-born talent? Perhaps it's "a productive exhibition of personal style;" that is, the ability to perceive the most desirable physical and emotional nuances of an activity and then harness them into a coherent whole that uniquely expresses who you are.

It's hard arguing that natural-born talent doesn't exist when considering the fluidity of Tiger Woods' golf swing, the lustrous timbre of Luciano Pavarotti's voice, or even Jure Robič's ferocious style of bicycle racing. Talented people are so enthralled by how completely their activities express who they are that they're motivated to engage in long hours of focused practice, which creates a cycle of ever-improving performance.

Scholars have been at this chicken-and-egg argument for some time, but regardless of their position on whether talent or practice comes first, most agree that exceptional performers approach their training in a unique way. When O'Keeffe and Kaiser talk about all the "hard work" they devote to ultradistance cycling, these athletes underplay the zeal with which they push themselves to excel.

Take Les Handy, my faithful driving partner during the 2009 race and himself an accomplished endurance athlete. When he found himself snowbound in his Colorado home one Christmas, he hauled out his indoor trainer and set it up in his living room, determined to do a 12-hour training ride—a Christmas gift only a hardened cyclist could love. He jumped off his bike every few hours and updated his Facebook friends on his progress: bodily sensations, power output, calories consumed, distance covered, and so forth. Les wasn't just putting in mindless hours listening to Christmas carols; he remained highly focused on his workout. He monitored his activity continuously, striving to improve. Throughout the day sympathetic endurance athletes responded to his Facebook postings with their own suggestions based on the data he reported.

Unbeknownst to him, Les was engaged in a special form of training called "deliberate practice."

Professor Anders Ericsson coined this term along with a few colleagues in 1993 and went on to pioneer the expert performance movement, a group of scholars seeking to answer a seemingly simple question: what makes a person really good at something?

Two adherents of this movement, Stephen Dubner and Steven Levitt, write that, "Deliberate practice entails more than simply repeating a task—playing a C-minor scale 100 times, for instance, or hitting tennis serves until your shoulder pops out of its socket. Rather it involves setting specific goals, obtaining immediate feedback and concentrating as much on technique as on outcome." Professor Ericsson points out that deliberate practice is not inherently motivating or enjoyable. It's grueling, repetitive work during which the subject must maintain full attention to things like performance feedback, bodily sensations, and emotional state.

Welcome to the world of exceptional people achieving great things.

THE WAY JIM REES WORKED TO ESCAPE HIS TRAUMATIC PAST and become one of the best British ultracyclists offers a fine example of how deliberate practice produces results. These days Rees has a cohesive self-identity, but that wasn't always so. It took years of deliberate practice for him to become the resilient, confident man he is today.

Rees was a cocky, aggressive kid who knew no limits. He still remembers watching an Australian public-service television campaign designed to instill a health-conscious mind-set in young people. One spot opened with an overweight couch potato named Norman sitting at home on his lounge chair watching sports on television. Norman sat there muttering to himself and criticizing the athletes for their slack play. The punch line of the spot was, "Have a go, you mug!" (Translation for non-Australians: "Hey Norman, you bum, get out there and give it a try yourself!") This colloquial slogan had a big influence on young Rees. "It was about bringing a winning attitude to everything you do and never quitting," he explained to me before the 2009 race.

Unlike O'Keeffe and Kaiser, Rees was an all-around athlete in school—football, cricket, running, swimming—and got picked for all the teams in spite of his brashness. He even tried out as a professional footballer after moving to the United Kingdom in young adulthood. When he didn't make the cut, he started competing in triathlons and excelled before eventually coming around to ultradistance cycling.

His path was anything but smooth. He married young and had three children with his first wife, who like him had grown up in an abusive household. But unlike Rees, she never managed to overcome her feeling of victimhood. As a mother of three, she became depressed and suicidal. She was in and out of the hospital, and Rees was under so much stress he lost his passion for sport. Their marriage eventually ended, and Rees has since remarried. His second wife, Tracey, gives him plenty of support to pursue his dreams. Rees' life experiences taught him much about overcoming victimhood. He came to terms with his own childhood abuse, his failed marriage, and the ensuing separation from his kids. Along the way he crafted a life philosophy centered on what he calls "mental fitness."

"I could have played the victim; after all, I was abused, adopted, and abandoned. But instead I chose not to let my story weigh me down," he explained. "We can always find excuses why not. 'Oh, I was adopted,' or 'I was an only child,' but we can also turn this thinking around: '*Because* I was adopted, I'm stronger and more resilient.' It works both ways."

Rees incorporates the story of his life and his RAAM achievements in his coaching and motivational work. In his keynote speeches he points out that he's just a "normal guy" who has the mental discipline to overcome hardship, let go of the emotional baggage, and abolish limiting thoughts and feelings. Free from self-imposed constraints he sees unbounded possibility, and this motivates him to bring tremendous focus and intensity to achieving his athletic goals. His professional life and charitable pursuits are aimed at inspiring others to do the same—particularly children. Because of his own challenging childhood, he relates to kids who have lost hope and are afraid to dream.

Rees worked hard to escape his frightening family situation when he ran away as a young teenager. He worked hard to create a new life for himself, and to become a virtuous person despite how roughly people had once treated him. And by working so hard on these things, he wound up in a place where he could work even harder to become an accomplished ultradistance cyclist.

All of this involved deliberate practice. Rees trained his mind to abolish self-doubt and see opportunity instead. Because he didn't get a lot of encouragement as a child, he worked hard to behave in a way that made others feel good about themselves. Rees did this by practicing the correct ways to think and behave, making mistakes, and improving each time. He then incorporated these winning life strategies into his RAAM training.

Columnist David Brooks writes in *The New York Times* about the role of deliberate practice, observing that, "Public discussion is smitten by genetics and what we're 'hard-wired' to do. And it's true that genes place a leash on our capacities. But the brain is also phenomenally plastic. We construct ourselves through behavior…it's not who you are, it's what you do." Deliberate practice isn't just about mastering a skill or profession. As Rees discovered, sometimes it's about re-wiring your brain, changing your attitudes and thought patterns, and saving your own life in the process.

DESPITE HOW HARD HE WORKED to make sense of his past, Rees still has issues to sort out. For one, he hasn't reconciled his grandiose desire to break the British RAAM record with the common-man public image he cultivates. He certainly hasn't figured out how to reconcile his personal athletic goals with his desire to spend more time with Tracey and his now far-flung family. "Is RAAM my way of dealing with some of the stuff that happened to me as a kid?" he mused. "Am I running away from something? Do I need to mangle myself in RAAM to try to get to know myself at a deeper level, or is this about being Peter Pan—a grown kid who just wants to play?"

In the middle of Missouri on this day, in the throes of his third solo RAAM, Rees wasn't reflecting on *why* he was doing the race, but *how* he was racing it. His immediate conundrum was this: could he square his behavior during the race with his desire to leave a positive "fingerprint" on everybody he came in contact with?

Possibly because of his childhood traumas, Rees is keenly aware of how his behavior affects others. He's constantly challenging himself to be more empathetic, perceptive, and supportive of others. "How do I show up, especially when the pressure is on?" is a question he frequently asks. During RAAM, sometimes not so well. Rees argued with his crew in each of his RAAM bids.

Because he's so self-aware, when he goes off on a crew member it tortures him afterward. In his motivational speeches Rees asks his audience, "What fingerprint do you want to leave?" On this day the question was turned around on Rees. Near Jefferson City, Missouri, he called a crew meeting in the middle of the night to sort out the simmering conflicts that were hindering his race. Nearly two-thirds of the way to Annapolis, it was time for Rees to decide what fingerprint he would leave on his energetic, devoted young helpers.

Jefferson City is one of the more dramatic time stations in RAAM. First the racers pass directly under the grand Missouri State Capitol building, which rises from bluffs a few blocks from the Missouri River. Its nearly 250-foot-high dome topped by a bronze statue of the goddess Ceres is visible for miles. Then they cross the "Big Muddy" itself—the magnificent Missouri River, which served as a path for Lewis and Clark, the expedition dispatched by Thomas Jefferson in 1804 to open up a trade route to the Pacific Ocean.

Team Rees had enjoyed these landmarks in daylight the previous year, but Rees was so much faster this year that he clocked into Jefferson City around 2:00 AM, just in time for a sleep break. It had been a long, 23-plus hours of cycling through the second half of Kansas and most of Missouri in high humidity and temperatures that often exceeded 100 degrees. As in the southwestern deserts, Rees had wrapped himself like a mummy in white bandages soaked in his trusty evaporative cooling liquid. Despite having to contend with narrow-shouldered roads jammed with high-speed traffic, he had cracked jokes all day long and well into the night.

Rees' gaiety masked some not-so-funny undercurrents. He was still the fifth man on the road, but on this day Kaiser had made up a few hours on him. Now the pesky American was nipping at Rees' heels less than an hour back, and Rees' pace was slowing. He would cover fewer than 300 miles on this day, his lowest 24-hour tally since climbing the Rockies. He was starting to slip off a 10-day pace, let alone the British-record pace that was a couple of hours faster.

When Rees sensed he was slowing earlier in the day, he pressed crew chiefs Phil and Martyn for information. He wanted to know what speed he needed to maintain to salvage his record bid, how far back Kaiser was, and how his time station splits compared with the previous year's. He became frustrated when Phil and Martyn were unable to give him definitive answers. *Don't they realize I need this information to maintain my motivation?* he thought.

He was still laughing and joking on the outside, but he was also growing increasingly annoyed at his all-rookie crew.

There was more. He was still upset at Phil for having turned a five-minute phone break into a 30-minute delay back in Pratt, Kansas. And why were the crew changes taking so long? And how come the crew still hadn't replaced his juicer after it stopped working a few days ago? He craved his high-potency vegetable concoctions and the best they could offer him was disgusting pureed baby food. And what was up with Robin and Kate?

Robin was Rees' mechanic, a nice, adventurous young man from Colorado who had served on a RAAM crew before. Kate was Rees' videographer, a cute, shy woman who produced films in Bristol, England, and who seemed shell-shocked by the rigors of living out of a crew vehicle. Improbably, the two had struck up a romance while Rees was out there racing. This wasn't the first romance ever to blossom on a RAAM crew; after all, this is just the sort of thing that happens when a bunch of energetic young people cram themselves into a car for a cross-country adventure.

Back in Kansas a day or so earlier, Robin and Kate—who were serving on different shifts—had demanded that Phil and Martyn tweak assignments so they could work the same shift. They even threatened to mutiny unless they got their way. So Robin was reassigned to Martyn's crew to be with Kate, while Kevin (Rees' chiropractor) was shifted over to Phil's crew. This move created new problems. Now Kevin was serving on the same shift as Rees' nutritionist, Lindsey. On the one hand this was good because Kevin had a knack for calming Lindsey down when she locked horns with Rees. On the other hand, Kevin supported Lindsey's point of view about what, when, and how much Rees should be eating and drinking.

Rees had grown increasingly exasperated about the rigid way Lindsey was regulating his food and drink. *Can't she see I'm retaining water?* he thought to himself. *All she has to do is look at the edema in my arms and legs. My electrolytes are out of whack and I keep having to beg for more salty snacks. And why won't she give me that Snickers bar I asked for two hours ago?*

As an exhausted and bedeviled Rees rolled past the Missouri State Capitol building in the middle of the night, he called a crew meeting in an effort to get things sorted out. It was shift-change time so both follow-vehicles were there, as well as the motor home where Rees would nap.

Everybody on Team Rees waited for him to get settled, wondering whether Rees would soothe frayed nerves or open new rifts.

Phil was thinking that Rees was acting too much like a big kid. "He tries to push you and get as much as he can from you," Phil told me after the race. "When he finally hears 'no' he goes off sulking."

Martyn wished Rees would trust the crew more to make the right decisions. "It's hard to know how to push him, or even how to help him sometimes," Martyn explained. "His answer is always, 'Ahhhh, young grasshopper, I know better.'"

When Rees opened his mouth it was clear he wasn't happy. He told everybody he was "massively demotivated" by the way the crew had been handling things. He needed his chiropractor Kevin to focus more in his aching neck and less on other melodramas. He needed his nutritionist Lindsey to relax and give him more freedom to make his own decisions about food and drink. He needed everyone to show his crew chiefs Phil and Martyn more respect. Then he lit into Martyn about not being able to tell him what he needed to do to stay on British-record pace. Martyn replied, "Okay, we're on it." Then Rees exploded. "You're obviously *not* on it. When you *are* on it, you'll be able to give me the stats!" he bellowed. He implored everybody to pull together, think more clearly, and work faster and smarter so he could keep his time off the bike to a minimum. Before Rees shuffled into the back of his motor home for his sleep break, he acknowledged how exhausted everyone was and thanked everyone for how hard they were trying.

As he was dozing off he wondered whether his crew really understood how hard it was to compete in RAAM. He regretted the sharp words, but he was worried. He had been on British-record pace for almost 2,000 miles but he knew in the morning he'd have to pick up his speed to stay there. He fretted about whether he could fend off Kaiser's attack and hold onto fifth place.

But he had another concern that was too frightening to contemplate right now—his neck was starting to go. He had nightmarish flashbacks about his 2007 race, when he was forced to ride for days wearing a backpack-like scaffold to hold his head up. It was an absolutely miserable experience. He didn't know whether he could stand wearing a brace again this year.

"My neck was buggered by that point," he recalled gloomily after the 2009 race. "It put me out of sorts and got me pissed off." By the time he got to Jefferson City his head was drooping forward slightly and he had to exert conscious effort to hold it up—the unmistakable signs of dreaded Shermer's Neck. Rees knew he wasn't leaving the best fingerprints on his devoted team members, but he had other things to worry about.

By now it was 2:30 AM. The Jefferson City streets were deserted and the traffic lights all around town were blinking yellow. Everybody on Team Rees was resting quietly, some in the motor home, and some slumped on the follow-vehicle's seats. But nobody was having a particularly peaceful sleep.

Days Eight and Nine: Marooned in Ohio

Ohio and Illinois, June 24 and 25

At about the time that Lt. Col. Tony O'Keeffe had dropped out of the race on the evening of June 22, Janet Christiansen was a few hours farther up the road trying to keep cool in the cornfields of Kansas. Her goofy sense of humor was melting away in the record-breaking heat, but the weather was the least of her problems. She had been leading the women's field for days now, but her rival—the Brazilian Daniela Genovesi—was suddenly on the move. Christiansen's crew chief Bill Osborn was worried, though his concerns didn't have anything to do with Genovesi. He was focusing on his rider for now. "I didn't think she could last another day unless we solved this problem," he told me after the race.

The problem involved the awful saddle sores Christiansen had endured for the past four days. Osborn was concerned about infection and worried that Christiansen's discomfort was eroding her will to fight on. Coming on the heels of her meltdown the previous year just 250 miles from Annapolis, everyone on her crew hoped the Osprey wouldn't lose her resolve this time around.

Aside from her saddle sores, things had been going well. She was keeping ahead of her previous year's time splits, her race plan was intact, and despite a few rough spots her support team was working well together. "The Osprey is kept entertained by crew members singing Broadway tunes in five different languages," Christiansen reported.

Christiansen and Osborn had methodically tried everything they could think of to soothe her wounds. They swapped her saddle, adjusted her seat height, applied a variety of emollients and salves, and tried different types of padding—to no avail. Just as Osborn had run out of ideas, he picked up a tip from another racer's crew. When Team Osprey stopped for a break in front of a Wal-Mart somewhere in central Kansas, he wandered up and down the aisles looking for salvation. Just as he was about to give up he found the exact ointment he was searching for.

Once they had covered her abrasions with the recommended liquid bandage and threw on some antiseptic cream for safe measure, her condition began improving and Osborne could relax.

The Osprey reached the Missouri border in the middle of the night on June 23 feeling so good she decided to ride past the time she had earlier chosen for her sleep break. As she crossed the Mississippi River on the morning of June 24, in spite of her dwindling lead she felt an enormous sense of accomplishment for having reached the two-thirds point on her way to Annapolis.

By now she had been racing for almost eight days and nights and she was bone tired. "Dealing with edema and sleep deprivation were my biggest challenges going into this year's race," Christiansen explained. By the time she arrived at the Mississippi, she was suffering from both. Her edema was under much better control than the previous year, but still she had to cut the toes off her cycling shoes to accommodate the swelling in her legs and ward off the burning sensation on the balls of her feet.

"Last year my edema was really bad," she explained. "Bill said when I got off the bike my hands looked like catchers' mitts. They were talking about putting me in the hospital. Luckily I could still shove my feet in my cycling shoes." Christiansen says that female ultracyclists are more prone to edema than their male counterparts. She believes this is in part a hormonal reaction to the byproducts of muscle breakdown. "The medical doctors and exercise physiologists don't have a good handle on it," she said. "I take antihistamines, sleep with my legs elevated, and use massage to get the cell waste out of the muscles. But swelling is still a real concern."

Whatever she was doing to control her swelling was working this year. As for her fatigue, Osborn was now watching her closely for signs that she might be falling asleep and losing control of her bike. Once she had crossed the Mississippi and entered Illinois in the afternoon on June 24, Osborn saw something that put him at ease. As they rode along Route 40—one of the original coast-to-coast U.S. highways from the 1920s—an injured kitten limped onto the road. Christiansen spied the animal immediately. She jumped off her bike to see if she could help, but the animal swatted at her and wouldn't permit her to come near. As she walked back to pick up her bike, she glanced over at her crew mates in the follow-vehicle, shrugged her shoulders, and then got going again.

The incident cheered Osborn. "What it showed me was that she wasn't a zombie on the bike," he said. "She still had good awareness and reaction time, and that was nice to see."

Osborn was awfully proud of his rider. Christiansen's attitude and motivation were as strong as ever. "She was still in a good mood, still cracking jokes. She raced RAAM the way she took on life. Her desire and spirit are what will always stick with me," he said.

Osborn was right. She was still having fun out there, listening to show tunes over her PA system, laughing with her crew, and coming to the aid of injured animals. All of this while leading the women's race and covering about 265 miles per day through the hottest, most humid weather the Plains States had seen in years. Her goal was to finish in 12 days or less, and she was on track to get the job done.

REES WASN'T FEELING QUITE AS SPRIGHTLY as Christiansen on this June 24 afternoon in southern Illinois. About six hours behind Christiansen on the road (about 100 miles), Rees was battling the effects of sleep deprivation. Rees had been struggling with this problem for days, and back in the Plains States he really had a scare even though he jumped five places from 10th to fifth during that time. At that point he had still been holding the pace required to finish in 10 days. If he could only goose his pace a bit he'd have the British record, something he'd sought for years.

But how? It wasn't as though he could dial back on his sleep because he was hardly getting any at all. He experienced vivid hallucinations as he raced along in the narcotic prairie heat. At one point he thought he saw soccer star David Beckham running along in front of him, desperate to get his hands on some Viagra and imploring Rees to help. Hallucinations aren't always scary for the racers, but they always are for their crew members.

Rees' crew chiefs Phil and Martyn feared he might fall asleep on the bike so they were on the lookout for warning signs: weaving in the road, head bobbing, or slowed reactions to traffic or navigation instructions. "At night I watched Jim's head dip up and down every five minutes, and it was scary, because I suspected he was falling asleep out there," Phil remembered. "But when I yelled 'Wake up!' over the PA system he insisted he wasn't dozing off. My decision making was challenged because of my own sleep deprivation, so I began doubting myself." Pulling a racer off the road is a difficult decision, but by Day Seven a racer's life is in his crew chief's hands.

Happily for Phil, Rees began trusting him more and more as the race progressed.

At one point Rees' exhaustion had became so complete that Phil did order him off the bike and Rees collapsed in the driveway of a house in rural Kansas, too tired to climb into his motor home or change out of his dirty cycling kit. Lying there like a passed-out drunk, Rees didn't look anything like the sophisticated and debonair man who had shown up in Oceanside a week before. The homeowner arrived minutes later, and as he tried pulling his car into the garage, he spied a prostrate Rees on the ground in front of him, out cold. The man leaped from his car and noticed Phil standing near the motor home.

"Is that guy dying?" the man asked accusingly, nodding in Rees' direction.

"Nope, just sleeping," Phil answered cheerily.

Now in Illinois two days later, Rees had been racing for 168 hours—seven days—since leaving Oceanside. He had gotten less than 10 hours of sleep during this time and was coming apart, just like all the other racers were at this juncture. But Rees was in rougher shape than most because he had gotten even less sleep than the others, and he was cycling now in that gauzy half-dream state that terrified RAAM crews.

"C'mon Reesey, wake up!" Phil shouted into the microphone. His voice boomed from huge loudspeakers mounted atop his vehicle, but the cyclist riding just 15 feet in front of it didn't seem to hear.

"Jim, time to put a little more speed in, you can do it, mate! Concentrate!" Phil shouted. Rees was cycling very slowly now. He was also weaving all over the road, almost crossing into oncoming traffic. His head flopped down and then jerked up. Rees was struggling to stay awake.

This is how they die out there, Phil thought. For the first time he was afraid something terrible might happen to Rees, as it had to Bob Breedlove in the 2005 race. Breedlove died instantly when a 15-year-old driving a pickup truck smashed into him on a desolate road in Colorado. There were no witnesses. The police said Breedlove had fallen asleep and crossed into oncoming traffic, but his family maintains the speeding teenager had swerved into Breedlove's lane coming around a bend.

Breedlove was well known in the ultracycling community and his death was mourned around the world. But it didn't come as a shock; sleep-deprived RAAM cyclists cheat death every hour of every day that they're on the road.

Oh God, if something happens to him, how am I going to tell Tracey? Phil thought. Phil knew he had to be assertive, lay down the law, and get his cyclist off the road.

"Okay, time for a rest Jimbo. Just a short one," Phil's insistent voice rumbled over the loudspeakers. Phil heard Rees' raspy voice over their two-way radio. "I'm *not* falling asleep. We're *not* stopping," he growled into the microphone affixed to his helmet. At this point Rees was still hoping to break the British record. Phil pulled his follow-vehicle up to Rees and managed to persuade his rider to take a short rest.

The vehicle pulled ahead of Rees and stopped along the shoulder of a rural road somewhere in Indiana, 2,300 miles into the race. Out popped Lindsey, Rees' nurse and nutritionist. Next came Robin, his bike mechanic. Phil jumped out last, opened the door of the minivan, and pulled the massage table out, setting it discreetly under a tree and out of sight from passing cars.

Rees rolled his bike off the road and Phil jumped to catch it and steady his rider as he slowly climbed off. Rees shuffled stiffly about, his gaze soft and unfocused. He walked over to his crew and thanked Lindsey, Robin, and Phil for their support. His head was cocked slightly to one side and pointing downward as his neck muscles continued to weaken.

Lindsey led him by the arm over to the massage table, gently stripped off his cycling shorts and jersey, and gave him a sponge bath as if she were working at her hospital north of London. Then it was Phil's turn to massage Rees' aching neck and legs. Rees was asleep the whole time.

After Phil woke him up, Rees let out a long sigh, pulled on a clean pair of cycling shorts, and sat up ready for some food. Lindsey spooned some fresh fruit into his mouth. "How are you feeling?" Lindsey asked as she slathered him with sunscreen, putting her face close to his to get his attention. "Fancy a chicken sandwich?"

He tried focusing his mind on his competitive predicament as he sat there chewing. As Rees had feared the previous night in Jefferson City, Kaiser passed him this morning just before they crossed the Mississippi. Rees is fond of saying, "You can't argue with reality," and right now reality was winning.

"I raced until Jefferson City," Rees remembered. "Then after that, once my neck problems came on, I just managed my position." Two days before, Slovenian veteran Marko Baloh had lost his will to fight when the charging Austrian Gerhard Gulewicz passed him to claim third place; now Baloh languished fully eight hours behind Gulewicz. Rees didn't realize it at the time, but just as Baloh had given up his goal of a podium finish, Rees was letting go of his dream of breaking the British record.

THOUGH CHRISTIANSEN WAS DELIGHTED to have reached the Mississippi leading the women's race, she was surprised by how rapidly her sparkly Brazilian foe was closing. From around midnight on June 22 to midnight the next day, Daniela Genovesi had managed to cut about four hours from Christiansen's once-comfortable six-hour lead. The Osprey had led the race since Arizona. All of a sudden her position didn't look nearly as commanding.

Shortly after crossing the river on the morning of June 24, Christiansen's lead was down to an hour—just over 10 miles. Feeling feisty and on form, the Osprey wasn't interested in relinquishing first place. She pushed hard throughout an afternoon of intense racing through the southern part of Illinois, mostly paralleling Interstate 70 on straight, pancake-flat rural roads that cut through neatly tended agricultural fields. Christiansen even managed to clock the fourth-fastest time split of the entire field into TS35 in Greenville, Illinois.

As the sun began sagging low on the horizon behind them, the two leading women reached TS36 in Effingham, Illinois, a town that boasted one of the world's largest crosses. A religious monolith easily visible for miles around, the cross was carefully designed to top out at 198 feet, just under the 200-foot aviation limit. "You have to have a light on top if it's 200 feet. And there's no way in heck that we would do that," explained a town official.

Christiansen didn't even try searching out the massive cross. Her lead was now only 10 minutes, or about two miles. She decided she could handle losing the lead she'd held for so long. After her heartbreaking DNF the previous year, the most important goal was to finish, and doing it in under 12 days would fulfill her wildest dreams, no matter how she placed.

A few minutes after cruising through Effingham, Christiansen heard her crew chief's voice in her earpiece: "Here she comes. We're dropping back to let her follow-vehicle through." In an instant, Genovesi pulled alongside Christiansen. Genovesi spoke little English, so even though racers are allowed to ride side by side for up to 15 minutes during a pass, Christiansen wasn't expecting much chitchat. Genovesi glanced over at her, flashed a big smile, and pulled ahead. Christiansen couldn't believe how strong, alert, and unblemished her rival appeared.

By the time they passed through the next time station about 75 miles farther in Sullivan, Indiana, Genovesi's lead had swelled to almost an hour.

As Christiansen was drifting off to sleep a few hours before dawn on June 25, she wondered where on earth Genovesi had come from. Her crew chief Bill Osborn was wondering the same thing. As he pored over time station splits posted on the RAAM website, he noticed something shocking. While she was closing on Christiansen the previous afternoon, Genovesi had laid down the fastest time split of the entire field—men *and* women—in the roughly 50-mile segment into TS35 in Greenville. And she had recorded the third-fastest split into TS37 in Sullivan later that night. Osborn was dubious. Even though Christiansen had led the women's field for most of the race, his racer had only managed to notch the fourth-fastest time splits on two occasions.

Even more incredible to Osborn was that Genovesi had raced the entire 170-mile stretch from TS34 at the Mississippi River to TS37 in Sullivan faster than anybody else. She even smoked the mighty Jure Robič by over an hour, and Robič was on RAAM-record pace, no less. Genovesi's effort wasn't simply an anomalous burst of speed through a single time station.

According to her reported splits, she had bested the entire field during 12 long hours of racing through this 170-mile stretch that spanned *three* time stations.

Christiansen hadn't done a shabby job, either; she had completed this 170-mile section with the fifth-fastest time. But to Osborn, the Brazilian's performance seemed a bit too miraculous. He simply didn't believe the split times Team Genovesi had reported to race headquarters.

As he drifted off to sleep, Osborn promised himself he would share his concerns with race headquarters in the morning. He would ask them to put some race officials on Genovesi to see if they managed to spot any funny business going on. He was confident they would.

ALONG WITH GENOVESI, AMERICAN RIVALS KEVIN KAISER AND CHRISTOPHER GOTTWALD also blitzed the field on Days Eight and Nine. Demure Kaiser wasn't acting very meek at this point in the race. He had begun Day Eight just outside Jefferson City in sixth, nipping at the heels of veteran Jim Rees while Rees was getting ready for his "all hands" team meeting later that night. By the end of the following day he was blazing a trail through rural Ohio, almost six hours ahead of Rees.

Fueled by grape soda, pizza, and pickles, Kaiser had pared back his sleep during this two-day stretch and raced for 22 hours each day. Kaiser underwent a transformation in the Ozarks. "He became the commander out there," a crew member recalled. "He'd call the follow-vehicle and say 'This is what we're going to do.' He was decisive and forceful and called all the shots."

Meanwhile, the aggressive stage racer Gottwald was in the full throes of executing the secret race plan that had worked so well for other pros before him. He was banking much more sleep by indulging in long breaks, then racing faster for shorter periods of time. As the finish line drew near, Gottwald began reducing his sleep and now he was coming on strong.

Gottwald's charge had begun back in Kansas on Day Six. Before that, "I was sleeping four or more hours a night and my crew got nervous when I fell so far behind," he said. "But they didn't understand my race plan, and because of all that sleep, I was feeling great." Then Gottwald cut his daily sleep allotment to three hours.

"I could've been in first place if I hadn't gotten so bored in Kansas," he declared with the bravado he often displayed when talking about his cycling accomplishments. "After seven hours in the saddle, my mind just starts wandering and I need a break."

Gottwald knew his crew would have to snap into action if he was going to continue attacking. "I challenged them: 'If I make a move, which of you will stay up all night to make sure nobody passes me while I'm down?'" he recalled. Gottwald needed his crew to start spying on the racers immediately in front and behind in order to gauge how hard he needed to push his pace.

Gottwald is a competitive guy, and he was gunning to be the first American and the first rookie to finish the race. His reconnaissance told him that his main rival for both of those titles was Kaiser.

Kaiser was six hours behind Gottwald when they had first entered Kansas after midnight on Day Six. As Kaiser moved up the field he remained stuck just behind his cocky rival through much of Kansas, sometimes so close he could see Gottwald up ahead on the same stretch of road. By the time these two Americans crossed from Kansas to Missouri late at night on Day Seven, they were in sixth and seventh places, both a couple of hours behind Rees in fifth.

"Gottwald's a much faster rider but he stopped a lot and didn't seem to be enjoying Kansas," the ever-modest Kaiser said. "His team scrambled when I passed him at night while he was asleep, but he could've kept himself in front if he'd just kept going."

Gottwald had begun Day Eight in 10th but climbed up to seventh by the end of Day Nine, charging up the field just like Kaiser had. By this point Gottwald was the one on poor Rees' heels, though he still yo-yoed between three and seven hours behind Kaiser, who had edged past Rees earlier. Because his sleep breaks were still longer than Kaiser's, Gottwald wasn't fazed by his herky-jerky progress.

Though Kaiser and Gottwald had blitzed the field, they hadn't quite been able to keep pace with race leaders Robič and Wyss. But they were solidly in the next echelon, covering about as much ground as third-place Gerhard Gulewicz. The two leading Americans had traveled farther on these two days than even the Slovenian ultracycling great Marko Baloh, who was fading fast after ceding third place to Gulewicz a few days before. Just as amazingly, the women's leader Daniela Genovesi kept pace with these two storming Americans, covering almost as much distance on these days as they did—even though by then she had been racing one day longer.

As Day Nine wound down, the endgame for the 2009 race was coming into focus. There are always three marquee races-within-the-race in solo RAAM: the men's race, the women's race, and the race to be the first rookie. The men's race was down to a historic showdown between Jure Robič and Dani Wyss, which was now expected to be the closest men's battle in the history of RAAM. In addition to the competitive fireworks, it was likely there would be fireworks of a different sort, too. Team Robič continued to pester race officials about equal treatment and hurl cheating accusations at Team Wyss.

Though Daniela Genovesi was making a spectacular charge, the women's race remained close. As in the men's race, Janet Christiansen's crew chief was concerned that their rival might not be playing fairly. It appeared as though there would be fireworks here, too.

The race for top rookie (and top American) was down to Kevin Kaiser and Christopher Gottwald. Kaiser held a slim lead but they were both chewing up the field, with Gottwald coming on even stronger than Kaiser. It was also going to be a tight race for the honor of being the first rookie finisher.

EVERY CONTESTANT EXPERIENCES VIOLENT WEATHER at some point during RAAM, and 2009 was no exception. There had already been dust storms in the Utah deserts, frigid rains in the Rockies, and even a tornado in the Plains that sent a few racers scurrying to their follow-vehicles. Since the racers are outdoors almost continuously, dealing with extreme weather is a big part of the race. A racer needs proper clothing, good race planning, and a little luck to get through it all. He also needs the proper attitude, because Mother Nature can be cruel to a cyclist exposed to the elements for as long as RAAM cyclists are. Just past Oxford, Ohio, several racers learned this lesson all over again.

By late evening on June 25, Janet Christiansen was trailing the surprise race leader Daniela Genovesi by almost two hours. An hour behind Christiansen was a charging Kevin Kaiser, followed by Jim Rees, who had recently ceded his position to Kaiser and was yet another hour back.

As Christiansen crested a hill outside of Oxford on this muggy summer's evening, she was feeling terribly sleepy. Once Genovesi had passed her, Christiansen's crew chief Bill Osborn noticed that his racer began showing signs of severe sleep deprivation. He labored to keep her awake with chatter, music, and anything else he could think of.

Then something happened that brought back some pep: she felt a few drops of refreshing, warm rain. But these weren't normal drops; they were the kind of drops that signal a deluge—drops that felt like plump, overripe blackberries as they landed. Just then the wind gusted and towering lightning bolts lit up the now-purple sky. As the first thunder claps rolled over her, the deluge began.

The thunderstorm quickly intensified and lightning came down all around. Soon Christiansen could only guess at where the road was by the reflections of mailboxes on either side. She felt energized and excited to be riding through such a spectacular storm, and there was a big grin on her face as she squinted to make out what was ahead of her. The Osprey told herself that as long as she could follow the road, she would keep racing. Along with the mailboxes, she used the refracted, disorganized headlights of approaching vehicles to help discern the way forward and pedaled on.

Then Christiansen felt pinpricks in her arms and legs. The rain had turned into pea-sized hail and the road surface quickly iced up. Christiansen's follow-vehicle pulled alongside her and Osborn motioned for her to stop. He yanked her off the bike and hurried her into the van as darkness fell.

"Rather be safe and be able to continue than take a chance that could end the race," Osborn explained. "Whether she's first or second is down on her priority list."

Osborn decided to be productive during the weather delay by having his racer take a sleep break this evening rather than waiting until her usual 3:00 AM nap time. If she got going again in the wee hours of the morning, she'd have to ride for nearly 24 hours before her next 3:00 AM break to get back on track. He was confident she could rise to the challenge.

As Christiansen fell asleep to the rhythmic sound of hail on the windows, a man ran through the deluge toward her van in the darkness. He pounded so hard on the driver's window that Christiansen thought they'd been hit by a car. "Get this van out of here!" he yelled at Kat, Christiansen's on-duty crew member who had also been dozing in the driver's seat. It took Kat a moment to get her bearings, and then she realized she had mistakenly stopped in the man's driveway. She waved him off and pulled her vehicle away and out of sight. She was pretty groggy, but Kat was certain of one thing: the angry fellow had been as naked as a jaybird.

Even though he had been about 20 miles behind Christiansen when it hit, the Ohio storm was so massive that it also affected Rees' race. Like Christiansen, Rees wanted to race through it. He was losing hope of beating the British record, but he desperately wanted to make it to Annapolis in under 10 days.

The storm had something else in mind. Rivers of water swamped the roadway and stopped Rees in his tracks. He dismounted and tried walking in knee-deep and then waist-deep water coursing down Oxford's streets, the result of a nearby stream that had swelled its banks. *This isn't going to work*, he thought. Like Christiansen, Rees had to pull over and wait. The storm raged for three hours longer, producing incessant lightning and booming claps of thunder that made the ground shake.

Rees managed to get an early nap just as Christiansen had done. But the weather forced a longer stop than Rees had planned, and he knew it meant he was slipping even farther behind his goal pace.

Gottwald was also waylaid by the flooding, but he didn't mind a bit. Even though he was back in seventh place, he had planned on taking a longish sleep break that night anyway. His secret race plan incorporated more rest than Rees' did, so he slept soundly and without worry. *The next day I'm going to give everybody a real surprise,* he thought as he drifted off.

Rees got going again in the middle of the night. Because the roads were such a mess, his navigator made a wrong turn that cost him another hour or two. All told, Rees figured that storm-related delays had cost him nearly five hours that night. With about 30 hours of racing left, it was doubtful he'd be able to claw back the time he had lost.

After relinquishing his goal of beating the British record, his secondary goal of finishing in less than 10 days was now also in jeopardy. Still, he was well ahead of the pace he had set the previous year, so at least his fallback goal of beating that mark remained intact.

As for Christiansen, she surmised that her rival Genovesi had been just far enough up the road that she had missed the storm and hadn't been delayed. So Christiansen knew her chances of retaking the lead were gone. As dawn broke, Genovesi would be about five hours ahead.

The deluge had put a measurable crimp in both Christiansen's and Rees' race plans. Yet neither of these resilient RAAM veterans cracked or felt sorry for themselves. When the skies cleared, they both mounted their bikes without any fuss or self-pity, grateful for the chance to continue racing. Christiansen had struggled with her morale the previous year, but she wasn't going to let anything bother her this time. In fact, both Rees and Christiansen said that the Ohio storm was one of the most awesome and beautiful sights they'd experienced during the race.

14

Day Nine: Final Ultimatum

Pennsylvania and Maryland, June 25

Back on the morning of Day Eight, crafty challenger Dani Wyss had caught sight of his prey—the Slovenian titan Jure Robič—as they approached Blanchester, Ohio. This otherwise forgettable small town boasted one memorable feature—the world's largest horseshoe crab in the guise of a rounded community pavilion. This monstrosity dominated the grounds of a Baptist church that claimed 60 people could sit within its dark-brown shell for weddings and other ceremonies. A wooden post propped up a spiky 20-foot-long tail that pointed straight up in the air.

Wyss hadn't noticed this bizarre sight as he plowed down Blanchester's forlorn, five-block-long main street the previous day. The only thing in his sights had been the back of Robič's maroon follow-vehicle. Wyss was just able to make out the faint sound of Slovenian turobofolk music that had been emanating from the massive speakers moored to its roof.

Wyss had finally reeled Robič in and wasn't about to let him slip away again. Thanks to the one-hour penalty differential, Wyss' crew chief Christian Hoppe knew that all Wyss had to do to win the race was to keep Robič close. But Hoppe also knew Robič had the potential to uncork one final, vicious attack that could leave his racer in the dust. *Let him try,* Hoppe thought. He recalled the 2007 race when an untouchable Robič had vanquished Wyss by nine hours, but he felt his racer was much faster and stronger now. Wyss was already way ahead of the pace he had set in his two previous RAAM efforts.

They still had about 500 miles of racing ahead of them. The ultracycling community drew in its collective breath anticipating the battle to come, and coverage from RAAM media fanned the flames. "Over the next 24 hours, we are set for a heart-stopping race as the riders get closer to Annapolis," they reported. "Will the penalties come into play? Will Robič pull away? Will Wyss actually catch Robič and pass him? Do not go away. You don't want to miss what this race has in store!"

The day before had been a historic one. Starting in Blanchester, over the next 20 hours the two leaders remained within sight of each other for almost 300 miles of furious racing through Appalachian Ohio and West Virginia. At one point that afternoon, Wyss had slipped by to briefly claim the lead when Robič punctured a tire. This probably came as a relief to Robič, who had been stalked by Wyss for days. *Let him set the pace,* Robič thought. *Let's see how long he lasts.* On the other hand, Robič was miffed that Wyss had passed him while he wrestled with a mechanical issue—something that cycling etiquette frowns on. Just one more thing to heighten the growing enmity between these two men.

Since third-place Gerhard Gulewicz was 12 hours back, he posed no threat; the final 24 hours of the race would be a strategic chess match between the two leaders. The endgame could unfold in one of three ways. Because Gulewicz wasn't a factor, Robič and Wyss could both afford to ease up together, playing a game of chicken and saving their energy for decisive attacks and counterattacks much closer to the finish line. Alternatively, one of them could attack early in an effort to build a gap that would demoralize his opponent. In the third scenario, both racers would establish a strong but sustainable pace, each hoping the other would simply fade away as the cumulative effect of racing for more than seven days and nights took its toll.

Now that Wyss had passed him while he changed his flat, Robič could finally observe Wyss for himself. As they raced through the rolling rural roads of southern Ohio, the defending champion studied his adversary, trying to ascertain what he had left in his legs.

Robič felt he had a number of advantages that would help him prevail. The first was his much greater experience; racing in his seventh straight RAAM, he had seen and done it all. Also, he was confident he could withstand the cumulative effects of severe sleep deprivation better than Wyss. He had had only seven hours of sleep up to this point, yet his mind was clearer than it had been in many of his previous efforts. He knew each of them would get one last rest break, and he hoped that Wyss' would last longer. Even though Wyss had surprised the reigning champion by sticking with him through the Rockies, Robič still believed himself to be the better climber. With the Appalachian Mountains just ahead, Robič held out hope that he could break Wyss in this final series of climbs.

Robič knew his most formidable advantage was his mental toughness. For example, in 2004, Robič beat back an attack by Mike Trevino to win his first title. Just six weeks later he entered Le Tour Direct, the most diabolical ultracycling race in Europe. This race was called "the nonstop Tour" because it traversed many legendary mountain stages visited by the Tour de France. Racers faced more climbing in this 2,500-mile event than in RAAM—fully 140,000 feet, almost five times the height of Mount Everest.

Robič also won Le Tour Direct, finishing in just under eight days and vanquishing the best ultracyclists on *two* continents that year. Commenting on this feat, two-time RAAM champion Pete Penseyres said, "That's just mind-boggling. I can't envision doing two big races back to back. The mental part is just too hard." Hans Mauritz, the co-organizer of Le Tour Direct at the time, agreed. "For me, Jure is on another planet," he said. "He can die on the bike and keep going."

All told, Robič raced for 17 days and nights during that six-week period, covering 5,500 miles and climbing 250,000 feet. That's almost 50 miles straight up. Done all at once, that much climbing would have catapulted Robič beyond the troposphere, even beyond the stratosphere, to the outer reaches of the mesosphere—the least-studied layer of the atmosphere because it's way, way higher than planes can fly but just a tad too low for orbiting spacecraft.

DESPITE ALL THE ADVANTAGES ROBIČ FELT HE HAD, as the miles ticked away and the leaders crossed from Ohio into West Virginia, Wyss kept pace. *At least he isn't attacking,* thought Robič's longtime crew chief, Uroš Velepec. *That means he can't. He's as spent as we are.* But Team Robič didn't spot any signs that the Swiss challenger was weakening, either. Most observers out on the race course that evening felt Wyss had the upper hand. The Swiss challenger looked relaxed and almost serene even as the tension mounted. He was still enjoying himself because he had nothing to lose.

Robič had everything to lose, and it showed.

The Slovenian champion had never raced RAAM for enjoyment or with a smile on his face. This four-time winner attacked the course viciously. It was his *job* to win RAAM. During the race he was at war—with himself and the rest of the field. His internal challenge was all about pushing himself beyond his limits. His crew had always played an important role, exhorting him to dig deeper, cheering him on, even shouting insults at him, whatever it took—even when Robič was so weary he wanted to die. "When I am tired [my crew] can take me to the edge, to the last atoms of my power," he once explained to a journalist. But this year was different. Robič was facing the gravest challenge of his RAAM career, and he seemed especially edgy.

That evening in West Virginia, Robič's crew member Matjaž Planinšek reported, "On the climb towards Ellensboro, Jure is constantly attacking his opponent and trying to break him." In the soft twilight this beautiful Appalachian region of steep wooded hills, narrow valleys, and winding streams offered gorgeous views around every bend. But the raging battle on the road was so all-consuming that nobody noticed.

As midnight drew near and Day Eight came to a close, the two leaders were struggling over endless Appalachian rollers as they passed through the tiny town of Grafton, West Virginia. None of these ascents were as long as the ones in the Rockies, but the 130-mile stretch into Grafton involved more climbing than any similar expanse on the entire route. Robič and Wyss climbed about 11,000 feet during this almost nine-hour slog—over two miles straight up. Mighty Robič was pouring it on now, trying to bury Wyss in this last mountainous section. Still, Wyss hung on—haunting Robič, stalking him, tormenting him like an evil shadow that would not be shaken.

Wyss stopped for a break somewhere past Grafton after midnight at the start of Day Nine. Robič's crew chief Uroš Velepec had a decision to make. Should they stop as well, or keep going in order to open a lead on Wyss? Velepec convinced his rider to rest as well, arguing it was unlikely Wyss' stop would last long enough for Robič to make much headway.

Better to take the time to put on some warm clothing for the long, chilly night ahead.

Neither racer slept.

As his masseur worked over Robič's ruined legs, the champion received an update on the penalty situation that had been brewing for days. Robič's spies had been watching Wyss and they were certain they'd spotted him violating traffic regulations. Then, as Wyss got rolling again in the middle of the night, Robič's crew claimed some bystanders had seen Wyss roll through a red light right in front of a race official without receiving a penalty. Someone posted a mysterious comment to this effect on RAAM's own race blog.

Throughout the afternoon and now deep into the night, the atmosphere on Team Robič couldn't have been more different from Team Wyss'. Even though they were under intense pressure, everybody on the Swiss challenger's crew still seemed to be enjoying themselves. Robič's Slovenian soldiers weren't having much fun at all. They were livid about what they believed to be biased officiating and paranoid that the race organization was out to get them. They complained loudly to the race officials who were now shadowing them (and Wyss) continuously.

The heart of the contretemps between Team Robič and the race organization involved the penalties Robič had received for what his crew considered minor technical infractions having little to do with how he was racing his bike: one for "illegal peeing" at the starting line, one for passing another rider on an interstate in Arizona after they claimed to have been given the go-ahead from an official, and a third for failing to return to the original spot after getting lost in Indiana. These penalties had added one hour to Robič's finish time. Wyss didn't have a single minute of penalties yet, so in order to win the race Robič had to cross the line in Annapolis 57 minutes ahead of him (in Oceanside Robič had started three minutes after Wyss). Everybody on Robič's crew was weary, and the effects of sleep deprivation fueled their collective paranoia and stoked their feelings of frustration and anger.

Robič's cognition was also compromised. Sleep researchers at an English sleep research laboratory note that, "Sleep deprivation impairs decision making involving the unexpected, innovation, revising plans… and effective communication." The champion wasn't capable of calmly and dispassionately absorbing the information his crew shared with him, let alone coming up with a rational decision about what to do. He was entirely dependent on his crew, and because of his profound fatigue he was also highly suggestible. It was no surprise that he became as paranoid and infuriated as his team was. His total exhaustion had completely obliterated his coping mechanisms.

As Robič willed his weary body to climb back onto his bike after the break in Grafton, he was fixated on the three penalties he had received. *How could they treat me like this?* he thought to himself. *I've worked so hard, and now they're trying to take away my victory with cheap penalties. I can't let them. I won't let them.*

Race owner and president Fred Boethling had been notified that Robič's team was complaining loudly about penalties and officiating. As the race grew tighter, Boethling realized that the penalty controversy wasn't going to fade away.

Boethling had been in control of RAAM for about three years and had made great strides in professionalizing race management and operations. But by all admissions, RAAM was still a work in progress. This year, for example, Boethling had struggled to recruit the full complement of experienced race officials necessary to effectively cover such a sprawling competition. "I need to build a reliable pipeline of up-and-coming officials," he explained to me afterward. "It'll take a few years, but my goal is to establish an apprenticeship program using RAAM qualifying races as a proving ground."

He had managed to secure 13 pairs of officials, most of whom he knew to be reliable, some of whom he wasn't so sure about. It hadn't been easy. Race officials sacrifice two weeks of their lives for only a pittance, live without creature comforts from the inside of a car, get very little sleep, and work long, hot, tedious days and nights. As with RAAM crew members, they do it for the love of the sport and the adventure.

The previous day, when Boethling and his race director saw how close the men's race had become, they had decided to move their best officials to the front. Both Robič and Wyss would be shadowed continuously during the final 24 hours, and Boethling had even decided to go out on patrol himself during the final several hundred miles of racing.

Boethling had reviewed the events surrounding each of Robič's penalties and was convinced they were legitimate. He felt ready for the confrontation he expected would come.

Having finished the race himself a few years before, he knew something about what Robič and Wyss were feeling. Boethling appreciated what this moment meant to these two warriors. Out of respect more than anything else, Boethling promised himself he would do everything in his power to ensure the integrity of the result.

AS ROBIČ AND WYSS WATCHED THE SKY SLOWLY LIGHTEN UP ahead of them for the last time on the road, they were finally out of the Appalachians and entering Maryland when dawn broke. These men knew the winner would be crowned by nightfall, but they were both so spent they could not imagine how they were going to make it through another day. They commanded their addled minds to stay focused on the moment: the sound of their own breathing, the sensation of turning the pedals, and the undulations in the road ahead.

All that work in the mountains had paid off for Robič. He had squeezed out a 10-minute lead by early morning, just 225 miles from Annapolis. A few hours earlier Robič's team member Matjaž had wondered, "Can the great king once more show his powers or will the new prince show us how to win the RAAM in future?" Then he exhorted his rider to "write history today."

It was June 25—Statehood Day in Slovenia—the day Robič's country had won its freedom as an independent nation in 1991 after a successful plebiscite months earlier. Robič felt a wellspring of nationalistic pride rising inside him. On this day especially, he wanted to make his people proud. He felt it was his *responsibility* to do so. Statehood Day was a national holiday in Slovenia, and Robič's website drew more than 20,000 visitors on this day—one out of every 1,000 Slovenian citizens.

RAAM's website was also being pounded by mesmerized ultracyclists all over the world. "This is unbelievable," one fan posted. "Hollywood couldn't have scripted a more dramatic finish. These athletes both deserve the win."

The two men were digging deep. They were both on pace to just about match the fastest time ever posted for RAAM—this on a course that had much more climbing than the year the record had been set. Despite their staggering exhaustion they were managing a steady pace over the rolling terrain of northern Maryland as the rural countryside gradually gave way to the sprawling exurbs of Baltimore–Washington, D.C.

After clawing up four short but devilishly steep climbs into TS48, Robič's lead on the road had crept up to 13 minutes by midmorning. This after racing for almost 190 hours—eight days straight—and covering 2,850 miles. But because he carried 60 minutes of penalty time, his 13-minute lead didn't amount to much. There were 180 miles left; could he gain enough time in the roughly 11 hours of racing that remained? The RAAM "10-percent rule" suggests it's possible to catch another racer as long as he's no farther away than 10 percent of the remaining distance to the finish. Including penalties and the fact that Wyss had started three minutes before Robič, at their current speed Wyss' effective 44-minute lead worked out to 7 percent of the remaining distance.

It was theoretically doable.

But by now Robič knew that Wyss would not simply fade away. It would be up to Robič to wrest the victory away from his foe with one last ferocious attack. But carving out this 13-minute lead on the road had already taken Robič to the limit this morning. How could he find another 44 minutes in these final 11 hours? His crew chief Uroš Velepec exhorted the defending champion just as he had done innumerable times before. If anyone could reach into Robič's soul and find that one last spark of energy—that one last reason to conjure more power from his quivering legs—it was Velepec.

Just then Boethling heard that some of Robič's crew members wished to meet him at TS49 in Rouzerville, Pennsylvania, about 130 miles from Annapolis. He headed there along with his second in command, his son Rick, as well as his most trusted official, George Thomas. Boethling had conscripted Thomas to be an official just a few days before, after Thomas finished a shorter version of the race that had ended in Taos, one-third of the way to Annapolis. Thomas was a wizened ultracyclist and a RAAM finisher many times over. Boethling respected his judgment and knew he would need his best assets to monitor the Robič-Wyss showdown.

TS49 was situated along a quiet country road lined by trees so tall and full they completely shaded out the sun, making it feel more like a dark forest than a suburban byway. When I arrived, Robič's motor home was already there, parked in a small lot in front of a rustic, wood-paneled restaurant. Except for a few of Robič's team members, the place was deserted.

I stood in front of the restaurant waiting for the leaders to pass. Tree branches swayed gently in the breeze and bird calls came from every direction. I knew this calm would soon be broken by music blaring from the racers' loudspeakers. I also knew that even if I jumped up and down and waved and yelled, neither man would offer as much as a glance in my direction.

Robič came through first, around 1:30 in the afternoon. Three of his crew mates stood in formation shoulder to shoulder, anticipating their racer's arrival. They threw their arms up in unison as he passed, cheering, "Jure, Jure, Jure!" He didn't even turn his head to acknowledge his friends, and within seconds he was around the bend and out of sight. Wyss blew by a few minutes later, having eaten a bit into Robič's lead and almost daring Robič to mount a final attack. With just 130 miles to go, the race would be over in eight hours.

Boethling and his two colleagues showed up shortly after the leaders had passed by. A couple of Robič's crew members greeted Boethling and they stood together awkwardly. Robič's big, strong helpers all wore coordinated T-shirts in camouflage green bearing the Jure Robič team logo. Seeing the scowls on their faces, I knew what was about to come. The RAAM contingent faced these intimidating soldiers fully prepared for a showdown.

"Robič's crew had developed a reputation for bullying officials back in 2004, when he and Mike Trevino were going neck and neck," George Thomas recalled. "They had accused Trevino of cheating and it really messed up his head. He almost pulled out as a result." RAAM legend Danny Chew was reporting on the race that year and observed, "That neither Trevino or Robič knew anything about the allegations drives home just how protective crews are of their riders."

Team Robič needed to force either of two things to happen, and fast. They had to convince the RAAM officials to waive Robič's penalties, or they had to prove that Wyss deserved some penalties, too. They still wanted to believe their racer could win without these concessions, but they weren't taking any chances.

"We cannot accept the penalties," barked Robič's teammate, looking at George Thomas, the official who had been shadowing Robič. "The penalties are not fair. Jure is the fastest man out there. He deserves to win this race."

Thomas calmly ticked off the rules that Team Robič had violated. Without making eye contact, he started with the illegal move on the interstate in Arizona, then the failure to return to the spot where they had become lost in Indiana. The two sides went back and forth for a while. *It's you guys who compromised Jure's race*, Thomas thought. *These errors were crew mistakes. Now you're trying to make us look like the bad guys.*

Robič's representatives huffed and sighed and shuffled their feet, clearly frustrated. "But the *peeing*! Surely this is not a penalty. Jure was not even racing yet," one claimed. Robič's fellow soldiers were fighting with all the ammunition they had. "Okay, okay, give Jure a fine, a ticket for public urination. But you cannot give him a time penalty for this. Where is it written?" another asked.

Boethling stepped in at this point. "I'm sorry. It was an unsportsmanlike thing to do. Jure should have known better," he said firmly. These RAAM officials weren't going to back down. At that point, Robič's side pulled out a video recorder. "Now you must see this," a crew member said. "It is Dani cheating. We have proof. He cheated many times, but you give him no penalties."

Robič's videographer thrust the camera into Boethling's hands. Boethling, his son, and Thomas huddled together and squinted at the screen, watching in silence. The video had been shot from behind Wyss by about two city blocks. In the footage, he rides up to a busy four-way intersection and the light changes to red as he draws near. Just as he reaches the intersection, a vehicle blocks the camera for a moment. When the view clears up, Wyss is turning right at the red light, then immediately doubling back toward the original road and turning left onto it, completing his return to the race route that kept going straight ahead.

Thomas spoke first. "We've seen this before. We analyzed your tape earlier," he said. "One of our officials is trained in video analysis and he studied your footage frame by frame. Sandy's assessment came back inconclusive. I can't help you here."

The video does seem to show Wyss making a right turn at a red light, pulling an immediate, illegal U-turn, then turning right to return to the race course, avoiding the need to wait the red light out. But RAAM officials didn't feel the footage made an indisputable case.[*]

---

[*] Robič's video of Wyss can be found on YouTube and elsewhere on the Internet.

"We even agreed to look at this footage without your side completing the required complaint form," Thomas said. "Believe me, we're trying to work with you here." Looks of disgust congealed on the faces of the Slovenian soldiers. In desperation, Robič's crew members began ticking off other penalties they felt Wyss had unfairly avoided.

Eventually, Thomas put an end to the bickering. "Submit everything," he said. "We want all of it. The video of Wyss and also all the video you shot of your racer during the last 24 hours. That's the only way we can do this fairly."

Robič's representatives complained this was impractical, not stipulated in the RAAM rules, and just plain ridiculous. With only eight hours left, they didn't have time for games. They stomped away totally unsatisfied.

FROM THIS POINT ON, THERE WOULD BE NO MORE CLIMBING. The final challenge for Robič and Wyss was navigating about 100 miles of gently rolling terrain through densely populated suburbs. Both men would be racing at their limits, and navigators would have to be on their toes; there would be lots of turns and ample opportunity to guide their racers astray. Any mistake at this juncture would be disastrous.

Then there was the "penalty box" at TS51, located in the parking lot of a bicycle shop in suburban Mount Airy, Maryland, just 50 miles from the finish line. Here the racers would be forced to sit while they served whatever penalties they had accumulated during the race. For most racers, serving their penalty time offers a festive respite, a time to relax and savor their accomplishment along with their crew members before the final couple of hours of racing. Racers forced to stop here often use the time to have a bite to eat, take some photos, and clean up before their rendezvous with the celebratory crowd in Annapolis.

But for race leaders, the penalty box can be a nightmare; for Robič, it would be an inescapable catastrophe. He would have to sit there for an hour while Wyss raced on.

After the confrontation with race officials a little while earlier, Robič's slim lead had all but evaporated. The "10-percent rule" suggested his chance of winning had slipped away, too. Why hadn't this titan—this invincible, untouchable ultracyclist—been able to build a one-hour lead on Wyss over the final 20 hours of racing? Was it simply that at 44 years old, Robič didn't have the ability to put in a short, intense burst of speed against a man five years his junior? That seemed implausible; even at his age, Robič was still winning just about every ultra race he entered. The previous year he had vanquished the field, winning RAAM by almost a full day. That same year he also crushed the field in the prestigious Race Around Slovenia, beating 26-year-old Christoph Strasser by a wide margin.

A more likely explanation is that both of these men were on such a blistering pace that they were already pushing the limits of human endurance. Extra bursts of speed weren't physically possible. It was also likely that the penalty controversy had affected his concentration and Robič was too emotionally spent to summon the "last atoms" of his power this time around.

Robič coasted into the bicycle shop parking lot at TS51 in the soft twilight around 6:30 PM with Wyss only a few minutes behind. With 50 miles to go, this was the closest men's race in history and Robič still held a slim lead, if only on the road. Then, yet another misunderstanding threatened to push Team Robič completely over the edge.

The race rules are a bit murky on this point, but Robič was under the assumption that *all* racers were required to stop at TS51 and call headquarters to verify their penalty status, even if they didn't have any penalties on file. So Robič was astonished to see that Wyss hadn't turned into the lot along with him. Wyss was gone.

Boethling was there awaiting Robič's arrival. As soon as the champion rolled to a stop Boethling was swarmed by Robič's crew members as emotions boiled over. Crew chief Uroš Velepec and Matjaž Planinšek both let Boethling have it. "Jure is still in the lead! He's faster than Wyss, yet he is not winning the race. I've been involved in sports for almost 30 years," Velepec said. "The treatment Jure received is the biggest disappointment in my career as a sportsman and coach. It's unacceptable to mistreat a four-time champion the way you have." Then Velepec dropped a bombshell. He stuck out his chin and looked straight at Boethling. Pausing for a moment, he declared, "We have decided to quit the race in protest. We will not go to Annapolis."

While this confrontation raged just steps away, Robič was slumped in a lawn chair as if forgotten. He stared blankly at the ground, not making eye contact with anyone.

Boethling took in Team Robič's criticism without anger or defensiveness. He felt sorry for Robič and his crew—they were so tired and under so much pressure. He was disappointed in them, but not angry. He knew it was pointless to carry on a public debate with Velepec, so he shooed away the crew members and press. He slowly strolled over to where a sullen Robič sat with his head in his hands.

Boethling had known Robič for years and was fond of him. He appreciated Robič's passion and easy smile and felt he was a good representative for the sport. As Boethling approached, he watched the four-time champion carefully. They were together now, alone and out of earshot.

"He certainly looked tired but not totally spent," Boethling recalled later. "Studying him closely, it seemed to me that he was mentally exhausted. I reminded him that we enforce what we see, uniformly and fairly. I told him that if he left the race at this point he would be letting himself and his fans down." Boethling suggested that "he serve out his penalties, get back on his bike, and ride to Annapolis."

Boethling stood in front of the greatest ultracyclist ever and looked down at him. Not getting a reaction, he tried a different tack. "If you don't finish the race, Jure, you'll regret it," he offered in a gentle, avuncular tone. Robič continued staring at his feet, expressionless. "Either way, I expect to see you in Annapolis. And I want you to congratulate Wyss like the true champion and sportsman you are." Boethling took his leave, hoping his words had an impact. He got back in his car and headed to Annapolis to crown the winner.

AS SOON AS WYSS' CREW CHIEF CHRISTIAN HOPPE let his racer know Robič had stopped racing and the pressure was off, everything started hurting and Wyss felt overpoweringly weary. The final 50 miles seemed to go on forever—past strip malls, over freeway intersections, and through innumerable traffic stops. Still, Wyss drank in the glow of his last sunset on the road as Annapolis drew near.

At least he didn't have to fear hearing the sound of Slovenian turbofolk music growing louder behind him.

Darkness fell as Wyss approached Annapolis, so he couldn't enjoy the sights of this historic town with its picturesque harbor. He missed the boats bobbing in their dock slips, the tourists strolling with their ice cream cones, and the sight of the historic 1772 Maryland State House, a gracious Georgian structure topped by a golden dome and a lightning rod designed by Benjamin Franklin. Tonight, all he could see were the taillights of the official RAAM pace car that led him into the finishing chute. At 9:25 PM, he broke the tape and rolled across the line as the 2009 RAAM men's champion.

In front of about 100 cheering spectators, Wyss stopped his bike and climbed off gingerly, an ear-to-ear smile on his usually placid face. He squinted under the klieg lights, searching out the familiar faces of his teammates.

This mild-mannered man didn't pump a fist in the air or raise his arms and let out a scream. His young, attractive crew members were acting out his exuberance on his behalf. He hugged each of them, and then slowly climbed onto the stage to accept his medal.

Eight days and six hours after departing Oceanside, Wyss had reached the Atlantic Ocean victorious. He had beaten Jure Robič and bested his own 2006 winning time by a remarkable 31 hours, turning in the second-fastest finishing time in the history of the race.

Wyss was too exhausted to communicate clearly in English, but this German speaker did manage to stammer some words of thanks. Then he was whisked away by his energetic crew members and into a waiting van.

As quickly as the crowd had massed when word of Wyss' imminent arrival spread, it dispersed just as rapidly. Within minutes, the klieg lights went dark and Annapolis Harbor fell silent again.

15

Days 10 and 11: Tough Love

From Ohio to Maryland, June 26 and 27

As he prepared to attack the formidable Appalachian Mountains that would go up and down all night long, Marko Baloh learned that his friend and countryman Jure Robič's had withdrawn the previous day. At the time, Baloh was in no shape to reflect on the implications of this shocking news. He was a whopping 14 hours behind Gerhard Gulewicz, the rampaging Austrian who had passed him earlier—a gap of more than 200 miles on the road—and his motivation was shot. It wasn't any comfort to him that Robič's withdrawal meant that unless disaster struck, Baloh would finish on the podium in third place. Baloh was disappointed with himself for falling so far behind his Austrian rabbit and for missing his goal of finishing in nine days.

His crew mates were discouraged as well. They had watched helplessly as Baloh's motivation faded after Gulewicz passed him a couple of days earlier. Baloh had called a crew meeting the following day, appealing to his wife Irma to play a more active role in coaxing back his fighting spirit. Irma tried lighting a fire under her husband, but the gap to Gulewicz just kept growing.

During the first half of the race, Baloh's time splits had frequently ranked among the fastest of the entire field. After ceding his position to Gulewicz, Baloh had managed to record the fifth-fastest time only once, back in Jefferson City on Day Six. During Days 10 and 11 his splits generally ranked in the lowest third of the men's field. In spite of the fact that Baloh was slowing relative to the field, the next man on the road was still almost 18 hours behind. Even if he crawled the rest of the way to Annapolis his competitive position wasn't at risk. Only his ego was.

Baloh was winding his way slowly through the Appalachians in the wee hours of June 26 when his crew chief Andrej tried a new ploy: he told Baloh that Gottwald was closing, a fib designed to get him kicking. But Baloh didn't—or couldn't—heed the warning. Instead he stopped frequently in the darkness and dithered away time off his bike. His crew mates encouraged him to hurry up and get going again, but Baloh kept finding reasons not to: he needed different gloves, a special snack, a change of tires. "I don't know how to push the button in the last few days of RAAM," he explained to me weeks later. "It's a mental issue. I needed Irma's motivation more than anything."

Baloh had plenty of excuses to take frequent breaks. One was the dreadful saddle sores that had blossomed during the second half of the race. Another was the edema in his extremities. There was more: as he held the handlebars, the bruise on his palm was growing more painful by the hour. On top of this, by now he could barely move his numb fingers because of nerve compression in his wrists.

Numb hands aren't as painful as saddle sores, but they provide their own unique form of torture. A racer's hands become ravaged by the constant pressure of holding up his body weight as the race progresses. Constant wrist flexion causes the ulnar and median nerves to swell and scar, leaving the racer with limited control of his fingers. It can take six months or longer for a racer's hands to get back to normal again, during which time he's forced to rely on loved ones to help him dress, lace his shoes, and cut his food—just like a small child.

As Baloh knew well, nerve damage was also a vexing challenge during the race. To even out their cadence over undulating terrain, cyclists shift gears anywhere from once every 10 seconds to once every few minutes— perhaps 50,000 times during RAAM. Several of the best-financed Europeans—Dani Wyss and Gerhard Gulewicz among them—invested in push-button electronic shifting systems because they knew the simple act of engaging a mechanical shifting paddle would become an arduous task. Unfortunately, Baloh hadn't.

ON THEIR SECOND-TO-LAST NIGHT ON THE ROAD, Baloh's crew chief Andrej devised a last-ditch, diabolical plan for encouraging his racer to stay on his bike and race. Given his frame of mind, Andrej concluded the sight of the motor home was too enticing to Baloh. Every time his racer spied it, he found some excuse to stop and climb inside. So Andrej decided to keep the motor home hidden from sight. This way Baloh would have to race all night long because he wouldn't have a comfortable place to take a break.

As Baloh labored through the Appalachian rollers longing for his motor home, his on-duty crew members played dumb when he demanded to know where it was. As a result Baloh had to take his breaks outside, wherever he could find a safe, comfortable spot. It was a chilly, damp night and Baloh wasn't happy. What was most disturbing about this pitiful sight was just how undisturbed his crew members seemed to be as they watched Baloh lying outside in a field along the roadside.

Baloh fought the road all night long. He felt terrible and unloved, but he didn't complain. He just kept riding. After sunrise on June 27, Baloh was finally through the last mountain range. He was completely exhausted and wanted more than anything to climb into the motor home for an hour or two of sleep. Instead, he sprawled outside and soaked up the sun's warming rays. *If only this sunshine could give me more energy*, he thought as he drifted off for a short power nap. As he lay there, 250 miles down the road his adversary Gerhard Gulewicz became the second man to break the tape in Annapolis.

Baloh collected himself again, determined to pick up his pace and race the rest of the way without another sleep break. That evening he hit a torrential rainstorm as he fought through the section into TS48 with those four short but steep climbs that every racer cursed. He did these climbs in heavy rain, still unable to take shelter in his motor home. He cycled through the night, past the Gettysburg battlefield and onto crowded byways of the Baltimore–Washington, D.C., metro area. He wasn't laying down a terribly fast pace at this point, but at least he wasn't finding excuses to get off his bike.

Baloh squinted into the rising sun as he watched his final dawn break on the horizon ahead. Soon he was picking his way through suburban neighborhoods as Annapolis drew near. He had finally been allowed inside the motor home to freshen up, and now he was giddy in anticipation of reaching the finish line later that afternoon.

Alex, a good friend and fellow cyclist from Slovenia, waited for him at a gas station a few miles from Annapolis Harbor. Alex also worked as a civil servant at the agricultural ministry in Slovenia, and he had cycled all the way from Canada just to be there to greet his countryman. Baloh jumped off his bike and embraced him. Surrounded by Irma, the kids, his loyal crew mates, and now Alex, Baloh's big, strong heart overflowed with love and gratitude.

Escorted by an official RAAM vehicle, Baloh and Alex rode the final few miles side by side. Baloh's follow-vehicle crawled behind them sporting a giant blow-up orca whale on its roof, as it had done throughout the race. The loudspeakers on either side of the orca played a song chosen especially for this moment.

I sat in the official RAAM escort car that led Baloh and Alex as they approached the finish line. As they rode along at a leisurely pace, they chattered and bantered as if on a weekend pleasure ride. Baloh looked content. Each time he stopped at a traffic light he shook his hands, trying to draw some feeling back into them, but otherwise he showed no discomfort. Tourists waved at him and honked their horns in appreciation as he drew closer to Annapolis Harbor. He seemed pleased by all the attention.

Baloh was the third man to finish in the early afternoon on a pleasantly sunny day in Annapolis. He succeeded for the second time in four tries, this time landing a spot on the podium. It was a dream fulfilled, not only for him but also for loyal crew members like Andrej who had supported him year after year. At the finish line, the devoted dad swept up his kids in his long, thin arms and he and Irma enjoyed a tender family embrace. This humble but powerful ultracycling great was smiling, but he didn't even raise his arms in celebration.

I marveled at how good Baloh looked as he crossed the line. He was sharp, unblemished, and somehow seemed perky. Though he had surely lost his resolve, the race hadn't wrecked Baloh physically as it had Gulewicz.

When Gulewicz finished in second place the previous afternoon, he had trouble dismounting his bike. He was dirty and sweaty and his stomach was badly distended. It was reported that he gained eight kilograms (15 pounds) of water weight during the race. Gulewicz had gone on a rampage as Annapolis drew near. During his final 40 hours of racing he had been off his bike for barely an hour. Gulewicz thought he was hallucinating at the finish line because he suddenly saw his father standing in front of him. "Papa, Papa," he said over and over again as he tenderly embraced his dad, who had flown from Austria to surprise him. Then he shuffled stiffly to the podium to accept his finisher's medal.

The finish line was an entirely different experience for Baloh. After he broke the tape some 23 hours later, he hopped off his bike with ease and hugged and kissed Irma and the kids. His daughter placed his mascot—a yellow Tweety Bird doll—on his aerobars. Baloh strode smoothly and easily toward the stage. His long legs still looked strong and steady, and he had not a drop of sweat on his brow.

Baloh took the microphone and shared his feelings with the small crowd of well-wishers and amused tourists. "I was not really that satisfied with my race," he said, pausing as if pondering if he really meant what he had just said. "I had maybe slightly bigger goals. I was hoping to be closer to nine days." Ever the gentleman, Baloh ended his brief statement by adding, "My hat goes off to the three men ahead of me." Of course, he had included Robič in this group, even though his countryman had not officially finished.

In a show of respect for this crowd favorite, all three of the men ahead of him were there for his arrival: the newly crowned champion Wyss, the vanquished Robič, and the second-place Gulewicz. These three had finished racing a day or more ago, so they wore civilian clothes and looked fresh and rested. Moments earlier, Robič had demonstrated his respect by shaking Wyss' hand and congratulating his rival, though few words were exchanged and they both looked uncomfortable. Boethling caught the moment out of the corner of his eye, and was pleased that Robič had greeted the new champion. After hugging his friend Baloh, Robič slipped away as quickly as he had arrived, disappearing into the crowds strolling along the boat docks of Annapolis Harbor.

After Baloh and his wife had been bundled into their minivan and whisked off for a well-deserved rest in a real hotel bed, Baloh's crew member Matic came over to me anxious for a word. We sat in a crowded bar in front of a large plate glass window that framed the pretty harbor while Matic savored a beer. "I think Marko held back," he said. "Come on, did he look like he left everything out there?"

As Baloh had discovered, a racer's crew members can get tough to spur their charge down the homestretch. Crew members are only human, and it frustrates them when they think their racer isn't giving his all late in the race. Like Baloh, American rookie Ben Popp also received rough handling in the final days of his race. The father of twin boys had surprised everyone by coming through the Rockies in seventh place. He had briefly reclaimed that position at the two-thirds point near the Mississippi River, but by the time Baloh was finishing in Annapolis, Popp was 300 miles back mired in 10th after battling through the toughest part of the Appalachians. Popp had ditched his goal of finishing in 10 days a while ago.

The previous day his crew mates had demanded that he do what they asked. They insisted they should manage the race plan and decide on Popp's sleep breaks—his brain was too fried to do this effectively for himself. His wife Megan had to convince her husband to cede control. "Ben, you have to listen to these guys. They're professionals," she reminded him. After this confrontation, Popp's mind seemed to shut down. Popp was now the hardware, and his crew was his software.

Popp suffered mightily through his final night on the road. "The last night was just terrible, miserable, and scary," his father-in-law Bob recalled. Like every other competitor, Popp dreaded the four steep climbs into TS48 late that night. Bob worried that Popp was moving so slowly he might actually topple over. But Popp summoned whatever reserves remained and got through the last bit of torture the RAAM course had to offer. Having endured about four hours of climbing, after midnight on June 28 Popp's crew chief allowed him to rest before they entered Pennsylvania. Everybody dreamt of reaching Annapolis later that day.

BY DAY 10, GAPS BETWEEN THE REMAINING RACERS were too large to overcome, and the leader board was pretty much locked in place— except for one marquee race. As he had promised, airline pilot and former pro racer Christopher Gottwald had put his secret plan into action in an effort to capture rookie of the year and first-American accolades. He had cut back on his sleep breaks and was now eating up the road.

When dawn broke on Day 10, Gottwald had just regained his pace after being waylaid by the same monster storm that had delayed Christiansen and Rees in Ohio. As he had done every morning during the race, he first collected his crew for a group prayer. "It was a good reminder that this wasn't about glorifying me," Gottwald explained. "It was about my charitable cause, and how I could use my God-given talent to help others." Then he raced strong all day. By early evening he had catapulted past Rees as the two men reached the Appalachians. That night Gottwald even managed to smoke his American rival Kevin Kaiser in the mountains, erasing the small-town pharmacist's five-hour lead in West Virginia alone.

"I had nothing left in my legs," Kaiser explained. In his defense, Gottwald's withering attack would have bested most of the men in the field.

Gottwald and Kaiser raced within sight of each other into TS45 in the heart of the Appalachians just past midnight on June 27. Stopped a few miles before the time station, Kaiser's crew member Gary Carter recalled that, "Gottwald was such a gentleman. He walked over to Kevin to check up on him and gave him a hug. It kind of choked me up."

Gottwald remembers it differently. "With Kevin, it was interesting," he told me after the race. "We suspected he was cheating. I was closing fast on him the day before in Ohio when that giant storm hit. Somehow he managed to get through the flooded roads while I got stuck, and he put big time on me. That was my first red flag. In the Appalachians, I kept thinking I was about to reel him in but somehow he'd pull ahead. Or I'd blow past him and then he would suddenly reappear. When I finally caught him and saw he was pulled over, I walked over while he was sitting in his van. He and his crew acted weird. I spoke with him and he seemed—just peculiar."

Gottwald also accused Team Kaiser of calling in a time station split well before they had actually arrived, a ploy that can be used to obfuscate a racer's actual position and create an opportunity for him to jump in his follow-vehicle for a quick push up the road. These were explosive charges, but Gottwald never lodged a formal complaint with race officials or produced any proof of his post-race claims.

Gottwald was able to increase his lead over his American rival throughout Day 11. He finally let himself dream about what it would feel like to be the first American and the first rookie to finish. He had earlier received a 60-minute penalty for failing to attend a mandatory pre-race meeting, so he needed to build a hefty lead over Kaiser to cement his victory.

After the Appalachians, Gottwald put extra distance between himself and Kaiser through just about every time station. He was more than four hours ahead of his American foe by the time he rolled into the penalty box at TS51 in Mount Airy around 11:00 PM. "After sitting at Mount Airy serving my time, I asked for my time trial bike and put on my skin suit," he recalled. "I got a massage, and I was ready. My plan was to cook it all the way to Annapolis, because I was concerned that Kaiser was going to try to pull something and get past me somehow."

As Gottwald pounded down the homestretch, the rest of the field was holding on for dear life. This race was extracting a brutal toll by now, and everybody else—racers and crew alike—was beyond exhaustion on this last, long night.

HAVING WAITED OUT THE TORRENTIAL RAINSTORM IN OHIO, Janet Christiansen mounted her bike in the wee hours of June 26 headed toward West Virginia and her rendezvous with the Appalachians. Slogging through hilly southeastern Ohio all afternoon, the Osprey finally began feeling the effects of severe sleep deprivation. Christiansen's crew pulled out all the stops to keep their racer alert; they donned pirate outfits, clown costumes, and luau dresses and stood on the side of the road cheering. They played her favorite show tunes and read messages from friends over the loudspeakers. A crew mate's father even offered a poem about her RAAM challenge to inspire her in these final hours.

Closing in on the West Virginia border, Christiansen couldn't help thinking about her experience the previous year. She was near the spot where 12 months earlier she had lost her resolve and dropped out of the race, just 250 miles from the finish line after racing for almost 12 days straight. She knew it would be an emotional experience to cross into West Virginia and make it safely through the Appalachians.

The specter of collapsing close to the finish line had haunted Christiansen since her first 500-mile ultracycling race years ago. "That year, I was afraid to take too many electrolyte pills because during my Ironman races, salt caps made me queasy," she recalled. "But the Ironman takes less than a day to finish, and I didn't realize I needed to do things differently. So I stopped sweating and lost that nice, cooling effect in the desert heat. It wasn't just hot, it was painful. I forgot to put sunscreen on. I forgot to take my contacts out, and when I did they were so dry I scratched my cornea pulling them off. Everything just hurt. Then we ran out of water."

During that fateful race, Christiansen came over the final climb and fell apart only 20 miles from the finish—after 480 miles and 35 hours of racing. She threw her bike down, collapsed on the shoulder of the road, and started sobbing. Her crew didn't know what to do, but her three-year-old nephew did. He had been along for the ride with an Etch A Sketch in tow. Pulling the device onto his lap, he started fiddling with the knobs, drawing a dinosaur. "This will cheer Aunt Janet up," he promised the incredulous adults, his angelic face reflecting total faith in his mission.

Soon enough Christiansen was helping him draw and having fun in the process. After a few lighthearted minutes of play she pulled herself together, got back on her bike, and finished the race. Her effort nabbed her second place in the 40-and-over age group.

Thanks to the more upbeat attitude she brought to this year's race, Christiansen was cautiously optimistic about her chances of making it safely through the West Virginia mountains. She reached them in the early evening of June 26 after 10 days of continuous racing. When she spied the "Welcome to West Virginia" sign, she put her hands to her face and grimaced in mock fear. She kept laughing and joking all evening long, trying to stave off the nervousness that gripped her now that she was nearing Annapolis.

As darkness enveloped her and she felt the chill mountain air, the Osprey was only a few time stations away from the spot where she had dropped out the previous year.

West Virginia's state motto is "Mountaineers Are Always Free." Route 50 cuts through the heart of the Appalachians and offers everyone a chance to play mountaineer. The road winds and climbs over countless peaks and valleys. Racers are transported back in time as they glide past sleepy hillside hamlets and through dense forests. Majestic stands of ancient hemlock and hardwood give the roads a cathedral feeling, blocking out the sun and with it any sense of the outside world.

The switchbacks on Route 50 are so treacherous that the racers had to be on their toes. But they had another worry as well: since this is logging country, gigantic logging trucks regularly thundered along this winding, shoulderless road. By all accounts, truckers didn't like sharing their turf with slow-poke cyclists. One RAAM contestant claimed a truck driver had tried to knock him off the road by swinging his load into him—twice. It missed, but not by much.

Christiansen wasn't concerned about the lorries or enchanted by the ancient hemlocks lining the road. She was consumed by a single sensation—her profound, grinding weariness. She had been racing for nearly 24 hours straight, and she was having unsettling hallucinations. She saw men in military fatigues jogging alongside her and spied invisible llamas and other animals watching her go by.

As she and her crew discussed when and where to stop for a nap, her driver became violently ill with a stomach bug and her navigator had to take over. The navigator was now the only functioning crew member, and she was a first-timer. This poor soul had to drive, navigate, and keep Christiansen alert—which she did by singing show tunes for a few harrowing hours. This was a recipe for disaster, because it's almost impossible to follow the route book and drive at the same time. Luckily, this rookie crew member had practically memorized the race route and didn't need to follow the turn-by-turn instructions.

Thanks to these heroics, at 3:00 AM after fighting through the toughest climbs the Appalachians had to offer, the Osprey had reached her planned rest spot, some 375 miles from Annapolis. As she crawled into the cot wedged in the back of her minivan, she knew that in the morning she would pass the location where she had dropped out the previous year. She also knew that the next night—her last on the road—would be even harder. With a bit of luck, the day after that she would finish in Annapolis.

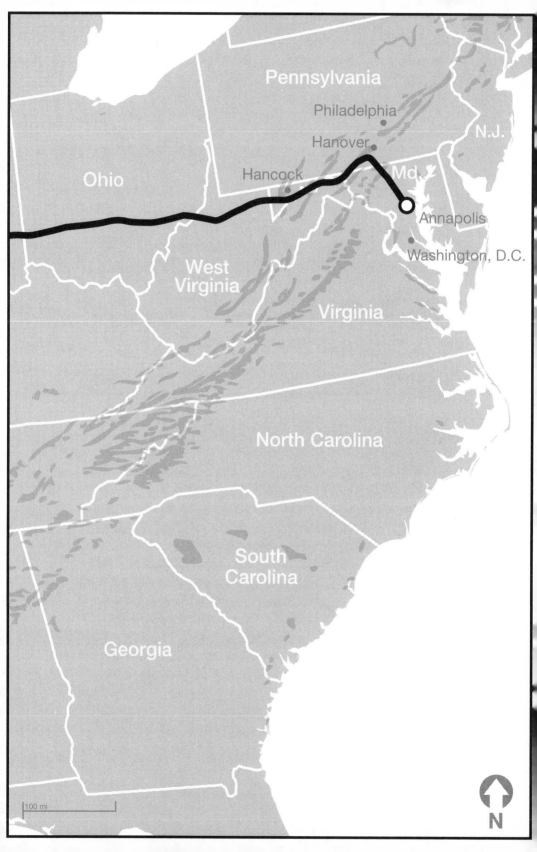

16

Day 12: Guts and Glory in Annapolis

Annapolis Harbor, June 28

There were still a dozen solo racers on the course just after midnight on Day 12. Dani Wyss, Gerhard Gulewicz, and Marko Baloh had already finished. Half of the 28 soloists had DNF'd by now, including several race favorites: the four-time champion Jure Robič, Christoph Strasser, Franz Preihs, and Michele Santilhano. This year RAAM had done what it always does—brought some of the most accomplished and hardened ultradistance cyclists in the world to their knees.

Around 3:00 in the morning former road racer Christopher Gottwald crossed the line as both the first rookie and first American. His time of 10 days, 12 hours was good for fourth place.

While Gottwald was loading his bike into the van for a trip to his Annapolis hotel, Kevin Kaiser was closing in on Mount Airy, cycling in the middle of the night only 75 miles from the finish line. "My crew started celebrating back in West Virginia, but I wasn't feeling the love yet. I got excited when I hit the Mount Airy time station," he said. "I wanted to finish early in the morning because Annapolis would be quiet at that hour." Kaiser did exactly that, breaking the tape around 8:30 that morning. His wife was there to meet him, along with his sister and brother-in-law. He was as surprised to see them standing there as Gulewicz had been to see his father fresh off a plane from Austria.

"People can't fathom the magnitude of this effort—how hard, how big this race is," he explained. He choked up recalling the scene at the finish line. "I was so happy my family and friends were there so they could appreciate the enormity of it all."

It was hard to tell by his placid demeanor, but in his own way this introverted man was overcome by his triumph. He was weary and his body had been pulverized, but he couldn't imagine being anywhere else at this moment—the most perfect moment ever. Kaiser lingered at the finish line. He had enormous respect for race veteran Jim Rees and knew Rees was only a couple of hours behind him. When Kaiser had passed Rees back in Illinois, they cycled together for a time and chatted. "I told him it was an honor to ride with him and that he was an inspiration to me," Kaiser said. Now Kaiser wanted to congratulate his fellow traveler.

Rees pulled into TS51 in Mount Airy at about the time Kaiser's race was concluding in Annapolis. When this British veteran coasted to a stop to serve his penalty time, he was a different man from the one who had set off from Oceanside. He had been racing for more than 10 days. During this time he had managed less than 15 hours off the bike and he was unraveling, just like all the other surviving racers were by now.

Rees was probably the most urbane and articulate racer in the field, but these characteristics had been stripped away. His cognition was slower, and his needs were more basic. He was utterly dependent on his crew for eating, clothing, and safety. Rees had been transformed by his transcontinental journey along the back roads of America.

After dismounting in Mount Airy, Rees steadied himself and gazed around at his crew glassy-eyed. His neck muscles were failing so his head was tilted forward. He shuffled over to his motor home and peered through the door as if looking for something, but then turned around empty-handed.

He tried engaging in conversation with his crew, but his thoughts were choppy and disconnected. The zipper on the front of his jersey was puckering. Didn't it look awful? He wanted something to eat. How about ice cream? His teammates worried that he was wasting time off the bike, so they tried hurrying things along.

Rees got a massage, a change of clothes, and something to eat. Then he was off again with Annapolis in his sights. He was cranky and ready to be done with this infernal race, and he grew impatient with the dense suburban traffic and red lights in his way. Down the homestretch most racers' brains are mush, and many become convinced their crews are leading them around in circles only miles from the finish line. Rees was one of these, and he became cross with his crew because he couldn't believe it was taking so long to reach Annapolis.

Despite his difficulties, Rees was one of the lucky ones. Many of his competitors had already succumbed; racers had been pulled off the course with pulmonary edema, broken bones, failing neck muscles, hallucinations— all manner of ailments, some life-threatening, others simply agonizing.

Rees finished his third solo RAAM around noon, the only Briton to ever accomplish this feat. He pumped his fist in the air and whooped as he crossed the line. He hadn't broken the British record and he had missed his 10-day goal by a dispiriting 21 hours. But he had bested his time from the previous year by almost half a day and earned himself a sixth-place finish. Rees had indeed become a faster cyclist this year, and that was something to celebrate.

Rees looked absolutely shattered, but within seconds of crossing the finish line he managed to pull himself together. After dismounting, he hugged and kissed his crew. Then he jumped up three small steps and onto the stage. This battered ultracyclist almost instantly morphed back into the provocative, clever motivational speaker he was in real life.

"This motley collection of friends has done an amazing job supporting me from one end of America to the other," he said, pointing to his crew members while stifling a sob. "It's down to them that I'm here on stage for the third time." Typical of Rees, he then began psychoanalyzing himself. "Normally I'm a reasonable guy, but when it gets hot and I get miserable, I can be fairly unpleasant," he admitted. "This shows up quite a bit, unfortunately. My crew handled it extremely well." He choked up again when he thanked his wife Tracey, home in England, "for putting up with me."

In spite of his fatigue, Rees hung around afterward bantering with Kaiser and others in the crowd. I watched as he took time to chat patiently with two teenage girls who happened to be there quite by accident. Rees had raised money for Team Inspiration during his race, his charity dedicated to "inspiring children to achieve greatness." He explained to the girls how RAAM teaches people that "anything is possible." Even after just finishing a Herculean effort, Rees was eager to encourage these kids to reach for the stars.

Finally, he collected his crew and repeated a ritual he'd performed each year at the finish line. As a group they walked to the edge of the pier and pulled out a bottle of ocean water they had collected from Oceanside. One by one, they poured their Pacific Ocean water into the sea on the other side of the continent.

Rees cleaned up at his hotel and then returned to Annapolis Harbor later that evening. His crew chiefs Martyn and Phil were there also, enjoying a beer in a crowded pub. But Rees wasn't with them. He was sitting alone in a serene, candlelit wine bar reading a book. I met him there because he explained he needed to talk to somebody from the "outside world" beyond his RAAM crew. He was clean-shaven, wore a pair of smart-looking glasses, and was stylishly dressed. Seeing him sitting there, one never would have known what this man had just put himself through.

After enjoying a glass of wine he was ready to share feelings that hadn't come out on stage earlier in the day. "It was a struggle with such a green crew," he explained with a sigh. He didn't look tired, but there was an air of exhaustion in his voice. "I had to ride Phil and Martyn hard. And my nutritionist and I fought a lot. Then my chiro got caught up in the drama and lost focus, so my neck started to go. All of this took a toll." Then he admitted he wished he had broken the English record.

Rees seemed disappointed with himself and his crew, even though as a three-time finisher he had just accomplished something no other Briton had ever done. I felt bad for him, and was pleased to be able to offer an outlet for him to share his feelings. It would be a while before this thoughtful man could fully process everything that had transpired during the race. Now wasn't the time. As I bid him good night, Rees ordered another glass of wine and returned to his book, thinking of home.

THE FINISH LINE WAS BUSY ALL AFTERNOON LONG. After Rees, three more solo racers glided down the chute over the next few hours and into the waiting arms of their teammates, friends, and family.

Just before Rees had finished earlier that morning, the energetic, loquacious American Ben Popp began serving his penalty time in Mount Airy. He sat in a lawn chair joking with his crew and devouring an enormous pastry. His crew mates Owen and Peter tossed a Frisbee in the parking lot. Everybody on Team Popp seemed relaxed and content, and Popp seemed to have his wits about him. Soon enough it was time to get back on his bike for his final hours of racing. He crossed the line later that afternoon in ninth place, 11 days after leaving the Oceanside Pier.

He was limber and alert when his bike coasted to a stop. Except for a bit of stubble on his face and some swelling around his eyes, like Baloh, Popp was largely unblemished. The first thing he did was place a call to his twin boys. Then he posed for photographers, looking like someone who might have just stepped off the cover of a men's lifestyle magazine.

As the evening's orange glow began painting the corners of the Annapolis sky, word came that Janet Christiansen was nearing the finish line. The previous afternoon she made it through Gormania, West Virginia—the town where her race had prematurely ended in 2008. As she continued through the Appalachians at sunset, a small fox jumped out of the brush and ran ahead of her for about a hundred yards before diving back into the woods. Christiansen considered it a good omen—even the animals were helping shepherd her onward toward Annapolis.

But her final night had been awfully rough on the Osprey. Her knees felt like they were about to come apart, her hands were painfully swollen, and she was falling asleep on the bike. Even worse, her neck muscles were weakening and starting to fail. "This is the hardest thing I've ever done," she moaned as she buried herself on those four steep climbs into TS48 around midnight.

Bill Osborn was horrified by Christiansen's incipient neck failure, but relieved at the same time. "If this had happened yesterday she probably wouldn't still be riding," he said. Ever the dedicated crew chief, Osborn had decided to stay with his racer all through the final night and as long as it took that next day to guide her to the finish.

Her night shift crew pulled out the instruction sheet Christiansen had prepared to help them through a situation like this. It was titled "Instructions for When Janet Loses Her Mind." It explained all the psychological ploys and motivational tricks the crew should use to calm her down and keep her on her bike, including what jokes to tell and what music to play. Mercifully, her crisis passed, but just to be certain, her crew member Kathryn locked the van doors around 3:00 in the morning so that her rider couldn't retreat inside every time she stopped for a quick nature break or rubdown.

By then the Osprey had been racing for a little over 11 days and still held out hope of reaching Annapolis inside of her 12-day goal. "She had gone for about 24 hours without a break by that time. I was pushing her because I knew it would be touch-and-go trying to beat 12 days," Osborn explained. "But then she started weaving all over the road. I had to put her down."

Christiansen finished her final nap just before sunrise and then got back to business. Later that morning she was just over 100 miles from Annapolis when she heard that RAAM rookie Daniela Genovesi had become the first woman to finish. This news didn't bother Christiansen. By now she knew she'd finally finish solo RAAM, one of only 26 women ever to accomplish this feat. But she commanded herself not to think ahead. *Just keep the pedals turning over,* she thought. *Anything can happen out here. It's not over yet.*

Then she received her second good omen while passing a horse farm in Pennsylvania. Her crew pointed out a herd of thoroughbreds, and as she approached, these gorgeous horses broke into a gallop and paced her for the length of their pasture. The spontaneous display sent Christiansen's confidence soaring, and she finally permitted herself a brief roadside celebration and group hug.

Christiansen crossed the line around 7:30 PM, a scant five hours over her 12-day goal. As she stumbled off her bike in the fading light, Osborn ran over to steady her. He hugged her tightly and whispered, "I'm so proud of you."

She looked even more wrecked than Gulewicz did after he had finished, and like Rees she struggled to hold her head up. She held her body stiffly and moved with difficulty, but she was beaming and her eyes sparkled brightly. In a show of respect and sportsmanship, Rees came over and congratulated Christiansen for a job well done—the only male finisher to do so.

After a few minutes of merriment, Osborn held Christiansen gently around the waist and escorted her to the stage. She mounted the steps with difficulty, but her huge smile never left her face.

"I had a lot of doubts about this year's race," she explained in a croaky voice, standing in front of the small crowd. She looked emaciated and bedraggled and she had even forgotten to remove her helmet. Her voice might have been weak and her words halting, but her thoughts came out clearly. "My body was still beaten up from last year's attempt. But we learned from that. The ideas we tried worked well this year. I might have been fitter and stronger last year, but I was smarter this year." Her voice cracked with emotion when she shared the highlight of her race. "It was coming down the finishing chute just now and remembering how bad it was last year," she said. "So much weight has been lifted off my shoulders. It took me 6,000 miles, but I finally finished."

17

Aftermath

THE RACE ACROSS AMERICA TAKES ON A MYTHIC QUALITY TO those who get close to it.

Mere observers are irresistibly, almost ghoulishly, fascinated to see how each racer copes with his misery.

Crew members care for their racer, and through their experience of his suffering, they deepen their own understanding of compassion, which literally means to suffer with someone else. They end up forging a bond with their racer that can be unnervingly powerful and intimate.

The racers endure an astonishing amount of physical and mental punishment. They experience the agony of breaking through personal limitations. They risk their lives and sometimes push themselves to the brink of madness. We are compelled to ask why they do this.

Joseph Campbell, an American mythologist and author, describes one life-affirming myth that's shared by every culture going back as far as recorded time. It offers a way to understand the allegorical meaning of this race and the racers' motivations.

In this myth, an ordinary person receives a "call to adventure" that compels him to leave an everyday world that he's psychologically and spiritually outgrown. He journeys into a dreamlike arena—a dark forest, a desert, a foreboding place. Along the way he encounters a teacher who instructs him in skills he needs to successfully achieve a goal that is now revealed to him.

The protagonist is challenged to his limit by a series of terrifying and demanding trials before finally reaching and overcoming one final ordeal.

Through these struggles he experiences a euphoric transfiguration and is forever changed. Unencumbered by personal limitations, he discovers new powers and purpose. He then sets off to re-enter his normal world.

His last task, Campbell says, is to share his discoveries, which promise a boon to his society that will somehow restore its vibrancy. He encounters many who are incapable of comprehending. Finally someone hears the message and arises as the next adventurer.

RAAM contestants are a modern-day equivalent of the adventurers and seekers in this archetypal myth. Each racer has his own reason for undertaking his mythic journey across the continent, but all are drawn by an irresistible call to adventure. Through their experiences, they develop insights into their own psyches and gain new powers that can benefit us if we are willing and open.

"Pain is self-revelatory," seven-time Tour de France winner Lance Armstrong writes. "There's a point in every race when a rider encounters his real opponent and understands that it's himself. In my most painful moments on the bike, I am at my most curious and I wonder each time how I will respond. Will I discover my innermost weakness or will I seek out my innermost strength?" The 15 men and women who finished the 2009 race all reached the deepest source of their strength. Watching them do so, we are obliged to re-examine our own limiting thoughts and beliefs.

IF YOU'RE ACQUAINTED WITH A RIDER before RAAM begins, it's pretty easy to predict how he'll be affected by failing to finish his solo race. For example, Lt. Col. Tony O'Keeffe, the military leader whose friends describe as the most inspirational person they know, bounced right back after withdrawing because of Shermer's Neck in Kansas. "My self-worth isn't attached to my result. I loved the race, I learned a lot, and I want to come back," he told me a few weeks after returning home. "If I had made it across in less than 10 days, maybe not. But I'm already setting up my training schedules for next year's RAAM."

O'Keeffe doesn't internalize failure. He doesn't even use the word. Every missed goal is just another opportunity to learn and improve. "Because RAAM is so big, friends can't really understand. They just assume you'll be fine," he said. "But RAAM makes me work hard; this is not easy for anybody."

O'Keeffe used his DNF as a teaching moment, a clear sign of the depth of his character and the strength of his leadership. "This was my first DNF ever and it took everybody by surprise," he explained. "[My wife] Jackie and [crew member] Randy understood immediately, but it took a while for the other guys to see that my decision was motivated in part by my assessment of the risks our team faced. It was simply too dangerous to continue."

Whether this was the real reason or not, even in failure O'Keeffe saw himself as a role model and teacher. He aimed to return the following year in his third RAAM bid and clearly relished the challenge. "My personality is such that if I'm given something or if I get something easily, I don't cherish it as much. The things I worked the hardest for, they're irreplaceable," he said. Indeed, O'Keeffe did return in 2010 and made his crossing without a hitch. He finished his second solo RAAM in 10 days, eight hours—good enough for fourth place. Team O'Keeffe took great care of their rider the following year, and "kept me from hurting myself." He added, "I'm just delighted," as he stood at the finish line, looking perky and unblemished by 10 days in sun and wind and nasty weather.

LIKE O'KEEFFE, THE TATTOOED AUSTRIAN FRANZ PREIHS had a similar reaction to his early DNF after his knee swelled up in the Rockies. The year before that he had raced with a broken collarbone and finished in fourth place, so his resolve was unbelievably strong. "Look, I'm only 31 years old," he said as I sat with him and his wife Michaela in a suburban Vienna restaurant about a month after his withdrawal. "My DNF didn't shatter me or destroy my motivation. I don't think about it, and I don't look back very much." There was no remorse in his voice.

Having participated in sports all his life, Preihs "devotes everything" to his goals. He still enjoys enthusiastic support from his wife and parents for the lifestyle he has chosen, and that's all he needs to continue. "My father always wanted me to be a pro skier, but being an Austrian there was just too much pressure, and when I quit my father didn't talk to me for a year," he says. "But now he's totally behind me."

Preihs acknowledged that his DNF would make it more challenging to attract sponsorship money for another go, but he was undaunted. "I felt so much pressure from my sponsors to win this past year," he said. "So in one sense my DNF benefits me. Since I might not be able to attract as much sponsor support at least the pressure will be off."

It turns out he had called it correctly. Preihs wasn't able to raise enough money to return to the U.S. the following year, but this didn't stop him from competing altogether; he took second place in the 2010 ultracycling world championships in Austria just one week before RAAM started in California.

There has never been any doubt in Preihs' mind about his eventual return to the race. "Even if I have to pay my own way, I'm going back next year, and the year after that," he said. "I want to do RAAM every year for the next 10 years. I bought my first bike in 2003, and qualified for RAAM four years after that. This is something I was meant to do. I have no worries or doubts about how it will go." Preihs has already had remarkable success in his short time as a competitive ultracyclist, and his love affair with RAAM showed no sign of cooling off.

GIVEN THEIR PERSONALITIES AND LIFE PHILOSOPHIES, it didn't surprise me that O'Keeffe and Preihs had quickly decided to return and that they hadn't let their DNFs get them down. Likewise, considering how miserable he was during his aborted race, it wasn't a surprise that the brainy research scientist Patrick Autissier didn't want anything to do with RAAM ever again. "Life will move on, and I'm sure there will be many more challenges in the future," he explained several months later. Autissier still felt guilty and embarrassed about his meltdown in Arizona after only two days of racing. "I realize now that I should never have done the race," he told me. "I dipped heavily into my own savings to pay the bills. My wife Anne-Cecile has forgiven me and we've become closer as a result. But I now see that I was focused on my passion, my ego. I'm disappointed with myself for the DNF, and also for being so self-centered."

Unlike O'Keeffe and Preihs, Autissier was having doubts about his future in ultracycling. "I might come back, because I hate to end with a DNF," he said. "Maybe when I'm 60? Right now I need more balance in my life."

Autissier hadn't yet found closure. But he did find comfort knowing that through his efforts over three RAAM tries, he had raised money for charities he believed in. In thanking all his supporters over the years, he wrote, "You have all been a big part of my dream, and thanks to you, some people in need have hope for a better life." At least that was something.

MICHELE SANTILHANO, THE SOUTH AFRICAN ÜBER-ATHLETE, had also used RAAM to garner visibility for a charitable cause—the scourge of child sex trafficking—but that hadn't been enough to help her overcome a balky quad muscle and an unhelpful crew. A few months on, her RAAM DNF still felt like an open wound.

Before RAAM, her greatest athletic disappointment happened 23,700 feet up Mount Everest. She described that day as the worst of her life. Her RAAM DNF was certainly excruciating, but being older and wiser, it didn't destroy her quite as comprehensively as failing to reach the Everest summit had done. Still, she was miserable about not finishing and upset about how things had gone with her crew. It turns out that anger was a healthy emotion for Santilhano. "I've signed up for every long-distance cycling event and clinic I could find!" she reported a couple of weeks after returning from RAAM.

Santilhano was determined to improve as an ultracyclist. "I learned a lot through my DNF, and I realize now that I wasn't ready for RAAM," she told me later that summer. Santilhano wasn't sure if she would enter RAAM again, but she knew she wanted to become a stronger cyclist. So despite the fact that she worked full time as a nurse, she decided to cycle across the country unsupported later that year, roughly following the RAAM route. Santilhano mapped out her transcontinental trip, dividing it into several weeklong sections. To improve her cycling endurance and power, she began working with coach John Howard, the Olympic cyclist turned Ironman triathlete who finished second in the inaugural RAAM event.

"The reason for my transcontinental ride is to train for a possible return to RAAM, and to rediscover my love for the bike and my joy," she said. "The Race Across America has now become my ride across America."

Indeed, Santilhano found everything she sought. She crossed the country in pieces throughout the summer and fall, fell in love again with the adventure of long-distance cycling, and rediscovered her happiness and confidence. "Wow, what an incredible privilege," she blogged from somewhere in Colorado. "I'm meeting the most incredible people. My heart is full; my love for cycling just keeps on growing and here by the grace of God I ride."

Santilhano was healing and growing more sure of herself. Later that year, she was delighted to learn that her aborted RAAM attempt had inspired others. "A lady I work with bought bikes for her entire family, and an obese work colleague used my effort to help her recommit to her weight-loss program. Wow, that blew me away," she said.

The winter after her DNF, Santilhano publicly committed to doing the race for a second year in a row. She now trusted herself to make the right decisions, and this time she really would ride across the country on the strength of the love, joy, and inspiration she found through cycling.

In 2010, Santilhano prevailed. She finished RAAM with just a few hours to spare before the official time cutoff. "It was an amazing experience," she said. "I never once felt in real distress. My crew was fantastic. I want to get right back on my bike and go climb some more mountains."

PERHAPS BECAUSE OF HIS AGE, THE AUSTRIAN GOLDEN BOY Christoph Strasser had the most trouble of all accepting his DNF brought on by pulmonary problems in the Rockies. "I was doing okay emotionally during my hospital stay in the U.S., but as soon as I landed in Austria and saw my mother at the airport I fell apart," he told me later that summer as we sat together in an airy restaurant in his beloved Austrian mountains. After refusing my earlier entreaties, Strasser was finally ready to talk about his failure to finish the race.

"After RAAM, I was exhausted and grieving and didn't do anything for weeks," he admitted. He didn't even unpack his bikes for weeks afterward, and it took him a long time to gain the courage to read the post-race guest comments on his website. He canceled his plans to do the Race Around Austria later that summer, and didn't have any time frame for when he would return to the competitive circuit.

"I would like to go back to the U.S. and race someday," he said hopefully. "My entire crew wants to come with me; our crew spirit was the best part of the race." But he seemed uncomfortable. "I'm still trying to figure out what happened out there," he finally said. "My lung problems. It's complicated, and the medical research on pulmonary edema isn't helpful. I'm trying to learn everything I can so this doesn't happen again."

That's the thing about this race. RAAM had struck down one of the brightest young stars in the ultracycling universe, and because he had pushed his body beyond the reaches of medical science, nobody could help him figure out how to prevent the onset of the debilitating pulmonary condition. Just like when he is riding his bike, Strasser was largely on his own.

As the winter snow covered the tops of Strasser's Austrian Alps, he was thrilled to learn that despite his RAAM DNF, his main sponsor Wiesbauer had decided to extend his contract. "I'm hoping to do RAAM again in two years' time," Strasser told me later. "I'm only 27 now. I have a lot of time. I want to gain more experience. Next time I'll be faster. My crew members and I are like brothers now, and together we can accomplish anything."

The following summer Strasser returned to competitive ultradistance cycling with a bang. He placed second in the Race Around Slovenia just behind Jure Robič. A month later Strasser won the ultracycling world championship in Austria for the second time, besting his countryman Franz Preihs. Strasser was back at the pinnacle of the sport, and he was impatient to get back to the U.S. to show everybody just what he could do.

MARKO BALOH LIVES ALONG A QUIET ROAD on a picturesque forested hillside overlooking Ljubljana, Slovenia, in a modest two-family home he built and shares with his parents. Aside from his mother and father, there's something else on the ground floor that he cherishes—a large storage room stuffed full of bicycles, wheels, and all manner of cycling gear. This room was the second thing he showed me when I visited him after the race; the first was his framed *Guinness World Records* plaque commemorating the world record he still holds for covering the greatest distance on an outdoor cycling track in a 24-hour period.

Baloh had recently returned from the U.S. after finishing RAAM for the second time in four bids. He had bested his previous time by an impressive 10 hours and finished in under 10 days. Thanks to Jure Robič's

DNF ahead of him, Baloh ended up on the podium in third place, although he doesn't give himself any credit for this accomplishment.

Within a week after returning home, Baloh was back on his bike. "Only 35 kilometers, easy, for regeneration. Felt quite strange," he said about this first ride. He also met his countryman Robič for coffee. "We talked about RAAM. Good memories for me, not so pleasant for him," he said.

Baloh was relieved to have broken the 10-day barrier, but he hadn't achieved his grander race goals. Despite having just accomplished something that only a tiny number of cyclists ever have, he felt disappointed afterward because he believes he's good enough to win. "When I crossed the finish line in 2006, I felt empty," he told me. "Well, this year was no different."

By now Baloh had reflected on why he faded after Gerhard Gulewicz passed him on Day Six in Kansas, but he still hadn't made much headway on the psychological conflict at the root of the problem. "It's a mental issue," he explained as we sat together around his small dinner table. "I couldn't articulate to my crew that I needed more motivation from them. I tried tapping into the energy I felt during the final few hours of my world-record 24-hour effort, but I don't know how." He flashed a wistful smile and shrugged his shoulders like he often does, then went quiet for a moment. Just then his wife Irma came over to the table to hear what her husband had to say about his performance during the race. Even though she was nodding her head while he spoke, when her eyes met mine they showed both doubt and bemusement.

Soon after Baloh had crossed the line in Annapolis, his masseur and crew member Matic offered his assessment of his racer's performance, one that differed markedly from Baloh's. "Marko isn't willing to lose his dignity and become an animal to win," Matic told me bluntly. "With his family there he doesn't have the killer instinct. When Marko is really ready to win he will come back *without* Irma and the kids."

Baloh hopes to return to RAAM in 2011 at the age of 44, and if he does, he'll have to decide whether his family should accompany him. He wants to win, and he might still be good enough to do it. But after his near-death experience in 2003 when he suffered that pulmonary embolism, he still hasn't decided how much he's willing to punish himself in order to be the best.

WHEN JANET CHRISTIANSEN QUIT A MERE 250 MILES from Annapolis in 2008, she knew immediately that she would return in 2009 to finish what she had started. In fact, she knew she'd be back less than halfway through that doomed effort. "I just wasn't happy with how it was going and I knew there was a better way to do it," she said. After leaving the race route she didn't go straight to a hotel room for a well-deserved nap and a good cry. No, a few hours after quitting she sat down and started making notes about things she could have done differently.

Before that ill-fated 2008 race, she had only just begun a new job back home in San Diego, and her colleagues had no idea what she had put herself through. So despite her crushing disappointment, she didn't receive any support or understanding at the office—only grumbling because she'd been gone for more than two weeks. Also, she had put so much time into her training that she had shut herself off socially. After her DNF, "There was nothing going on. Just nothing," she said. "The phone didn't ring. I had pushed everybody away, and I dreaded the weekends because there was nothing to do."

One year later, her co-workers had a deeper appreciation for the enormity of RAAM. Her company, ExpressLogic, had even contributed some sponsorship money to support her 2009 effort. When she returned to the office triumphant, they treated her to a celebration complete with balloons, cake, and flowers.

Several weeks afterward, Christiansen was clear about what came next. "I have a lot of plans after RAAM," she said. "I want to get back into running, buy a truck, and furnish my apartment. And I want to commit myself more to my work at ExpressLogic." The 48-year-old was equally sure that she wouldn't be returning to RAAM for the third year in a row. "My body is beaten up," she said. "RAAM just puts so much stress on your joints. This was my last major ultracycling race. There are other parts of my life that are getting starved out, and it's time to move on. This was my swan song. It's sad, and I'll be nostalgic. But I'll never do this again."

Her disappointment with how she felt she had been treated by the RAAM organization might have contributed to her decision not to return. "They seemed not to take the women's race seriously," she told me. "The women got no hoopla at the start, almost no media coverage, and even after we reported that we had seen Daniela Genovesi breaking rule after rule, RAAM didn't send officials back to take a look. They just told us to stop reporting the infractions."

Her crew chief Bill Osborn was even more upset about their unheeded allegations. "Genovesi drafted her follow-vehicle and let her media team provide [illegal] crew support," he claims. "Her shenanigans started within hours of leaving Oceanside, when she allowed her crew vehicle to follow her on a section where direct-follow support wasn't permitted. RAAM ignored it all."

Despite her bitter feelings, Christiansen planned on staying involved in RAAM, perhaps by mentoring other female ultracyclists or joining their crews. But several weeks after crossing the finish line, she was still just trying to recover physically as she savored her accomplishment as one of only 26 female finishers. Her success unleashed a flood of feelings that she was finally beginning articulate. "Let's see, elation? Much more than that," she said. "Vindication? Yes, but much, much more than that. Euphoria? I'm not a euphoria person. Completeness. Yes, I think that is it. I have never felt as fully satisfied with my efforts in any sport as I do now." The Osprey had returned and prevailed, and now she was ready to move on.

Or so she thought.

Soon enough, Christiansen sensed a familiar hunger stirring inside of her. Unable to imagine a life without competitive ultradistance racing, she realized that her self-identity was inextricably bound to this sport. After sitting out the race in 2010, she began telling friends she planned on returning in 2011. Her goal was to set the fastest finishing time ever for a woman over 50. It seems that there are two things Christiansen will never be able to leave behind: her need to always tinker and make things better, and her compulsion to race her bike over vast distances.

AFTER BREAKING THE TAPE IN ANNAPOLIS and waiting around to greet Jim Rees at the finish line, Kevin Kaiser finally retreated to his hotel for a nap before the finishers' banquet that evening. When his wife woke him for dinner, he seemed confused and asked, "Have we made it to Prescott yet?" In his dreams, Kaiser was still out there racing. It's not uncommon for racers and crew members to relive RAAM in their dreams. For several days afterward, they'll wake up in the middle of the night thinking they're still in the heat of battle.

At the banquet, the normally shy Kaiser seemed uncharacteristically at ease drinking in adulation from friends and family. The following day he returned home to Georgia, and when he went back to work in his pharmacy more accolades poured in. "It seemed as though every one of my customers had seen something in the paper about my RAAM success," he told me a few weeks after finishing the race. "It was really fun to have that recognition." Some days later a cycling buddy asked Kaiser to join him at a local tavern so he could treat Kaiser to a beer. Upon arriving, Kaiser was amazed to find two dozen of his cycling pals there to surprise him. Not a man to easily show his emotions, he choked up, completely overwhelmed by the attention.

"You're the man now," Doyce Johnson said as he toasted Kaiser that evening. Coming from Johnson, a respected local ultracyclist, Kaiser was thrilled. "Now the candle has been passed," added crew member Gary Carter as he picked up a candle from the table, pointed it at Johnson, then swung it in Kaiser's direction. Kaiser held court through a question-and-answer session, feeling so appreciated and grateful that he didn't want this magical evening to end. It was one of the finest moments of his life.

All the attention and respect meant the world to Kaiser. "I get a lot of motivation from people's reactions," he said. "I really enjoy the compliments other people give me, and I love seeing the look on their faces when I tell them that I'm racing hundreds or even thousands of miles."

Kaiser might be a reserved man off the bike, but during RAAM he threw himself into the race and it opened him up. "I want people to know that I have a lot of heart, and that's how I got across the country," he says. Like Jure Robič, Kaiser uses RAAM to help him express his humanity and connect to something larger than himself, an experience he was eager to repeat. "I decided pretty quickly to do it again," he said. "I need to take my wife on a vacation first, but then it's back to training. I would like a 10-day crossing. That's my goal." Kaiser was reaching way beyond his pharmacy job, way beyond his small city in Georgia, all the way to the sky. This goal animated him more than anything else possibly could.

In 2010, Kaiser succeeded in conquering RAAM again, becoming one of only 62 two-time solo finishers. He didn't manage to break 10 days, but this time he was the first American across the line. He might be a beast at heart, but this humble man told me afterward, "I consider myself an average, everyday rider that makes up for his lack of skills with hard work and perseverance."

LIKE KAISER, IT DIDN'T TAKE CHRISTOPHER GOTTWALD much time to decide to return to RAAM. After having executed his secret race plan to perfection and winning first-American and first-rookie honors, Gottwald was stoked. "This was the highlight of my cycling career," he said. "I am not able to convey the emotion. After my kids and wife, this is it."

Everybody around him encouraged Gottwald to come back and try to win the race, with his wife and devoted crew member Jessica acting as chief cheerleader. So a few months after returning from Annapolis, he declared he'd be doing it all over again. "I struggled about it from a spiritual perspective. I don't race my bike to glorify myself, but for the glory of others, to inspire them," he said. "So if this is my calling, why waste my God-given talent? It would be great if I could get a charity behind me, to show it's not an ego thing. I'm sensitive to the criticism that ultracycling can be a selfish lifestyle."

This time Gottwald was determined to win the race outright. He wanted to be the first American to do so since Allen Larsen back in 2003. He figured his biggest challenge would be in his mind, not his legs. "After six or seven hours I just need to get off my bike," he explained. "Maybe I need some mental coaching? I just get a little bored out there." Gottwald knew he would need to train himself to stay on the bike longer each day and reduce his sleep time. He just wasn't sure exactly how. "I'm almost 40 years old and it's not getting any easier," he admitted. "I have the confidence, so I better just go for it."

Gottwald didn't get back to RAAM in 2010. He's not comfortable with self-promotion, and as a result couldn't secure enough sponsorship money to cover the cost. As a full-time pilot with significant travel obligations, he describes his competitive cycling activities as "my hobby." But he's still talented enough to win races. One year after his RAAM triumph, he came in second in the National 24-Hour Challenge in Michigan, covering an impressive 484 miles—only 10 miles less than winner Chris Ragsdale. He thinks the outcome might have been different if he hadn't sustained a puncture when he and Ragsdale were going neck and neck near the end of the race. Gottwald remains as cocky and confident as ever about his RAAM prospects. He hopes he'll find a way to compete one year soon. He knows all he can do is be patient, keep racing, and let the hunger he feels inside keep growing.

IT WAS AN ENTIRELY DIFFERENT STORY FOR BEN POPP. "I'm not addicted to RAAM, and I'll never do it again," he declared sitting at home a few weeks after the race while his twin boys played in the next room. "It was a life's goal realized and a *huge* weight has been lifted from my shoulders." Popp hesitated as he tried to explain what drove him toward the Annapolis finish line once he began faltering in Kansas. Popp is a loquacious man whose words normally tumble out of his mouth like the coins from an old slot machine, so this was an uncharacteristic pause.

"I grew up thinking I'd be a doctor, but I never did well in school," he finally told me. There was some more silence before he went on. "I want people to accept me. By accept, I mean I want people to see me for who I am. I sense that people might think I'm lazy because I don't have to work and my wife's the doctor, not me." As a stay-at-home dad married to a successful physician, being a RAAM finisher helped Popp demonstrate his worth to others. This is the one reason he was so petrified by the prospect of not finishing the race. He needed to be a RAAM finisher so people would see him as the "go-go-go kind of guy" he knew himself to be. So even though he had a stated goal of making a 10-day crossing, Popp's only true goal was to finish safely and within the 12-day time cutoff.

But his crew mates had different ideas, and they had their hearts set on the 10-day mark. Popp had been on pace through the Rockies, but then his energy wilted in the baking Kansas cornfields. "We got really worried that Ben was going to go over 10 days, or worse, that he wouldn't make it," his father-in-law Bob recalled. "It was just so *hot* out there." Bob had expected Popp to push harder once he dropped a few positions in the Plains States. "I got really scared," Bob said. "I thought he was coming apart. We'd all invested so much, and Ben had done so much planning."

His magic cooling vest wasn't working as it had in the deserts a few nights earlier, so Team Popp resorted to using bags of ice placed under his clothing. He went through 30 pounds every five hours during the heat of the day. Popp slipped from seventh place to 10th. Crew members Bob, Larry, and Owen tried encouraging their rider to turn up his intensity, but Popp didn't heed their calls. Privately, he was telling himself he still felt okay precisely because he *wasn't* pushing too hard. Even though his crew was still focused on the 10-day goal, he reminded himself he just wanted to be an official finisher.

"My kids kept me within myself. Whenever I heard voices telling me to go catch the guy ahead of me, another voice would say, 'No, I have kids and a life and I don't train as hard as they do,'" he recalled. "I kept reminding myself that the main goal was to come home safely. And I knew if I pushed it, I increased the risk of not finishing. I couldn't bear the thought of having to explain to everybody back home why I had DNF'd."

Bob believed the mystery of Popp's slowing pace was Bob's responsibility to solve. "Things started going wrong and I felt it was my fault," he said. But Bob didn't know what more he could do. He became so nervous he couldn't eat or sleep. By the end of the race he was utterly spent, ill with a head cold, and six pounds lighter. "I learned a lot about myself out there," he said a few weeks later. "I was scared by the prospect of Ben not finishing because of my own fear of failure."

Sometimes fear of failure, humiliation, and guilt is enough to push a spent rider across the finish line, and that was certainly the case with Popp. He hadn't needed to be the first American, and he hadn't been trying to beat anybody. He had been terrified of the prospect of not finishing, and all he was trying to do was survive.

Now RAAM was out of his system for good and everybody could relax. "I accomplished a huge goal, put a huge collective effort together," he said. "I learned that if you're totally prepared, you can do anything. Now I can stop worrying about training and have some fun hanging out with my friends and raising my kids."

Popp is excited to "slowly and surely get back in the groove of a more ordinary life." He has no regrets about missing his 10-day goal or about his ninth-place showing. He's just thrilled and enormously relieved to be able to call himself an official RAAM finisher.

A MONTH AFTER SUCCESSFULLY COMPLETING HIS THIRD SOLO RAAM in a row—more solo finishes than any British man or woman in history—Jim Rees met me at a suburban London café on his way to be vaccinated for his upcoming family vacation to Egypt. He was excited to be taking his young son Sam to see the pyramids, but he was still looking backward as much as forward.

"It's been like purgatory since RAAM," he said as we settled down at a table. I saw anger and remorse in Rees, and this surprised me. Before I could ask my first question, he began questioning himself. "I'm still trying to make sense of it. Did I lay down the best time I could have? Why didn't I leave a positive fingerprint on my crew members?" he asked. "This year, I feel more broken by RAAM, and I turned more inward during the race. I was disappointed with how I handled stuff, barked at my crew."

He continued after a long, burdened pause, fidgeting with his cup and clearly uncomfortable. "I always struggle about whether my crew understands just how...*mangling* RAAM is. How RAAM strips you bare," he said. Rees is one of the most thoughtful, self-aware men I've ever met, and he was still tortured by his inability to reach closure. "I seem to always get bitchy and annoyed with my crew, but I wonder if they understand why?" he mused. "I'm hypersensitive about whether some of my crew gets how *hard* the race is for me. I want my crew to understand the enormity of this race—what RAAM does to you."

Rees never celebrated after the race. "Everybody was shattered and we just wanted to get home," he said. "The next day I was resting at the hotel and Kevin demanded that I come downstairs to help the crew pack up our gear. We were tired of each other and acting out." Weeks after the race, Rees still hadn't spoken with crew members Lindsey or Kevin. I realized that things on Team Inspiration must have been worse than I had thought.

"One lesson I've learned is that a professional crew is necessary to do really well in RAAM," he continued. "There was just too much infighting amongst the crew, too much time wasted fuffing around with things like crew changes and flat tires. And I really needed better information about my competitive position and pacing." Rees had tried putting things right during his middle-of-the-night crew meeting in Jefferson City on Day Eight, but by then it was too late.

Since Rees always challenges himself to be a better person, the most important lesson he learned had to do with his own behavior. "This race helped me re-learn lessons about how I affect others, and these lessons are painful," he said. "I didn't leave a nice fingerprint on some of my crew. Nirvana would be to have a RAAM experience where I show up in a way that I can be proud of afterward. But what I got upset about were crew mistakes, so you have to have the right crew first."

Rees was sure he wouldn't return to the U.S. for another go in 2010. But what about the year after that? "I really want to go back and continue to improve," he said, finally looking up again. "Reality is that my neck went out, I lost five hours waiting out that storm in Ohio, and my crew wasted too much time fiddling around. And you can't argue with reality." His voice sounded stronger now, even feisty. "If everything had gone smoother, I might have been able to beat the British record," he said. "I would like to do RAAM again, give it another go."

But right now Rees had to rush off to his doctor's appointment, so he didn't have time to sort out his future as an ultracyclist. His most immediate concern was with his family trip. After the race, Rees wrote, "If I've learned anything from RAAM it's that most people on the planet are barely scratching the surface of their own potential." Now it was time for Rees to fulfill his potential as a father and husband and get on with his family vacation. RAAM would have to wait its turn. Rees got up to take his leave, and his gaze shifted resolutely forward.

JURE ROBIČ WAS NAMED SLOVENIAN OF THE YEAR IN 2004 after his first RAAM appearance, catapulting the unknown ultracyclist from the small mountain village of Koroška Bela into the national spotlight. After winning RAAM over and over again, Robič's been in the spotlight ever since. Consequently, his voluntary withdrawal with only 50 miles to go rocked the ultracycling world during the 2009 event.

Immediately after that ugly scene at TS51 in Mount Airy, Robič retreated to his hotel in Annapolis. From there he posted a defiant press release on his website, along with an equally defiant and rambling video interview. Dressed in jeans and a T-shirt, he is remarkably skinny and his cheeks appear concave in the footage. His ruggedly handsome and deeply tanned face still sports thick stubble from days spent on his bike. His shaved scalp also bears curious-looking stripes of tanned skin that follow the contours of the ventilation holes in his helmet. He seems weary and maintains a blank expression throughout the interview.

"I have won RAAM four times and always followed all the rules," he says. "I am proud of that and know that I am the best racer in RAAM history. In spite of getting lost and adding six miles and one hour to my race, I rode my fastest RAAM ever, always staying ahead of my nearest competitor, Dani Wyss. None of my penalties gave me any advantage to be faster." He continued with a lawyerly argument about why each of his three penalties was undeserved. Then he explained what finally caused him to quit. "Wyss and his team were not subject to the same rules as my team and I were. We showed clear video evidence to the race officials of consistent infractions by Wyss and his team, but nothing was done. The race organization ignored infractions that clearly made Wyss race faster on a consistent basis," he said.

Robič scolded the RAAM organization and declared that he would not participate in the race again.

The day after his withdrawal, the dethroned champion greeted his countryman Marko Baloh at the Annapolis finish line and awkwardly congratulated Dani Wyss, who had also returned to cheer Baloh's arrival. Team Robič hung around Annapolis for a few days longer and then returned to Slovenia. But back home Robič was nowhere to be seen. According to a friend he was hiding out in a small town called Ptuj, waiting to learn whether the Slovenian Army would continue honoring his contract. After several days he was informed that his contract was intact, and Robič returned to public view.

Meanwhile, Dani Wyss posted an open letter on his website in which he shared his dismay with Robič's deeds and words. "Your accusations are embarrassing…your strategy of monitoring your opponents…is extremely disturbing," he stated. He went on to say that he hoped Robič's misinformed decisions were a result of the influence of his crew. He defended the illegal right turn captured on video by Robič's crew as an honest navigational error that was immediately corrected. Wyss maintained that he "had enough reserves to overtake" Robič as they neared Annapolis and that he had made a tactical decision to stay behind his Slovenian prey until they drew closer to the finish line. He ended by throwing the gauntlet down, challenging Robič to prove he was still the fastest ultracyclist in the world by besting Wyss' time of eight days, six hours.

Later that summer I visited Robič in Ljubljana, about an hour's drive from his home in the nearby Slovenian mountains. On this balmy night Robič sat by an open window in the small kitchen of a friend who was producing a documentary about Robič's life. Robič was in a restless mood, and up well past midnight. As soon as we sat down he skipped the pleasantries and looked me straight in the eye. "What did you think of how RAAM treated me?" he asked. As I mumbled a response, he continued. "We wanted them to look at the videos, to *do* something," he said. "If you want a race, you can do something, make a penalty to Wyss. It would have been a sprint to the finish, man to man. But they did not treat us like they treaded Wyss, and that's why we quit."

Then he went quiet, lost in thought. The anger was gone from his voice when he spoke again. "RAAM is my life," he said softly, looking down at his lap. "I am infatuated with RAAM, my feelings are deep and sincere, and it excites me beyond anything I can explain. I never stop thinking about it." When his eyes finally met mine they lingered there, as if making sure I could sense his pain. This mighty warrior looked lost and vulnerable.

"I would really like to go back because I have unfinished business there," he continued in a tired voice. He sat there quietly while his girlfriend watched television in the next room. He dearly wanted to return, but he was convinced the RAAM organization was out to get him, so he felt trapped. He reiterated his accusation that one RAAM staffer had acted as a spy for Wyss, reporting back to the Swiss challenger about how Robič was looking during the heat of their battle.

Robič was clearly in the mood to talk and desperately wanted me to understand. He is always trying to explain why he does what he does, how hard he works to achieve his goals, and how much pain—and joy—he feels during his races. We sat together for a long time that night. He talked about his upbringing and how he had to fight for everything he got, his addiction to RAAM, and how the race provides an outlet for his passion and a window into his essential nature. In the wee hours of the morning Robič finally rose to leave and his girlfriend joined him as we said our good-byes. As the door was about to close behind him, he suddenly swung around to make one last point. "Listen, I love my girlfriend," he said. "She accepts me and she understands what she's in for." Robič knew that whatever came next, he would throw himself into it with such force and fury it would frighten anyone close to him, including the ones he loved.

After his RAAM calamity, Robič didn't stop racing. In October he traveled to Australia to compete in the Crocodile Trophy, an extreme, multistage mountain bike race. At over 500 miles, it bills itself as "the world's hardest, longest, and hottest." Even though Robič doesn't do much off-road cycling, he finished fourth, vanquishing many of the most formidable extreme mountain bike racers in the world.

In the meantime the ultracycling world was having a sprawling, fervent debate about Robič's withdrawal, and online discussion forums were lit up by arguments on both sides.

Jim Rees encounters one of RAAM's early hurdles: racing across the Sonoran Desert in Arizona, where triple-digit temperatures test the mettle of even the sturdiest competitors. (Brendon Purdy)

Gerhard Gulewicz powers through Monument Valley in Utah, roughly 650 miles from the starting line in Oceanside, California.

Two of the race favorites—Marko Baloh and Dani Wyss—share the road with their support vehicles.

Ben Popp emerges from the Rocky Mountains with a well-earned smile.

Jim Rees reaches Colorado on pace to break the British record for a solo RAAM racer.

Tony O'Keeffe's crew sprays him down with water in an effort to keep him cool in Arizona's High Desert. (John Foote)

RAAM forces competitors including Daniela Genovesi (top), Franz Preihs (middle), and Marko Baloh (bottom) to find rest and treatment whenever and wherever possible.

(Brendon Purdy)

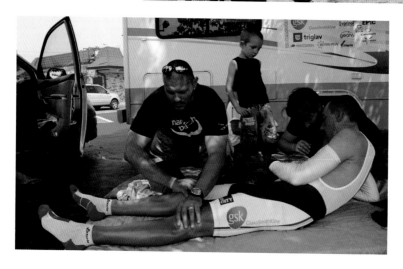

One of the most unusual and debilitating effects of RAAM is a condition where the neck muscles suddenly fail. To keep his head upright, 60-year-old American Paul Danhaus had to fashion a makeshift neck brace atop his handlebars. (Brendon Purdy)

After he was struck with this same condition in 2007, Jim Rees employed a scaffold to brace his head and continue racing.

After finishing the race in sixth place and sporting a T-shirt emblazoned with his message of inspiration, Jim Rees shares a hug with his crew chief Phil Roberton. (Alpine Photography)

Kevin Kaiser is all smiles after finishing his rookie RAAM attempt in fifth place. (Alpine Photography)

Gerhard Gulewicz sheds a tear after finding his father had flown from Austria to Annapolis, Maryland, to surprise him at the finish line. (Alpine Photography)

Overcome with emotion, Daniela Genovesi celebrates her RAAM victory with her crew. (Alpine Photography)

Despite lacking the strength to keep her head upright, Janet Christensen is thrilled to spend a few moments on the finishers' podium.

A series of challenges, both physical and psychological, compelled the seemingly unbeatable Jure Robič to withdraw from the race only 50 miles short of Annapolis. (probakster.si)

RAAM champion Dani Wyss happily sits for an interview after eight days, six hours, and one minute of racing.

"I had to watch the video a couple of times, but then it seemed clear that Wyss made a right turn at a red light, and that's against the rules."

"Seems like Robič can't handle not winning, so if he can't win he just won't finish."

"This year RAAM started out as a witch hunt to dethrone Robič...just read the biased pre-race articles."

"After watching these videos and reading Jure's comments I have a lot less respect for him than before."

Each side held its ground as the argument wore on, but there was one thing everybody could agree on: Robič's crew had let him down. Not only had his teammates' mistakes drawn costly penalties, but they had also fed Robič's paranoia during a time when he was emotionally vulnerable and completely dependent on them. It's difficult being on Robič's crew; there's a lot of pressure to win, a lot of scrutiny, and then there's Robič's volatile temperament. Perhaps he hadn't been able to persuade the best candidates to join his crew in 2009?

RAAM president Fred Boethling captured this sentiment well in an open letter to the ultracycling community. "My belief is that Robič's failure to win his fifth RAAM was a classic case of his crew not being up to the task," he said. "My sense is that Robič's decision to drop out was not his own, but that of his crew. When you look back, the majority of the penalty minutes accumulated by Robič were the result of crew error. My feeling is that at some level his crew was looking for an excuse for their own shortcomings."

In January, three months after returning from the Crocodile Trophy, Robič dropped another bombshell on the ultracycling world. He posted a video on his website announcing that he would return to RAAM after all. "I opted to come back because I feel obliged to overcome the farce of this past year and win again," he explained. "RAAM is a big part of my life and I don't want to leave that behind. I am at the peak of my psychological power and my goal is to set a new RAAM record by finishing in less than eight days." He had taken Wyss' bait and was determined to best Wyss' time and set a new record for the fastest crossing ever.

Several years earlier, Robič had told a reporter, "My passion is the way I'm living life now. I have loved cycling all my life. It's my way of life. I can't imagine a life without it. It's coming from the heart. I'm not doing it for the money or material things. It makes me happy and that's why I do it." If anyone back then had doubted Robič's devotion to RAAM—his obsession with winning this race—they didn't any longer.

As the new year came and winter began to bite in the Slovenian Alps, Robič commenced his new training season. He reported he was riding six and a half hours a day at a higher intensity than ever before. The worldwide ultracycling community was eager to see how Robič would fare six months hence. The following June he would step to the starting line near the shores of the Pacific Ocean for the eighth year in a row, prepared to tangle again with this beast of race and prove that even at the age of 45, he was still the one to beat.

Robič did as he promised. He won RAAM in 2010, collecting his record-setting fifth victory. (Wyss didn't return to defend his title.) He held the lead from start to finish, never once coming under serious threat and besting Gerhard Gulewicz yet again, this time by almost 12 hours. When he coasted into the penalty box time station at Mount Airy 50 miles from Annapolis, this time he did so with a big smile on his face. He lingered there for a while signing autographs, enjoying a slice of pizza, and doing an interview with RAAM media. "In big America, how a small Slovenian guy like me does this so many times…it's an amazing thing, you know," he said with a giggle and a shrug of his shoulders.

Upon crossing the finish line his crew ran over to him, draped a gigantic Slovenian flag over his shoulders, and led him to the stage. In an ironic nod to his Swiss foe from 2009, when handed the microphone he pointed out that while his almost all-new crew didn't have as much experience as in years past, "they worked like a Swiss clock." Robič had been slowed by atrocious weather in the Rockies, which prevented him from beating Wyss' time from the previous year, but to Robič that was a trifling detail.

At the finish line everybody speculated that Robič would be back in 2011 for his ninth consecutive attempt. His ultimate goal was to collect seven RAAM titles, the same number Lance Armstrong had garnered in the Tour de France—and one more than female title holder Seana Hogan's six. Robič had proved he was still at the pinnacle of his sport. The king of ultracycling had reclaimed his throne, and he had no plans of surrendering it again.

Epilogue

La Jolla, California, September 25, 2010

Yesterday, a little more than a year after the events chronicled in this book, something terrible happened that changed everything. Jure Robič was killed in a training accident. This invincible athlete and the main protagonist in *Hell on Two Wheels* died at the scene when he collided with an oncoming vehicle while barreling around a tight downhill turn on a quiet, unpaved fire road in the mountains a few miles from his home in the Slovenian countryside. Jure leaves behind a young son, Nal, and a huge number of grieving friends and admirers.

He was only 45 when he died and still at the peak of his athletic prowess, having won three ultradistance races in 2010: the 732-mile Race Around Slovenia in May, his record fifth Race Across America in June, and the 1,050-mile Tortour de Swiss in August. By many accounts Jure Robič was the world's greatest endurance athlete, dominating most of the races he entered throughout a storied career that included 100 victories and 150 podium finishes.

Jure's passion and courage touched everyone who met him, and the shock of his death sent the tightly knit ultracycling community into paroxysms of anguish. Hundreds of admirers cycled to his funeral in the mountains near his home in Jesenice, Slovenia, to pay their respects and offer condolences to family and friends, and more than 60,000 fans remembered him on a memorial Facebook page within days of his passing. It's hard to believe this indestructible king of ultracycling is gone; his death leaves a gigantic void.

I came to know Jure as I researched this book. He touched me deeply even though our encounters were limited. Nobody who met this attractive, charismatic man could ever forget him.

I've been trying to put it into words what made Jure so compelling to others. He toiled alone, away from fans and cameras, in a sport that is far outside the mainstream. Yet news of his death echoed around the world. This is in part because Jure worked hard to help people see his essential humanity and to understand what made him tick. Everybody wanted a piece of him, and he rarely waved his fans off. But I think it really comes down to this: Jure's persona spanned extremes, making each more accessible to the other. He was the toughest, baddest endurance athlete on the planet. But he could also be unnervingly vulnerable, surprisingly humble, and completely genuine. These personality traits rarely mix. But in Jure they did, which is why everybody who met him could relate to him and find something to learn from him.

I'm in shock that Jure is no longer with us. But even now—especially now—the story of this man's life and unique style of racing can still stir and astonish us. Jure, wherever you are, your power no longer turns a single set of cranks. Today you are the motivating force inspiring thousands to test their own limits and break through personal barriers, just like you did over and over again.

Appendix: The 2009 Solo Field

Name	Country of Origin, Racing Age	Previous Solo RAAM Experience	Biography	2009 Race Result
Autissier, Patrick	France, 47	3rd attempt – one DNF, one finish	Experienced swimmer, triathlete, and cyclist. Recognized as level-headed and cerebral. Scientist who uses himself as a research subject during RAAM.	DNF at 563 miles
Bachmann, Hermann	Switzerland, 57	Rookie attempt	Veteran ultradistance runner. Finished more than 20 Swiss Alpine Marathons (47 miles). Late-blooming ultradistance cyclist. Physical and massage therapist.	DNF at 1,614 miles
Baloh, Marko	Slovenia, 42	4th attempt – two DNFs, one finish	Top ultradistance cyclist and a world-record holder at 12h and 24h races. A civil servant and father of three known for his consistency and humility.	3rd place in 9d 22h 0m
Bradley, Bill	U.S., 49	Rookie attempt	Experienced Ironman/Ultraman triathlete and ultradistance runner known for his resolve if not his speed. Motivational speaker.	DNF at 884 miles
Briand, Dominique	France, 54	Rookie attempt	Acclaimed road cyclist with many age-group podium finishes, including some of the toughest one-day amateur races in Europe. Retired.	1st male over 50 in 11d 9h 40m
Christiansen, Janet	U.S., 48	2nd attempt – one DNF	Podium-finishing, veteran Ironman triathlete, stage racer, and ultradistance cyclist. Known for her tenacity and sense of humor. Software engineer.	2nd place in 12d 4h 57m

Name	Country of Origin, Racing Age	Previous Solo RAAM Experience	Biography	2009 Race Result
Clarindo, Claudio	Brazil, 32	2nd attempt – one finish	Cycling coach and experienced ultradistance cyclist, triathlete, and swimmer. First South American ever to finish RAAM (2007).	7th place in 10d 22h 11m
Cook, Michael	U.S., 39	Rookie attempt	Podium-finishing ultramarathoner and Ironman triathlete turned ultradistance cyclist. Healthcare software developer.	11th place in 11d 12h 21m
Danhaus, Paul	U.S., 60	Rookie attempt	Veteran ultradistance athlete completed 66 marathons, two 50-mile Ultras, and seven Hawaii Ironman triathlons. Veterinarian.	1st man over 60 in 11d 11h 51m
Garcia, Julian	Spain, 36	2nd attempt – one finish	Acclaimed ultradistance cyclist with 1st- and 3rd-place finishes at Le Tour Ultime (the "nonstop Tour de France").	DNF at 934 miles
Genovesi, Daniela	Brazil, 41	Rookie attempt	Personal trainer, world jiujitsu champion, and mother of three. Raced in many multiday, multistage mountain bike races. Untested ultradistance road cyclist.	1st place female in 11d 17h 41m
Gottwald, Christopher	U.S., 38	Rookie attempt	Pro criterium racer with the Colavita team in the 1990s. Untested ultradistance cyclist doing RAAM for charitable and spiritual reasons. Pilot and father of two.	4th place in 10d 12h 2m
Gulewicz, Gerhard	Austria, 41	4th attempt – one DNF, two finishes	One of the top full-time ultradistance cyclists in the world (road and mountain). Set a new world record for the fastest crossing of Australia in 2007.	2nd place in 8d 23h 10m
Kaiser, Kevin	U.S., 41	Rookie attempt	Mild-mannered pharmacist manager and veteran ultradistance cyclist. Dedicated student of RAAM history and race tactics.	5th place in 10d 17h 19m
Luikart, Scott	U.S., 47	Rookie attempt	Financial advisor and experienced ultradistance cyclist. Twin brother recently diagnosed with Parkinson's disease served on Luikart's RAAM crew.	DNF at 396 miles
Newey, Richard	United Kingdom, 44	Rookie attempt	Cat 2 road racer and mountain biker. Was a mountaineer before taking up cycling. Construction consultant and risk manager for London 2012 Olympics.	8th place in 10d 23h 56m

Name	Country of Origin, Racing Age	Previous Solo RAAM Experience	Biography	2009 Race Result
O'Keeffe, Tony	Canada, 48	2nd attempt – one finish	Lieutenant Colonel in the Canadian armed forces, veteran Ironman/ Ultraman triathlete, respected for his discipline, inspirational leadership qualities, and mental toughness.	DNF at 1,576 miles
Oyler, Peter	Canada, 39	2nd attempt – one finish	Athletic coach, multisport athlete, seasoned adventure racer, experienced Ironman triathlete.	DNF at 1,614 miles
Popp, Ben	U.S., 35	Rookie attempt	Athletic coach, multisport athlete, and Ironman triathlete with a background in Nordic skiing. Stay-at-home father of twin boys.	9th place in 11d 0h 28m
Preihs, Franz	Austria, 31	2nd attempt – one finish	Professional ultradistance cyclist. Late-blooming endurance athlete ran 54 marathons in three years. Rose rapidly through the ranks of ultradistance cycling.	DNF at 1,044 miles
Rees, Jim	United Kingdom, 46	3rd attempt – two finishes	Veteran Ironman triathlete turned cyclist. Keynote speaker, executive coach, and father of six. Known for his thoughtfulness, determination, and generosity.	6th place in 10d 20h 53m
Robič, Jure	Slovenia, 44	7th attempt – four 1st places, one 2nd place, one DNF	Greatest male RAAM champion in history, and possibly the greatest ultradistance endurance athlete ever. Renowned for pushing himself to the edge of mental breakdown during races. Full-time ultradistance cyclist and member of Slovenian armed forces. Killed in training accident in 2010.	DNF at 2,966 miles
Rudge, Daniel	United Kingdom, 42	2nd attempt – 1 DNF	Structural engineer and Brit living in Texas. Widely experienced endurance athlete, father of two, and aggressive charity fund-raiser during RAAM races.	10th place in 11d 5h 24m
Santilhano, Michelle	South Africa, 39	Rookie attempt	Pediatric oncology RN, mountaineer, adventurer, and widely accomplished ultradistance endurance athlete with accolades in swimming, running, triathlon, and cycling.	DNF at 884 miles

Name	Country of Origin, Racing Age	Previous Solo RAAM Experience	Biography	2009 Race Result
Strasser, Christoph	Austria, 26	Rookie attempt	Youngest entrant and a superstar professional ultradistance cyclist in the making. Youngest ever to win the ultracycling world championship in 2007.	DNF at 1,471 miles
Velez, Jean Marc	France, 47	3rd attempt – one DNF, one finish	Management consultant and longtime ultradistance cyclist. First Frenchman ever to finish solo RAAM (2007).	DNF at 934 miles
Wooldridge, Ann	United Kingdom, 50	Rookie attempt	Accomplished ultradistance cyclist with numerous high finishes, including course record for Sebring 24h in 2005, and 3rd female in Furnace Creek 508 in 2007.	DNF at 2,889 miles*
Wyss, Dani	Switzerland, 39	3rd attempt – one 1st place, one 4th	One of the top ultradistance cyclists in the world. Set a 24h world record in 2007 in Schötz, Switzerland. Only second racer to win RAAM in rookie attempt (2006).	1st place in 8d 6h 1m

* Finished unofficially after the time cutoff in 13h 6m 9m, but nonetheless set the UMCA transcontinental record for women over 50.

Acknowledgments

Here are two things you should know: first, the story of the 2009 RAAM was much larger than this book could possibly convey. Because my space was limited, I wasn't able to recount the travails of all 28 solo racers or even to share all the pivotal moments experienced by the racers I did feature.

There were many wonderful stories I regretfully had to pass over. Ann Wooldridge's amazing fortitude is one. In 2009 she set a new UltraMarathon Cycling Association record for the fastest transcontinental crossing by a woman over 50, even though she had missed the race's time cutoff and couldn't be recognized as an official RAAM finisher. Having taken a nasty tumble in Missouri, she came across the line battered and bruised. She was the embodiment of true grit.

Another was the heart and pluck of Paul Danhaus, only the fourth person over 60 years young to finish RAAM. Then there was the calm and peaceful way Claudio Clarindo made it across the country; I was impressed by how he managed to hold on to his center. I was equally captivated by the white-hot energy and verve of the female champion, Daniela Genovesi. And there were so many more.

Soloists weren't the only class of racers competing in RAAM. Amazing stories took place in the team divisions, too. For example, all the men on the winning eight-man team were Type 1 diabetics. On one four-man team, every racer was over 75 years of age (they finished). I wish I could have told their stories, too.

I encourage readers to search for the blogs and websites that many RAAM participants employ to keep their fans updated. It's also worth taking a look at the race coverage posted on RAAM's website, YouTube, and elsewhere.

The second thing I'd like my readers to know is that, from a journalistic perspective, covering this race was diabolically difficult. Before long the solo racers were spread out over 500 miles, and sweeping up and back through the field each day became impossible. Despite going without sleep like everyone else, try as I might, I couldn't be everywhere at the same time.

As a result, some of the events described in the book came to me second-hand, mostly through phone calls with crew members. If I didn't manage to see them on the road that day, I contacted every featured racer's team by phone, though there were a couple of occasions when dodgy mobile coverage prevented this. I made every effort to faithfully recreate the race action I didn't directly observe.

Before this, nobody had ever written a book that follows so many racers in such detail during an ultradistance race like RAAM. But the story of this remarkable race and these extraordinary athletes needed to be told.

THIS BOOK WOULD NOT HAVE BEEN POSSIBLE without the enthusiastic involvement of the racers who let me into their lives and trusted me to tell their stories. They all spent long hours with me and shared their feelings more freely than I ever imagined they would. Some of them have even become friends. For a tribe of outcast athletes so utterly mischaracterized by the media and even other cyclists, the ultracycling community really does want to be understood—and it showed.

Thanks also to Fred and Rick Boethling and the entire Race Across America organization for their trust and support and for insisting that the only way to gain an accurate understanding of the enormity of this race was to follow the entire event from coast to coast, enduring through-the-night efforts along with the racers (you were right, Fred!).

I am deeply grateful (and lucky) that my agent David Fugate of LaunchBooks shared my vision and was willing work with this first-time author. David was energetic and patient, and he had an intuitive sense for how to tell this story. I learned a lot from him. When I first started promoting this book concept, a discouraging number of agents and publishers told me that "a book about a bicycle race" could never succeed, especially if it wasn't written by Lance Armstrong. My agent David—along with Tom Bast, Adam Motin, and all the good people at Triumph Books—deserve credit for realizing this wasn't just "a book about a bike race" and for taking the leap.

I also want to acknowledge Dr. Judith Braun, who helped expand my understanding of the complex processes of human self-expression and self-revelation that occupy the deepest layer of this book's narrative. And this list would not be complete without thanking my coach, Bruce McAllister, for helping me to polish some of the initial chapters and for making sense of the arcane workings of the publishing industry.

My spouse Pat was my chief cheerleader, and along with family and friends, helped me overcome minor disappointments and celebrate achievements throughout this two-year project. We did it together, and that is the most rewarding thing of all.

Finally, I need to acknowledge the late, great Jure Robič. Nobody who met this passionate, humble man could ever forget him. I am particularly grateful for the hours Jure spent with me late one night in Ljubljana, Slovenia. He bared his soul and shared his deepest feelings just weeks after withdrawing from the 2009 race. Jure trusted me to treat the controversy surrounding his withdrawal fairly and with compassion, and his trust meant a lot.

Book Proceeds

ROAD CYCLING IS SAFER THAN CAR TRAVEL AS MEASURED BY fatalities per mile or per hour. Still, about 700 bicyclists are killed each year on the roadways of the United States, with an additional 500,000 visiting hospital emergency rooms. In the United Kingsom more than 150 bicyclists lose their lives every year, but Italy is the most dangerous country in Western Europe measured by fatalities per kilometer traveled. No matter where they ride, cyclists are vulnerable.

A portion of the proceeds from the sale of this book will go to supporting the following nonprofit organizations working to ensure the safety and well-being of people who ride bikes.

Adventure Cycling Association (www.adventurecycling.com)
Inspires people of all ages to travel by bicycle for fitness, fun, and self-dicovery.

California Bicycle Coalition (www.calbike.org)
An education and lobbying organization working to improve bicycling conditions throughout California.

League of American Bicyclists (www.bikeleague.org)
Promotes bicycling for fun, fitness, and transportation and works through advocacy and education for a bicycle-friendly America.

Notes

Introduction

Descriptions about the toll that RAAM takes on body and mind came from my own observations during the race, as well as from interviews and correspondence with racers and their crew members. Danny Chew's thorough reporting on the 2002 through 2005 races was also a valuable source. Chew won RAAM twice in the 1990s and then became an avid chronicler of subsequent races. His reporting can be found at http://www.dannychew.com. Several other sources helped deepen my understanding of the toll this race takes, including Kevin Wallace's race blog retrieved from http://teamrace.com/raam/ and an account of John Spurgeon's RAAM effort, "RAAM Tough," in the *Outdoors NW* website at http://www.outdoorsnw.com.

Finally, my own experience as a lifelong cyclist helped deepen my understanding of what solo RAAM racers are up against. Having logged 5,000 miles annually during my peak riding years, I am familiar with some (but thankfully not all) of the physical maladies that result from hours spent in the saddle.

The estimate of RAAM's caloric demands came from Knechtle and Jehle's "Energy turnover at the Race Across America," *Int J Sports Med*, Jul-Aug 2005; 26(6):499-503, as well as a *Runner's World* article by Amby Burfoot from July 2009, "Are Tour de France Riders the Ultimate Endurance Athletes?" The estimate of close to 1 million pedal revolutions to complete RAAM came from my discussions with RAAM contestants, as well as from John Forester's book, *Effective Cycling*, MIT Press, 1993.

In 1993, *Outside* magazine commissioned a panel of experts to rank the world's toughest endurance events. They employed criteria such as the "Mule Factor" (the distance involved), the "Forum" (how tough the course is), the "Anguish Index" (how hard competitors "have to work to convince themselves that what they're doing is only mildly insane and self-destructive"), and the "O Factor" (a combination of the event cost and the dropout rate). When compared to races like the Raid Gauloises, the Iditarod, the Vendee Globe Around-the-World sailing race, the Hawaii Ironman, and the Badwater Ultramarathon, RAAM out-punished them all. In a subsequent comparison RAAM slipped to the No. 2 spot, but this event is perennially judged to be one of the most punishing tests of endurance ever devised.

The oft-quoted comparison Wolfgang Fasching made between RAAM and climbing Mount Everest came from Danny Chew's 2007 race report retrieved from his website. Descriptions of Mount Everest and K2 dangers came from Alan Arnette's website at http://www.alanarnette.com/news/2009/12/18/the-deadly-side-of-everest, and Graham Bowley's *New York Times* article, "A Trek to Danger's Doorstep." The Everest fatality rate estimate came from an email exchange I had with Fred Boethling in May 2010 in which he compared a number of publicly available statistical sources.

Accounts of Dean Karnazes' 1995 Badwater Ultramarathon attempt came from Joshua Davis' January 2007 article in *Wired* magazine, "The Perfect Human."

Descriptions of the effects of sleep deprivation came from my own observations during the race as well as my discussions and correspondence with racers and their crew members. In addition, I was helped by two papers in academic journals: Christie Riggins' "Sleep for Athletes," *Physical Online*, November 2000, and Clete Kushida Anthony's "Sleep Deprivation," *Informa HealthCare*, 2004:316.

RAAM winner Franz Spilauer explained his fascination with seeing how far he could push himself in an interview published by Chris Kostman of AdventureCORPS, "Race Across America 1987 and 1988" retrieved from AdventureCORPS' website at http://www.adventurecorps.com.

Nancy Soloman's observation about how ultradistance athletes are transformed by their experiences came from a posting on her *Soloman Factor Blog*, "Courage is a Decision We Make Every Day" at http://www.nancydsolomon.com/?p=340.

Kirk Johnson's account of his Badwater Ultramarathon experience appeared in his book *To the Edge*, Grand Central Publishing, 2002.

Chapter 1: The Race Day Scene

David Halberstam wrote eloquently about the amateur culture of competitive rowing in his excellent book *The Amateurs*, Penguin Books, 1986.

Racers and crew members described how RAAM solo entrants prepared for the race in interviews and correspondence.

I quoted Daniel Coyle's insights about how cyclists go beyond normal conventions of toughness from his book *Lance Armstrong's War*, HarperCollins Publishers, 2006.

Observations about the nature of pain were shaped by Elaine Scarry's *The Body in Pain*, Oxford University Press, 1985.

Descriptions of each of the 2009 racer's backgrounds came mostly from my own interviews with them. I also relied on the racers' own blogs and websites, as well as Danny Chew's reporting on his website.

Chapter 2: The European Onslaught

The account of the early history of ultradistance cycling draws from Wikipedia entries on "Bicycle Racing," "Bicycle Touring," "Thomas Stevens," and "Tommy Godwin." Other helpful sources included David Mozer's "Chronology of the Growth of Bicycling and the Development of Bicycle Technology" on the International Bicycle Fund website at http://www.ibike.org/library/history-timeline.htm#chronology, a 2009 *New York Times* City Room Blog piece titled "Spokes: Gossip of the Cyclers, From the 1800s," and an entry in Dave Moulton's blog titled "The Tale of Two Godwins" retrieved from http://davesbikeblog.squarespace.com/blog/2009/11/30/the-tale-of-two-tommy-godwins-part-i.html. Modern round-the-world efforts are chronicled in "Round the World Biking? Who's the Quickest," a posting by David Atkinson retrieved from the road.cc website. Randonneurs USA published Bill Bryant's history of Paris-Brest-Paris, "A Short History of Paris-Brest-Paris" in 1999, and my account leveraged this work.

The modern history of ultradistance cycling was traced with the help of a *Wilmington Morning Star* story about the 1979 race titled "Bikers to Sprint Across the U.S.," and Michael Shermer's book chronicling early RAAM history, *Race Across America*, WRS Publishing, 1993. Fred Boethling, Rick Kent, and George Thomas also described this history in interviews with me. Other useful sources included official time and distance records kept by the UltraMarathon Cycling Association and the Race Across America.

The account of Franz Spilauer's 1987 and 1988 RAAM bids came from Tom Carter's article in *Bicycle Guide Magazine*, "Waiting to Attack," November/December 1988. The story of Rob Kish's life and RAAM accomplishments came from Chris Kostman's summer 1994 article in *UltraCycling* magazine, "Rob Kish, RAAM's Mystery Man."

Chapter 3: The Deepest Field Ever

The profile of Fred Boethling came from my interviews with him as well as from John Hughes' article "Fred Boethling: No More Training Wheels!" which was retrieved from http://www.ultracycling.com/about/boethling_profile.html. The description of cycling's all-important power-to-weight ratio came from Daniel Coyle' book *Lance Armstrong's War*, HarperCollins Publishers, 2006.

As with all the contestants featured in the book, profiles of featured racers came from interviews and correspondence with them; their own blogs and websites; the biographies they posted on RAAM's website; and official race statistics maintained by U.S. and European race organizations, and the UltraMarathon Cycling Association.

Chapter 4: Day One: Rolling!

Janet Christiansen and George Thomas helped me gain an understanding of the history of women's participation in RAAM. Also helpful were Candace Koska's "The Women of RAAM" retrieved from RAAM's website at http://www.raceacrossamerica.org and Danny Chew's race reports on his website. I also leveraged the statistics kept by the Race Across America organization.

The account of Seana Hogan's 1997 race came from David Houghton's The United States of Delirium website at www.unitedstatesofdelirium.com. The report of her 2004 induction to the UltraCycling Hall of Fame by Ed Fleming and John Hughes was also a good reference source.

Details about each racer's background are based on my interviews and correspondence with racers and their crew members, as well as the racers' own blogs and websites.

Adeline Goss was the inspiration behind the observation about the struggle between mind and body during RAAM. See her "Research at Badwater" on the seedmagazine.com website retrieved from http://seedmagazine.com/content/article/research_at_badwater.

Danny Chew's comments about racing at night came from his 2002 race report on his website.

Chapter 5: Day Two: Digging In

My accounts of the race action came from my own observations out on the course, interviews and correspondence with racers and their crews, the racers' own blogs and websites, and stories filed by RAAM media. Official time station statistics kept by the RAAM organization and retrieved from their website helped to complete the picture as the race progressed.

Before this book, nobody had ever attempted to tell the story of such a long ultradistance race following as many contestants as I did. The preparation this required was akin to what it takes to paint a room; the more care one takes, the better the result. It took me several weeks to reconstruct the hour-by-hour, day-by-day action as it unfolded over a field that was racing 24/7 and spread out over hundreds of miles. Eventually this work was condensed into a wall-sized chart that became my personal touchstone during the writing phase.

The story of Jure Robič's upbringing and early racing years came from my interview with him in Ljubljana, Slovenia, in August 2009. We spent many hours together that night, and Robič shared details about his life that even his close friends had rarely if ever heard.

The account of Robič's inaugural 2003 race was based on my interviews with him, as well as a blog entry on his website posted on July 1, 2003, titled "The True Story." As always, Danny Chew's race reports on his website were also invaluable. Daniel Coyle's 2006 *New York Times* article about Robič, "That Which Does Not Kill Me Makes Me Stranger," helped with some details of this race. Coyle's reporting about Robič's unique style of racing also came from this article.

Confirmation of Jure Robič's 24-hour world record came from the UltraMarathon Cycling Association.

Chapter 6: Day Three: Surprise!

Descriptions of the causes and effects of heat stroke came from Andy Shen's 2009 interview with cycling coach Allen Lim retrieved from the nyvelocity.com website at http://nyvelocity.com/content/interviews/2009/allen-lim-garmins-guru; Todd Balf's 2010 *Bicycling* magazine article, "Out on a Lim"; and an academic article written by Dr. Timothy Noakes, "Fluid replacement during marathon running," from *Clin J of Sport Med* 2003; 13:309.

As with all the racers profiled in the book, details about Jim Rees' life came from my interviews and correspondence with him, as well as material retrieved from his own blog and website at http://www.teaminspiration.org.uk.

The description of the Mount Everest death zone comes from Connie Levett's 2006 article, "The Deadly Business of Climbing Everest" that appeared in *The Age*.

Chapter 7: Crew Control

Comments from Robič's crew chief Miran Stanovnik came from Daniel Coyle's 2006 *New York Times* article, "That Which Does Not Kill Me Makes Me Stranger."

The description of the split-second decision making required during the Leadville Trail 100 running race came from Christopher McDougall's book *Born to Run*, Alfred A. Knopf, 2009.

Chapter 8: Days Four and Five: Extreme Extremes

When we met after his 2009 race, Robič explained to me how he tried to quit his RAAM addiction. I also used a quote on this subject taken from a RAAM newsletter article published before the 2009 race, "Jure Robič to Defend his RAAM Championship."

In researching this book, I was fascinated by the evolving academic research on how the mind responds to pain stimuli. My description of how personality affects responses to the cold pressor test came from Penny Lutkin's article, "Personality Correlates of Pain Perception and Tolerance" in *J of Clin Psychology*, v38n2 p317-20 Apr 1982, as well as Dana Albert's blog posting, "Cycling, Suffering, and the Cold Pressor Test," retrieved from his website at http://www.albertnet.us/2009/10/cycling-suffering-and-cold-pressor-test.html.

The role of the anterior cingulate cortex in mediating the pain response is described by Professors Rainville, Duncan, Price, Carrier, and Bushnell in "Pain Affect Encoded in Human Anterior Cingulate but Not Somatosensory Cortex," published in *Science*, August 15, 1997, vol. 277 no. 5328, p. 968-971.

Neuroscientist Patrick Wall played a seminal role in advancing our understanding of the pain response, and the wounded soldier example comes from his book, *The Science of Suffering*, Weidenfeld & Nicolson, 1999. Wall's description of the gate control model came from "All in the Mind," a radio interview he did with Natasha Mitchell broadcast by *ABC Radio International* on April 20, 2003. Physiologist Timothy Noakes' central governor theory was a provocative extension of Wall's research. Particularly helpful were findings from a research paper he authored along with St. Clair and Lambert, "From catastrophe to complexity: a novel model of integrative central neural regulation of effort and fatigue during exercise in humans," *British Journal of Sports Medicine* 2004; 38:511-514.

Atul Gawande wrote about how the mind perceives pain stimuli in "The Itch," which appeared in *The New Yorker* on June 30, 2008. I leveraged this work.

Art Beauregard described the running exploits of the Tarahumara Indians in his December 1996 paper "Running Feet" retrieved from the ultralegends.com website. In his book *Born to Run* (Alfred A. Knopf, 2009), Christopher McDougall profiles the Tarahumara culture and recounts the running lore of these indigenous peoples.

Chapter 9: Day Five: The Kansas Crucible

The account of Tyler Hamilton's injuries came from a *New York Times* article by Juliet Macur titled, "Hamilton Admits Taking Drug and Retires from Cycling," dated April 17, 2009.

The ghoulish reality TV show *Shattered* caused a stir in Britain in 2004. The description of what happened on this show relied on a news story carried by *The Independent* on January 14, 2004, titled "Counsellors lodge complaint with TV watchdog over reality show that may become a waking nightmare," as well as the Wikipedia entry "Shattered (2004 TV Series)."

Descriptions of ritual pain practices came from Ariel Glucklich's book *Sacred Pain: Hurting the Body for the Sake of the Soul*, Oxford University Press, 2003. Other useful sources were "Self-inflicted Pain in Religious Experience," retrieved from the HomieGFunk blog at http://faithfaq.com/pain.htm, and Charles Selengut's book *Sacred Fury*, AltaMira Press, 2004.

The pain-for-beauty passage leveraged Rachel Usala's "The Pain-Beauty Paradox," a student paper retrieved from Bryn Mawr's website at http://serendip.brynmawr.edu/ sci_cult/courses/beauty/web5/urusala.html.

Lance Armstrong's comment about how he copes with pain came from his autobiography co-written with Sally Jenkins, *It's Not About the Bike: My Journey Back to Life*, Berkley Trade, 2001.

Graeme Fife writes eloquently about how cyclists suffer while on the bike, and particularly helpful was his article "Glory Through Suffering" retrieved from the Rapha website at http://www.rapha.cc/glory-through-suffering.

The description of the cognitive techniques cyclists employ to cope with the pain of racing came from Jeffrey Kress and Traci Statler's "A naturalistic investigation of former Olymic cyclists' cognitive strategies for coping with exertion pain during performance," *J of Sport Behavior*, December 1, 2007, downloaded from the HighBeam Research website.

Jure Robič's explanation of his response to pain came from Daniel Coyle's 2006 *New York Times* article cited previously, while the other racers' responses were from my own interviews.

Chapter 10: Days Six and Seven: Collapse and Resurrection

The accounts of Marko Baloh's 2003 and 2005 RAAM bids came from interviews and correspondence with him, as well as Danny Chew's 2003 race report retrieved from his website.

The account of Michael Shermer's 1983 experience of sudden neck muscle failure came from Walter Libby and Sue Morris's "A Pain in the Neck," an article retrieved from the UltraMarathon Cycling Association website.

Chapter 11: Day Seven: A Race for the Ages

Details of Jure Robič's 2004 battle with Mike Trevino and his sleep deprivation training regime were captured by Danny Chew's 2004 RAAM race report retrieved from his website. Vic Armijo's June 19, 2007, story in *VeloNews* was the source of the Robič quote about his battle with Fasching being "a war."

In December 2009, I interviewed Susan R. Hopkins about her research on severe pulmonary edema, and her comments were from our discussion. The only documented cases of this malady came from a journal article published by McKechnie, Leary, Noakes, Kallmeyer, MacSearraigh, and Olivier, "Acute Pulmonary Oedema in Two Athletes during a 90-km Running Race," *South African Medical Journal*, 18 August 1979, p. 261. Dr. Hopkins' published debate on the existence of severe pulmonary edema can be found in "Pulmonary edema does/does not occur in human athletes performing heavy sea-level exercise," *J Appl. Physiol* 2010 Jan 7 [epub ahead of print].

Chapter 12: What Fingerprint Do You Want to Leave?

The literature on natural-born talent is intriguing and provocative. Several sources helped to lay out the arguments about whether natural-born talent is a predicate of exceptional performance, including Geoff Colvin's book *Talent is Overrated*, Penguin Group, 2008; a *New York Times* piece by Stephen Dubner and Steven Levitt, "Freakonomics: A Star is Born," from May 7, 2006; a David Brooks op-ed piece that ran in *The New York Times* on May 1, 2009; and an academic paper by K. Anders Ericsson, Ralf Th. Krampe, and Clemens Tesch-Römer, "The Role of Deliberate Practice in the Acquisition of Expert Performance," from *Psychological Review* 1993: Vol. 100, No. 3, 363-406.

Chapter 13: Days Eight and Nine: Marooned in Ohio

The account of Bob Breedlove's tragic death came from Alan Pendergrast's article "Wrecked" in *Outside* magazine, November 2006.

The description of the huge cross in Effingham, Illinois, was retrieved from the roadsideamerica.com website at http://www.roadsideamerica.com/story/10913, while the account of the gigantic horseshoe crab in Blanchester, Ohio came from the same website at http://www.roadsideamerica.com/story/13704.

Chapter 14: Day Nine: Final Ultimatum

RAAM media's account of the final stages of the Robič-Wyss showdown was retrieved from the RAAM website at http://www.raceacrossamerica.org/blog/blogs/blog2.php/2009/06/24/robic-and-wyss-dog-fight.

The account of Robič's amazing 2004 triumph at Le Tour Direct and Robič's comment about how his crew motivates him at the end of his races came from Daniel Coyle's 2006 *New York Times* article, "That Which Does Not Kill Me Makes Me Stranger."

In recounting the final hours of Robič's 2009 race, I relied on my own observations out on the race course and interviews with RAAM officials Fred Boethling and George Thomas. Also helpful were blog entries posted by crew member Matjaž Planinšek on Robič's website which was subsequently deactivated, as well as RAAM's official race blog at http://www.raceacrossamerica.org/blog/blogs/blog2.php/2009/06/24/champion-shuffle#comments.

Much ink was spilled with arguments on both sides after Robič's controversial withdrawal from the race. Robič and Wyss both issued press releases, Robič's crew members posted videos of alleged rule violations by Wyss as well as a lengthy videotaped interview of Robič taken in his Annapolis hotel the day after his withdrawal. RAAM president Fred Boethling wrote an open letter justifying how the race organization handled the situation, and a number of RAAM insiders shared their points of view.

I made every effort to recount what happened on the race course as accurately and honestly as possible. I took care to present the claims made by each camp so readers could hear their voices directly, and I sought to avoid speculating about events that could not be independently verified. I hope I accomplished these goals in telling a story that was complex and fraught.

Descriptions of the effects of severe sleep deprivation on decision making come from the work of Yvonne Harrison and James A. Home, "The Impact of Sleep Deprivation on Decision Making: A Review," *Journal of Experimental Psychology*, 2000, Vol. 6, no. 3, 236-249.

I interviewed RAAM finisher George Thomas about the reputation Robič's crew had developed over the years, and also relied on Danny Chew's 2004 race reporting retrieved from his website.

Comments from Robič's crew chief Uroš Velepec came from a press release dated June 26, 2009, and posted on his now-deactivated website, as well as my interviews and correspondence with Fred Boethling.

Descriptions of West Virginia's Route 50 were retrieved from Wulf Berg's Route 50 Coast-to-Coast website at http://www.route50.com/westvirginia.htm.

Chapter 15: Days 10 and 11: Tough Love

The estimate of 50,000 gear shifts during RAAM came from my email correspondence with Fred Boethling in May 2010. For those cycling devotees among us, he pegged it at 10,000 to 15,000 shifts on the chainrings, and 30,000 to 50,000 on the rear cassette, for a total of 40,000 to 60,000 overall.

Chapter 16: Day 12: Guts and Glory in Annapolis

Lance Armstrong's quote about pain being self-revelatory is from the autobiography he co-wrote with Sally Jenkins, *It's Not About the Bike: My Journey Back to Life*, Berkley Trade, 2001.

Chapter 17: Aftermath

The account of the hero myth comes from Joseph Campbell's book *The Hero with a Thousand Faces*, Princeton University Press, 1972.

Ben Popp's comment about getting back to an ordinary life comes from Cathy Peterson's interview that appeared in *The Bee* on July 8, 2009.

The arguments offered by Robič about why he withdrew from the race came from a press release dated June 26, 2009, and posted on his website which was subsequently deactivated.

Comments from Dani Wyss came from a press release posted on his website on June 29, 2009, and retrieved from http://www.wyssdani.ch.

Robič's comments about being infatuated with RAAM came from my post-race interview with him, as well as from a 2009 RAAM newsletter article, "Jure Robič Returns to Defend his RAAM Championship."

Robič's comments about his commitment to his lifestyle come from an interview he did with Danny Chew.

Epilogue

Accounts of Jure Robič's death came from an article by Bruce Weber in *The New York Times* from September 29, 2010, titled, "Jure Robic, Endurance Bicyclist, Dies at 45"; and a piece by Erin Beresini in *Outside* magazine from December 2010.

Book Proceeds

Statistics about the dangers of cycling on open roads came from the League of American Bicyclists in the U.S. and the Office of National Statistics in the UK. A wealth of bicycling safety studies are compiled by John S. Allen on his website at www.bikexprt.com. Ken Kiefer's memorial website (he was killed by a drunk driver in 2003) is a good source for safe cycling tips and can be found at www.kenkifer.com.

Index